Schleiermacher's Theology of Sin and Nature

"I have long been convinced that Friedrich Schleiermacher's account of original sin – its origin and its transmission – is superior to all others, including those constructed subsequently. To demonstrate the truth of this conviction, however, requires a specialist's knowledge of Schleiermacher combined with close knowledge of the history of philosophy and natural science. Daniel Pedersen has the needed expertise in all three areas and has brought them together to write a stunning book. Not only is it the finest book on Schleiermacher's doctrine of sin available in the English-language; it is, for me, the most significant constructive contribution to the Christian doctrine of sin in years."

– **Bruce McCormack**, Charles Hodge Professor of Systematic Theology, Princeton Theological Seminary

"An excellent and sorely needed contribution to discussion about the origins of sin. Pedersen (re-) confronts readers with Schleiermacher's claim that God is the author of sin and the cause of evil, in ways that open new questions of agency, normativity and tradition. That Pedersen is able to shed light on classical and modern accounts, examine Schleiermacher's position, and explicate implications across a range of doctrines is testimony to the high calibre of his scholarship. In Pedersen's feisty reading, Schleiermacher continues to disrupt familiar conceptions of God and human experience."

– **Esther D. Reed**, Professor of Theological Ethics, University of Exeter

"In this clearly written, accessible, and erudite book Daniel Pedersen provides a new interpretation of Schleiermacher's theology of sin and nature. The book shows how Schleiermacher was firmly committed to traditional theological notions, such as the priority of the good over bad, but that he relied on these notions to reach radical and unconventional conclusions. Notably, he denied that a historical Fall from paradise ever took place. Pedersen shows how Schleiermacher's account is ambitious both in its theological scope and in its engagement with the sciences of the time, including pre-Darwinian evolutionary theories."

– **Helen De Cruz**, Danforth Chair in the Humanities, St. Louis University

"One of the most strikingly modern features of Friedrich Schleiermacher's systematic theology (or Glaubenslehre), The Christian Faith, written almost two hundred years ago, is the treatment of the concept of sin, which lies close to the center of it. We are easily persuaded by Schleiermacher's scathing critique of traditional ideas of a "fall" of our first human ancestors, as I have found over the years in teaching. However, Daniel Pedersen's new book Schleiermacher on Sin and Nature identifies a much deeper and more positive line of thought motivating the critique. It is a conception of human history as completely governed by such laws of nature as we learn empirically, but with a salvific purpose of God behind the laws. In that conception there is no "fall" but there is progress, in different degrees in different individuals at different times, toward a religious consciousness of grace. And ultimately, as Pedersen reads Schleiermacher (rightly I think), there is salvation for all, after death – though that is a subject on which Schleiermacher is more reticent. In explaining Schleiermacher's thinking on these topics, Pedersen brings out how it was influenced by engagement with ancient and medieval as well as modern thinkers, notably including Plato, Aristotle, Augustine, Aquinas, Spinoza, and Leibniz. I strongly recommend Pedersen's book to anyone interested in engaging with Schleiermacher's thought on these topics. I consider it a major contribution to the history of theology, and also to systematic theology and philosophical theology."

– **Robert Merrihew Adams**, Clark Professor of
Philosophy, Emeritus, Yale University

"Schleiermacher's Theology of Sin and Nature presents an elegant, meticulous, and persuasive account of sin that is compatible with modern natural sciences on the one hand and with ancient notions of value, nature, and agency on the other. By these lights, this father of modern theology begins to look less Kantian, yet still distinctively modern and decidedly ancient. This project thus calls for a reconsideration of the prevailing historiography of modern theology. So too, it exemplifies the potential for fruitful conversations between theology and the natural sciences today. Like Pedersen's first book, The Eternal Covenant, this text will enlighten the novice and veteran reader of Schleiermacher and garner the interest of systematic, historical, and moral theologians broadly."

– **Emily Dumler-Winckler**, Professor of Constructive
Theology, St. Louis University

"How should Christians think about the origin of sin and evil, in light of evolutionary history? Schleiermacher's Theology of Sin and Nature presents a compelling defence of Schleiermacher's theology, as both deeply engaged with ancient and medieval Christianity and as providing unique, constructive resources for today. Pedersen proves a trustworthy and helpful guide through complex theological debates, and his clear and fluid prose makes for an enjoyable read. I thoroughly recommend this volume to both students and researchers in historical and systematic theology."

– **Joanna Leidenhag**, Lecturer in Science-Engaged
Theology, University of St. Andrews

"In this provocative work, Daniel Pedersen compels the reader to consider again the rather neglected doctrine of sin in the work of Friedrich Schleiermacher. With forensic care and rare insight, he exposits the contours, presuppositions, and implications of Schleiermacher's innovative treatment of hamartiology. But far more than this, Pedersen demonstrates Schleiermacher's account of human agency and failure to lie in unanticipated proximity to traditional Christian accounts and in remarkable sympathy with ancient philosophical ethics, yet to be radically removed from typical Kantian positions. The result is a work which requires the reader not only to reconsider their evaluation of Schleiermacher's work on sin, but also to rethink the very historiography of modern theology."

– **Paul T. Nimmo**, King's Chair of Systematic Theology, University of Aberdeen

Friedrich Schleiermacher (1768–1834), often considered the father of modern theology, is known for his attempt to reconcile traditional Christian doctrines with philosophical criticisms and scientific discoveries. Despite the influence of his work on significant figures like Karl Barth, he has been largely ignored by contemporary theologians. Focusing on Schleiermacher's doctrine of sin, this book demonstrates how Schleiermacher has been not only misinterpreted but also underestimated, and deserves a critical re-examination.

The book approaches Schleiermacher on sin with respect to three themes: one, its power to transcend an intractable metaethical dilemma at the heart of modern debates over sin; two, its intended compatibility with natural science; and three, a re-evaluation of its place, and so Schleiermacher's place, in the history of theology. It solves and dissolves problems arising simultaneously from natural science, confessional theology, ethics, and metaphysics in a single, integrated account using Schleiermacher's understudied thought from his dogmatics *The Christian Faith*. In contrast to the account sometimes given of modern theology as marked by a break with "Greek metaphysics," Schleiermacher's account is shown to stand in stark contrast by retrieving, not excising, ancient thought in service of an account of sin adequate to natural science.

This is a vital rediscovery of a foundational voice in theology. As such, it will greatly appeal to scholars of modern theology, theological ethics, and the history of modern Christianity.

Daniel J. Pedersen is Research Fellow in Systematic Theology at the University of Aberdeen, UK. His work focuses on modern theology, especially the thought of Friedrich Schleiermacher, and issues in natural science, especially evolution. He is the author of *The Eternal Covenant: Schleiermacher on God and Natural Science* (2017).

Routledge New Critical Thinking in Religion, Theology and Biblical Studies

The *Routledge New Critical Thinking in Religion, Theology and Biblical Studies* series brings high quality research monograph publishing back into focus for authors, international libraries, and student, academic and research readers. This open-ended monograph series presents cutting-edge research from both established and new authors in the field. With specialist focus yet clear contextual presentation of contemporary research, books in the series take research into important new directions and open the field to new critical debate within the discipline, in areas of related study, and in key areas for contemporary society.

Paradoxical Virtue
Reinhold Niebuhr and the Virtue Ethics Tradition
Edited by Kevin Carnahan and David True

Theology and Evolutionary Anthropology
Dialogues in Wisdom, Humility, and Grace
Edited by Celia Deane-Drummond and Agustín Fuentes

Racism and the Weakness of Christian Identity
Religious Autoimmunity
David Kline

Past and Present Political Theology
Expanding the Canon
Edited by Dennis Vanden Auweele and Miklos Vassányi

Schleiermacher's Theology of Sin and Nature
Agency, Value, and Modern Theology
Daniel J. Pedersen

For more information about this series, please visit: www.routledge.com/religion/series/RCRITREL

Schleiermacher's Theology of Sin and Nature

Agency, Value, and Modern Theology

Daniel J. Pedersen

Routledge
Taylor & Francis Group

LONDON AND NEW YORK

First published 2020
by Routledge
2 Park Square, Milton Park, Abingdon, Oxon OX14 4RN

and by Routledge
52 Vanderbilt Avenue, New York, NY 10017

Routledge is an imprint of the Taylor & Francis Group, an informa business

© 2020 Daniel J. Pedersen

British Library Cataloguing-in-Publication Data
A catalogue record for this book is available from the British Library

Library of Congress Cataloging-in-Publication Data
A catalog record for this book has been requested

ISBN: 978-0-367-18898-6 (hbk)
ISBN: 978-0-429-19905-9 (ebk)

Typeset in Sabon
by Apex CoVantage, LLC

For my parents

Contents

Acknowledgments

For valuable insight, advice, criticism, and encouragement, I would like to thank David Chao, Davey Henreckson, Ina Linge, Calli Micale, Jaqueline Mariña, Esther Reed, John Rose, Jeff Skaff, Derek Woodard-Lehman, Phil Ziegler, and anonymous reviewers.

Several more colleagues gave exceptional and invaluable thought and attention to most or all of the text of this work: Christopher Lilley, Charles Guth, Layne Hancock, and Paul Nimmo. My very great thanks to each of them.

In addition, I would like to extend special thanks to Bob Adams, who was instrumental in the improvement of this work, and extraordinarily generous in time and attention to it, and who, who so deeply inspired my work with his own.

This work would also not have been possible without personal support from John Perry and financial support from the Templeton Foundation's Science-Engaged Theology program. My sincere thanks to both.

And, finally, my greatest thanks of all to Christopher Southgate for all his help with this work in the form of his time, his attention, his criticism, his wisdom, and his friendship.

Abbreviations

GL   Friedrich Schleiermacher, *Der christliche Glaube nach den Grundsätzen der evangelischen Kirche im Zusammenhange dargestellt.* Second edition. Edited by Rolf Schäfer. Berlin: Walter de Gruyter, 2008.

1 Introduction

Schleiermacher's theology of sin and nature

Protarchus: Offer up a prayer, then, and think.
Socrates: I am thinking, Protarchus, and I believe that some God has
              befriended us.

– Plato, *Philebus*

It is often assumed that sin can be unnaturally bad only if it is impossible
to give a causally complete account of its beginnings: for to attempt to give
such an account is to treat what is bad as good by treating nothingness as
being, and so to offer an explanation of vice which is itself vicious.

Almost all traditional Christian accounts of sin share this assumption.[1]
And to decline it we are required, it is thought, to deny one or more of its
most basic premises: that being as being is good, that good cannot corrupt
good, and that, therefore, sin cannot have a natural origin, even in the will.[2]
Distinctly modern accounts of sin are typically thought to stand in contrast
to these traditional premises. Instead, to be modern means to hold to the
contrary: that to be and to be good are not necessarily the same, that value
is not ultimately natural and nature not analytically valuable, and that, in
the end, the will might even sin of natural necessity.[3]

These competing assumptions define debates over sin in the theology of the
last two centuries. Indeed, theology in modernity is marked by the disjunc-
tion. A choice must be made between positivism about value and skepticism
about nature's relation to the good on the one hand versus the convertibility
of the transcendentals and the deficiency of sin's determining causes – often
packaged with a burdensome natural history – on the other hand.

The choice between these two alternatives is of such concern because
it is of such consequence. In this one topic we find value and goodness,
agency and freedom, nature and grace so tightly entwined with one another
that even to begin to give a doctrine of sin commits the theologian to far-
reaching entailments. The doctrine of sin is, therefore, both fraught and
freighted. Its weight and its burden go hand in hand. And the starkness of
the choice between characteristically modern accounts and their traditional
discontents is a consequence of the genuine insight that so much depends on
claims and commitments made here.

In truth, however, neither kind of account is necessary and neither is sufficient. And it is Friedrich Schleiermacher's theology of sin which shows this to be so. He demonstrates how to transcend this stalemate by giving an account of sin and its origins which is, in principle, causally complete *together with* its relation to the natural world and to the good, including that blessed communion with God to which human nature is divinely ordered – an alternative which requires none of the naivety of the unqualified affirmation of the tradition, or the folly of its flat denial.

This work is about Schleiermacher's theology of sin and its relation to nature and the natural. In it I offer an interpretation and defense of Schleiermacher's incorporation of the best of what is ancient and what is modern to solve or dissolve problems arising simultaneously from natural science, confessional theology, agency, and metaphysics in a single, integrated account. In so doing, Schleiermacher shows us how to rise above some of the most vexing puzzles and problems facing both traditional and modern theological accounts of sin.

Tradition and modernity, value and nature

Having outlined the problem and Schleiermacher's promise to address it in broad terms, in this section we reexamine the problem more closely. I argue that the fundamentally different conclusions of traditional and modern accounts of sin are, somewhat counterintuitively, the consequence of an important shared assumption. Schleiermacher's refusal of this assumption, and how his declination plays out, is a running theme of this work.

Disagreement about sin and sin's origins appears intractable. On the one hand are theological traditionalists: roughly those subscribing to ancient, medieval, and Reformation-era accounts of sin and sin's origins, broadly in agreement with readings provided by any number of church fathers, though especially the well-developed account given by Augustine of Hippo. On the other hand are theological moderns: those theologians who, since roughly the turn of the nineteenth century, have abandoned the story of the fall of Adam and Eve from paradise as what Augustine called "an account of what actually happened."[4] These include the giants of Christian dogmatics like Barth and Tillich, to those such as theology-and-science specialists, seeking specific coherence between natural history and Christian theology. These categories are not, of course, neat. They are broad characterizations. But each camp agrees that, in general, its opposite is not only in error but also committed to some deeper, abiding conceptual fault.

The greatest of these disagreements is over how to conceive of and relate notions of *value* to notions of *nature*. This axiological and metaphysical dispute connects to sin first through questions of sin's origins and God's good creation, and second through questions of what it means for sin to be *bad*. Which is to say, sin relates nature to value both through origins and through ends. Here is how.

Traditional Christian accounts of the origins of sin hold that all inherit their sin, or tendency to sin, from the original humans, who were themselves sinners by no will but their own. Evil is explained by sin; and sin, in turn, is explained by fault. Such accounts provide enormously powerful explanations of the relation of nature to value.

On such accounts, natures norm. Things are most valuable when they exhibit the power and beauty intrinsic to their kind. That is, *what* things *are* determine what it means to be an excellent individual of a kind *x* – and hence what it means to be a vicious member of the same.[5] The very notion of the species in question implies its proper ends, the ends in reference to which all its activities are well or ill.[6] On such accounts what is natural is, by definition, what is in accordance with a determining terminal good or goods. Therefore, the determinate ends that constitute natures are the good which is logically prior to any privation or deficiency, and descriptions of facts *are always already* value laden. And, so, descriptions of nature and value are, as the medievals put it, *convertible*.[7] Nature and value are, at bottom, one and the same.

This philosophical commitment has theological consequences. In traditional Christian accounts of sin, it is intimately connected with a theological commitment to the goodness of creation: *in the beginning* the world was very good. The convertibility of nature and value results in the logical and chronological priority of the goodness of human nature such that the good deprived must have existed as natural before its privation.[8] Traditional accounts of sin, therefore, require a subscription not only to the priority of the good but also to the stronger claim that logical goodness and chronological goodness parallel one another precisely: what I will call the *principle of parallel priority*.

Accordingly, as much of the tradition has it, not only is sin unnatural but also *no* sin or sinner can have any natural *origin*. For every nature is created, and every created thing traces back to the *divine* nature. Sin, according to the tradition, cannot be so linked. All humans are sinners voluntarily, whether they be the first humans, who were so by no will but their own, or all others, who have inherited their disordered loves.[9] Sin is wholly unnatural, both with respect to our origins and with respect to our ends. It is perversity and nothingness and God has no part in its genesis.[10] The relation of God to sin must be *causally incomplete*. In other words, it must not be possible, in principle, for sin to be traced through any created nature to God. Therefore, supplying any created cause of sin threatens to disrupt this elegant, powerful, but delicate account which secures the normativity of natures and the priority of the good.

A range of findings in natural science propose to supply just such causes of sin and, consequently, threaten this very disruption. Traditional theologians must, on their own grounds, explain the unnaturalness of sin and do so in such a way that is true to the facts of natural history. But what we know from history and the natural sciences counts against any change in human nature from an Edenic state – *of any kind*.[11] Thus, theologians are forced to explain sin deprived of the resources that are needed to do the explaining well. Being determined to maintain the priority of the good and the normativity of natures, traditional accounts of sin must struggle to tell a story of a historical fall, or fall-like events (whether individual or social[12]), all because of their commitment to the principle of parallel priority: that, because the chronological and logical priority of the good *must* parallel one another precisely, the priority of the good and normativity of natures can be maintained only if there was, in fact, a sinless human past.

Enter *modern* accounts. In opposition to traditional accounts, they are characterized by theories of sin without recourse to a change in human nature.[13] Two broad sub-strategies emerge. First, there are those accounts which make sin ontologically basic to human beings as created. Reasoning from the premise that what is chronologically prior is natural, they conclude that sin must be natural in the sense that it is *constitutive* of what it means to be a human.[14] Second, there are those accounts which refuse the priority of the good and the normativity of natures altogether. Reasoning in the opposite direction, moderns instead conclude that, because there never was a prior time in which humans were without sin, there is no logically prior norming nature. Often the relation between origins and ends is left unclear. We are sometimes thrown back to freedom (typically conceived in libertarian terms[15]) or, worse, to straightforwardly positivist accounts of the relation of facts to values, which is to say, to the belief that there is no necessary relation.[16] Lost is a robust connection between human nature and human ends. And with that connection lost, many accounts of sin which cohere with natural history, or which offer causally complete accounts of sin's origins, struggle to articulate the relation of nature to the good, or else they neglect the task altogether.

The result is a dilemma. Theologians must either secure an adequate account of value at the expense of a sufficient account of sin's origins (often through dubious claims of natural and/or historical fact), or forfeit an adequate account of value in exchange for a causally complete account of sin. Criticism and defense of these alternatives are the hallmark of disagreement over sin in the last two centuries.

Let us, however, pause for a moment and take notice of something rarely, if ever, recognized. Upon inspection, what we find is that a striking accord lies behind this dilemma. Both kinds of accounts share an assumption about how nature must relate to value – if it is to relate at all. Namely, traditional *and* modern accounts of sin (and their variants) implicitly agree that the normativity of natures and the priority of the good can be sustained only on the further assumption of the *principle of parallel priority*: that the *logical* priority of the good requires the parallel *chronological* priority of the good. That is, both kinds of accounts agree that the unnaturalness of sin must apply equally to both sin's ends *and* its origins, and that, without unnatural origins, appeal cannot be made to the normativity of natures and the priority of the good. Traditional accounts thus strive to sustain a story of sin's origins which authorizes these further commitments, while modern accounts, declining a change in human nature, also feel obliged (or at least encouraged) to decline traditional axiological commitments. It is thus one and the same assumption that causes the defects of *both* traditional and modern accounts. If this assumption could be abandoned or emended, the debate in its current form could not exist. And if this principle and its alternatives could be made explicit, a way would lie open for two centuries of disagreement to be transcended.

It is on this point that the present work departs most from both romantic accounts of tradition and triumphal accounts of modernity. In fact, it does not support *any* existing meta-narrative of the relation of tradition to modernity because both traditional and modern accounts of sin and nature depend on precisely the same, shared, doubtful premise. It is this basic assumption about how nature, value, and sin *must* relate (if they are to relate) that generates the disagreement about sin and sin's origins that has come to appear not only characteristic of theology in the last two centuries but also a *necessary* characteristic. If it can be shown that this disagreement depends on this premise, and that this premise is dubious, then it can be shown that this disagreement is unnecessary. This is, perhaps strangely, good news to traditionalists and moderns alike. Far from rejecting either (or both), it can be shown that we are entitled to much of the best of the tradition *and* to much of the best of modernity – provided we rightly sort the wheat from the chaff.

This is exactly what Schleiermacher's account of sin and nature shows to be the case: that, in contrast to prevailing wisdom, the affirmation of the unnaturalness of sin with respect to human ends does not entail the denial of its natural origins. Which is to say that sin is a deficiency, but a specific deficiency, and a deficiency with causes sufficient to bring it about. Schleiermacher's account of sin and nature demonstrates just how to sustain this distinction in service of *both* an adequate account of nature *and* an adequate account of value. Hence, Schleiermacher's account of sin shows how to overcome intractable disagreement between traditional and modern accounts of sin by declining the premise which both traditional and modern accounts take to be necessary, the principle of parallel priority.

Schleiermacher's alternative account

Schleiermacher's account of sin and nature is deliberately fit for this purpose. It is no coincidence that the "father of modern theology" was concerned to criticize and improve older accounts of sin. It is no coincidence that the champion of an "eternal covenant" between science (especially natural science) and the Christian faith was troubled to free the doctrine of sin from scientific inadequacy and to improve it with scientific knowledge. And it is no coincidence that the church theologian and esteemed Plato scholar sought to do so without compromising his first principles and the ultimate unity of ethics and physics.[17] Recent accounts of sin of many kinds have not been fully satisfactory because neither traditional nor modern accounts have gotten to the bottom of *both* internal and external challenges together and at once. Schleiermacher has. And he has succeeded because he *sought* to do so without falling into the traps that have plagued so many accounts of sin. His is an account tailored to show the coherence of key Christian claims about sin and nature without sacrificing adequate notions of power, agency, and value, which is to say, without failing to connect sin to nature in respect to both ends and origins. Substantiating and defending these claims is the subject of this work.

The reader, however, could be forgiven for some initial skepticism. Is not Schleiermacher the purveyor of a will undetermined by nature and the natural in a Kantian vein?[18] Further, is his not *the* ancestral account of all socially grounded accounts of sin and sin's origins?[19] And finally, is not his account of the Christian faith in general, and therefore sin in particular, instead meant to *avoid* questions of natural science, and, therefore, the natural origins of sin?[20] On all counts, the answer is no. I say much more about all three in the following chapters, but for now let me address them briefly, in reverse order.

In regard to questions of the relation of the Christian faith to natural science, this work both relies on and supports my interpretation in *The Eternal Covenant*. In that work, I argued that Schleiermacher ultimately intends his "eternal covenant" to unify, not segregate, the Christian faith and natural science, and that this consequence follows from Schleiermacher's first principles as revealed in the concrete particulars of his doctrine of God and his doctrine of creation. Much of my argument in the present work refers to and deepens, and, in some places, depends upon these arguments made in *The Eternal Covenant*.

Three such claims advanced in that work have special relevance here. First, I showed that Schleiermacher gives an account of the God-world distinction where a thing is either part of the mutually determined and mutually determining causal nexus that is the world, or not; and that there is only one thing that is not: God.[21] This entails, according to Schleiermacher, that nothing but God satisfies the criterion of ultimate responsibility central to so many libertarian accounts of free will.[22] Second, I show that Schleiermacher's account of *divine* freedom is even more radical: that God only ever acts of *absolute necessity*, and that this kind of necessity accordingly redounds to all created things and their acts.[23] Consequently, there is never a genuine possibility which is not actualized; and *that*, in turn, implies that Schleiermacher cannot even have conceived of freedom as requiring the principle of alternate possibilities.[24] He cannot have done so because, according to him, *there are no unactualized possibilities*.[25] Finally, I argue that these strong claims are in service of a vision of the unity of ethics and physics, an account where value and power are each necessary conditions of a complete account of reality.[26] These claims serve to support the thesis advanced in the present work that Schleiermacher gives a causally complete account of sin's origins. And my interpretation of Schleiermacher on sin serves to support the claims of my former work in turn.

Other claims in this present work are purely internally supported. One is that Schleiermacher does not, in fact, offer a socially *grounded* account of sin.[27] I also argue, contrary to some, that it is a virtue of his account that he does not.[28] What makes this position particularly important is that many of the arguments Schleiermacher offers against a fall (either Satanic or Adamic – see Chapters 2 and 3, respectively) rely on premises which are as incompatible with the idea that sin *began* from the wills of large groups of sinners as they are with the idea that sin began from the wills of only one or two. Such arguments therefore also serve to eliminate socially *grounded* (as distinct from socially perpetuated and exacerbated) accounts of sin as adequate substitutes.

I argue, instead, that all sin is, for Schleiermacher, not only of ultimately natural origin but also naturally determined.[29] On the matter of freedom and its compatibility with determination, this work joins a running interpretive dispute in Schleiermacher scholarship. I disagree with one well-established interpretive tradition of reading Schleiermacher *principally* as a kind of Kantian, in particular with respect to matters of freedom, agency, normativity, and value.[30] Since it is a central point of my overall thesis that Schleiermacher's account is superior to others in part because he offers what is in many respects a more traditional (i.e., ancient, not Kantian) account of these matters, sustaining my interpretation is key to my normative claims. Throughout this work I refer to great past thinkers and some of their contemporary adherents whose thought is more recognizably echoed than Kant's, especially the thought of Thomas Aquinas, Aristotle, and, of course, Plato.

In order to support my claims, this work, like *The Eternal Covenant*, proceeds on the principle that use reveals meaning. That is, when we examine the specific content of Schleiermacher's doctrines and how he takes his arguments to work, and look to what uses he puts them, we come to understand more perfectly what he means by the explicit claims he makes and the underlying assumptions upon which he tacitly depends. This procedure best reveals and coordinates principles and content. Specifically, Schleiermacher's theology of sin, more than any other doctrinal *locus*, reveals his true commitments regarding agency and freedom, and is likewise crucial in understanding his overall account of nature, the natural, normativity, and the value of which sin is privative.

Having defended an interpretation of Schleiermacher's theology of sin through an examination of his first principles and their coherence with his contentful claims and their consequences, I also, where appropriate, defend the adequacy of Schleiermacher's account against objections, real and imagined, and advertise its virtues. This, perhaps more than anything, distinguishes this work from the weight of scholarship on the topic.[31] I aim to show that Schleiermacher's account is, at least on the whole, superior to other accounts in light of the probable truth of the matter: that sin is as old as human being. And my interpretation of the specifics of Schleiermacher's theology of sin and nature both supports and is supported by this evaluation. What I propose is an account of the relation of sin to nature and the natural as an organic whole: of *Schleiermacher's* means and ends, content and form. If so, this account is able to explain how sin is natural with respect to human origins, yet unnatural with respect to human ends, how a sufficient account of value can be sustained in light of what is an in-principle causally complete account. Since meaning and use are mutually informing, the sufficiency of Schleiermacher's account is evidence of his intent.

The result is an interpretation and defense of Schleiermacher's theology of sin and nature with consequences which go far beyond Schleiermacher scholarship. Schleiermacher, I argue, gives us a satisfactory account of the natural origins of sin while sustaining sin's unnaturalness with respect to human ends by offering an account of the sufficient causes of the deficiency that is sin as part of a teleologically directed providential order. In order to do so, Schleiermacher deploys sophisticated notions of agency, normativity, and value too often ignored or omitted from recent work on sin, especially sin in relation to nature. On these points Schleiermacher's account of sin and nature also provides superior options in dogmatics and theological ethics.

This consequence depends on my reading, which, as noted earlier, promises to join lively debates in Schleiermacher interpretation on matters of agency, freedom, and determination. But on sin specifically, the conversation is remarkably quiet. Only two book-length works on Schleiermacher's doctrine of sin have ever been written.[32] Relatively few articles have joined them.[33] Book sections are brief.[34] My interpretation does not wholly disagree with any one of these accounts, but disagrees in part with nearly all of them, and offers a more complete account than any. Describing Schleiermacher's account of sin well promises to inform our views of his theology as a whole.

This leads to a final aim of this work: an intervention in the historiography of modern theology. Many textbook accounts make mention of Schleiermacher's place at (or near) the head of something called modern theology, a purported movement which stands in contradistinction to the ancient and medieval theology informed largely by Greek natural philosophy and first principles.[35] The advent of modern theology, it is noted, is at least partly due to the authority of the new natural science, but it is also marked by its relation to the thought of Immanuel Kant, whose thought displaces older beliefs and categories.[36] Though both marks can distinguish modern theology, they do not always do so, or do so in the same way. For instance, in relation to natural science, modern theologians might be taken to recoil from questions of science, or they might seek to embrace them. Likewise, modern theologians might be seen as marked by their adoption of Kant, or merely their reaction to him. That nearly all theology after Kant was at least in some respect in response to him is not in dispute, but the degree to which Kant was affirmed is not consistent. And yet, many of the most important accounts of modern theology at least suggest that, as theological epoch-maker, Schleiermacher stands to Kant largely as enthusiastic adopter. By implication, modern theology is itself largely marked by the embrace of Kantian categories and commitments. And so, accounts of modern theology often begin with Schleiermacher and end with Ritschl – literally or proverbially.[37]

The interpretation I offer stands against this trajectory of historiographical tradition. This work showcases Schleiermacher's *arguments*. Schleiermacher's arguments are evidence of his commitments. His commitments locate his position in the pantheon of theologians. This location shows that much historiography is stereotyped and that Schleiermacher's place in the history of doctrine is often seen in error in two respects.

In the first respect, I show that Schleiermacher does not, and indeed cannot, subscribe to a libertarian account of the will, so characteristic of Kant and his later followers. This must be the case, I show, given Schleiermacher's criticism of traditional accounts of the fall of the Devil and the fall of Adam – criticism that relies on his own account of agents always and ever acting voluntarily *for antecedent sufficient reasons*. I combine this with Schleiermacher's explicit claims on the matter to demonstrate that, in fact, Schleiermacher does not hold any distinctly Kantian notion of freedom and agency, but rather follows that tradition of thinking about the will traced through thinkers like Spinoza, Leibniz, and Aquinas to Aristotle and Plato.

In the second respect, I show that Schleiermacher's account of sin is distinct from purely ontologically basic accounts. By ontologically basic accounts I mean those which appeal to fundamental conditions of creatureliness or finitude (or the like) as the cause of sin. Though often different in detail, these accounts all hold in common the implication that, because sin is inevitable, it is also *naturally necessary*. And such accounts face objections regarding the naturalness of sin which are at least as dire as the objections to any account of sin which depends on an indeterminate will (though, ultimately, the two kinds of accounts merge: the will simply becomes another ontological basis of sin). I demonstrate the contrast with Schleiermacher's account by emphasizing the deficient or privative account of sin he explicitly describes and necessarily implies. Sin is not natural, but is instead an inhibited, hindered, or arrested condition of humans' proper ends. By distinguishing Schleiermacher's account from ontologically basic accounts, I show that Schleiermacher also cannot be located in what is often taken to be the main alternative to the tradition of the indeterminate will as the ultimate origin of sin.

In response to both types of misreading of Schleiermacher, I argue that Schleiermacher does not belong clearly or straightforwardly to *any* existing story of modern theology, and that his account of sin and nature makes this evident. This is above all because Schleiermacher's way of being modern, though doubtlessly in light of Kant in some ways, and importantly formed by his engagement with natural science, was not less ancient (or medieval, or early modern) for it all. In fact, I show that the novelty of Schleiermacher's account often lies in deploying *more* Greek thought than older theologians. For instance, Schleiermacher pits Aristotelian accounts of culpability and change against Augustinian accounts of the fall of Adam; and he gives recognizably Platonic accounts of the condition that is sin, of the moral psychology of sin, and of the role of sin and evil in a world providentially ordered by the good to the ultimate end of sharing its goodness as perfectly as possible. In crucial respects, Schleiermacher's way of being modern is to be *more ancient*.

Approach and outline

Last, a word on the procedure and order of this work. As in *The Eternal Covenant*, the sole source I aim to address is Schleiermacher's dogmatics, *The Christian Faith*. Though it is possible, even likely, that Schleiermacher's teaching on agency, normativity, and value is consistent across his works, or some selection of them, I am not here interested in either advancing or denying that thesis, and what Schleiermacher has to say elsewhere is immaterial to the topic at hand: sin and nature in his theology. Accordingly, my argument proceeds solely from the text of *The Christian Faith*, from its stated claims and necessary implications to an interpretation and defense of the same work. My challenge to those wishing to advance unified accounts of Schleiermacher's thought across some, or all, of his works is to prioritize the concrete particulars revealed in his theology in their own accounts. I proceed on the confidence that the wisdom of my own approach is borne out in content.

I make my case over six main chapters. In Chapters 2–4, I examine Schleiermacher's arguments against traditional accounts of sin and its origins. These serve not only to clarify exactly what Schleiermacher is rejecting and how far his criticism extends, but also to establish the principles on which his own alternative account proceeds. In Chapters 5–7, I show how Schleiermacher proceeds on the same principles to design and justify his own account. In Chapter 8, I draw these threads together in support of the claims I have made here.

Chapter 2, "Schleiermacher on the Fall of the Devil," examines Schleiermacher's treatment of the Satan tradition of explaining sin. By this means, it considers Schleiermacher's account of the will, reason, agency, and responsibility, and offers insights into Schleiermacher's treatment of authority. We learn not only that but also *why* the fall of the Devil has no explanatory power and should be rejected.

Chapter 3, "Schleiermacher on the Fall of Adam," continues these themes, only this time with respect to the ostensible first man, Adam. In this chapter we see the arguments from the previous chapter repeated and extended, but we also see the introduction of arguments against the possibility that sin introduces *any* change in human nature. We conclude the chapter by introducing the premise that underlies these arguments: the principle of sufficient reason.

Chapter 4, "Schleiermacher on the Fate of Deficient Causes," examines Schleiermacher's appeal to the principle of sufficient reason in contrast to an important traditional resource with its origin in Augustine's thought: the appeal to *deficient* causes. We examine this crucial difference from the Augustinian tradition, see what enormous work it does for Schleiermacher, and see why someone, following Schleiermacher, might be attracted to it – or even, why one who believes in God as described by Schleiermacher might find subscription to this principle necessary. At this juncture, we begin to see how, and in what sense, the principle of sufficient reason bears on questions of sin, value, and agency.

In Chapter 5, "Schleiermacher on the Origins of Sin," we shift from Schleiermacher's criticism of the fall of the Devil and the fall of Adam to his own alternative account of sin's origins. We not only discover that he proposes a grand evolutionary-developmental account of sin's genesis but also see how his reasons, which are often appeals to characteristically Augustinian concerns, illuminate his account as one of sin as arising through causes sufficient to explain sin – sin that nevertheless consists in a deficiency of value.

In Chapter 6, "Schleiermacher on What Sin Is," we examine in detail Schleiermacher's description of the state that is sin, how it yields sinful acts, and to what effect. We see, yet again, that Schleiermacher's position approximates very closely to that of the Augustinian tradition despite being couched in Schleiermacher's technical vocabulary. We also look to questions of the nature of sin and how its exercise relates to sin as a social phenomenon. Throughout we see that Schleiermacher consistently subscribes to sin as a sufficiently caused deficiency.

In Chapter 7, "Schleiermacher on Sin and Evil," we finally turn to that most vexing problem for any causally complete account of sin: namely, how sin and the evil which follows from it relate, through their origins, to God. After making my case for the content and coherence of Schleiermacher's teaching, I defend it against some of the most common objections by showing either that they are made in error, or else that they are consistent with teachings from Schleiermacher's own Reformed tradition and hence accrue no special burdens in comparison. Finally, I reconnect the sufficiency of sin's causes to matters of value once again and argue that, far from being severed from the good, it is in the perfect teleological ordering of the world to our ultimate ends that the unity of power and value, and the unity of divine justice and mercy, is found.

Finally, in Chapter 8, I conclude by integrating the content of the previous chapters into an overall picture of Schleiermacher on sin and nature. I show not only how such an interpretation is sustained by the conclusions of the previous chapters but also how Schleiermacher's thought on the matter provides unsurpassed resources for considering sin in light of nature in both senses. I end by reflecting on Schleiermacher's place in modern theology, and how not only his concrete claims but also the basis of his arguments becomes evidence for a very different picture of the father of modern theology, and hence of the story of modern theology as a whole.

Notes

1 See, for example, Aquinas, *Summa Theologica*, I–II, Q. 75, a. 1, resp.; Athanasius, *Against the Heathen*, I.2–3; *On the Incarnation of the Word*, IV–V; Augustine, *City of God*, XII.6–8; Irenaeus, *Against Heresies*, IV.37.1, 39.4; Calvin, *Institutes*, vol. 1, 241–49; Zwingli, "On Original Sin," 1–10.
2 Augustine, *City of God*, XI.17; XII.3.
3 The most influential versions of these themes derive from Immanuel Kant. See, for instance, *Critique of Practical Reason*, 5:41; *Critique of Judgement*, §§11, 15, 23; *Religion Within the Boundaries of Mere Reason*, 6:44. For a critical diagnosis along these lines, see MacIntyre, *After Virtue*. For a different diagnosis, see Dupré, *Passage to Modernity*.
4 Augustine, *The Literal Meaning of Genesis*, I.1, 168.
5 For a contemporary defense of this view in light of its supposed incompatibility with modern natural science and disability, see Porter, *Nature as Reason*.
6 See MacIntyre, *After Virtue*, 67–73, 96–99.
7 See Aquinas, *Summa Theologica*, Ia, Q. 5, a. 1, resp.
8 See Smith, "What Stands on the Fall?" 48–64.
9 Augustine, *City of God*, XIII.3.
10 Augustine, *City of God*, XII.1, 3.
11 For instance, recent work on human origins argues that many of humans' most wicked tendencies have analogues in our chimpanzee cousins and are thus best explained as natural inherited dispositions. See, for example, Wrangham and Peterson, *Demonic Males*, and Dolhinow, review of *Demonic Males*. Of course, not all natural scientists agree. See Marks, review of *Demonic Males*. For a reply to these objections, see Wilson et al., "Lethal Aggression in *Pan* Is Better Explained by Adaptive Strategies Than Human Impacts," 414–17; For a more roughly analogous analysis involving a more distant primate relative, see Hrdy, *The Langurs of Abu*.
12 It is often thought that social accounts of sin's origins are an alternative to a historical fall. In fact, they are in most relevant respects the same in kind, explaining the beginnings of sin through the past voluntary acts of human beings, and thus actually *traditional*, not modern accounts for our purposes. For the most important contemporary account in this vein, see Suchocki, *The Fall to Violence*. For a recent attempt to merge social with natural scientific considerations, see Deane-Drummond, "In Adam All Die?" 23–47.
13 For an overview of the variety of accounts on offer, see McFarland, "The Fall and Sin," 140–59.
14 See, for example, Kierkegaard, *The Concept of Anxiety*; Niebuhr, *The Nature and Destiny of Man*; Pannenberg, *Systematic Theology*, vol. 2; Tillich, *Systematic Theology*, vol. 2.
15 See, for example, Clayton, *In Quest of Freedom*, 133–64; Peterson, "Falling Up," 273–86. Also see Hick, *Evil and the God of Love*, 262–91.
16 See, for example, Messer's criticism of Holmes-Rolston in *Selfish Genes and Christian Ethics*, 86–88. See also Messer's nuancing of his position in *Selfish Genes and Christian Ethics*, 104–9. For a selection of similar accounts, see earlier.

17 See Schleiermacher, *Introductions to the Dialogues of Plato*, 299; Schleiermacher, *Lectures on Philosophical Ethics*, Introduction, final version, §59; 150–51.

18 For a recent defense of this view, see Mariña, "Where Have All the Monads Gone?," 477–505.

19 For example, see Vander Schel, "Friedrich Schleiermacher," 251–66; Nelson, *What's Wrong with Sin?* 15–48; McFarland, *In Adam's Fall*, 39–42.

20 For a synopsis of this debate see Dole, *Schleiermacher on Religion and the Natural Order*, 140, 144.

21 Pedersen, *The Eternal Covenant*, 69–97.

22 For an explanation and defense of libertarian free will specifically in terms of ultimate responsibility, see Kane, *The Significance of Free Will*, 60–78; "Libertarianism," 5–43.

23 Pedersen, *The Eternal Covenant*, 98–126.

24 That is, Schleiermacher cannot have conceived of freedom in classic libertarian fashion. Further, as earlier, Schleiermacher also cannot have conceived of freedom as requiring the condition of *ultimate responsibility* instead of, or in addition to, the principle of alternate possibilities. Thus, Schleiermacher's account of freedom is incompatible with all species of libertarian free will.

25 See Schleiermacher, *GL* §54.2, 54.4; *The Christian Faith*, 213, 216; Lamm, *The Living God*, 150.

26 Pedersen, *The Eternal Covenant*, 151–79.

27 For example, see McFarland, *In Adam's Fall*, 39–42; Vander Schel, "Friedrich Schleiermacher," 257–58.

28 Again, see Nelson, *What's Wrong with Sin?* 15–18.

29 In contrast, see Vander Schel, "Friedrich Schleiermacher," 255–56.

30 For Kant's account of freedom in respect of specifically theological concerns, see Insole, *Kant and the Creation of Freedom*.

31 Criticism of Schleiermacher's doctrine of sin is plentiful. See, for example, Barth, *The Theology of Schleiermacher*, 195–97; Mackintosh, *Types of Modern Theology*, 83–85; McFarland, *In Adam's Fall*, 42; Wenz, "Sünde und Schuldbewusstsein," 9–56; Westhelle, "Original Sin Revisited," 385–93; Wyman, "Testing Liberalism's Conceptuality," 138–54.

32 Flöel, *Der Entwicklungsgedanke in Schleiermachers Lehre von der Sünde*; Vance, *Sin and Self-Consciousness in the Thought of Friedrich Schleiermacher*.

33 Walter Wyman is the most prolific author in the topic. See Wyman, "Sin and Redemption," 129–49; "Rethinking the Christian Doctrine of Sin," 199–217; "Testing Liberalism's Conceptuality," 138–54. See also Bader, "Sünde und Bewußtsein der Sünde," 60–79.

34 See, for instance, Christian, *Friedrich Schleiermacher*, 114–17; Nelson, *What's Wrong with Sin?* 18–29; Vial, *Schleiermacher*, 97–99.

35 See, for example, Grenz and Olson, *20th Century Theology*, 15–23, 39–51; Mackintosh, *Types of Modern Theology*, 4–5; McCormack, "Introduction: On Modernity as a Theological Concept," 1–19; Welch, *Protestant Thought in the Nineteenth Century*, vol. 1, 1–5.

36 See Grenz and Olson, *20th Century Theology*, 24–31; Mackintosh, *Types of Modern Theology*, 19–30; McCormack, "Introduction," 2–6; Welch, *Protestant Thought in the Nineteenth Century*, 30–48; Wilson, *Introduction to Modern Theology*, 27–37.

37 This despite the fact that almost all recognize that Ritschl defined himself against Schleiermacher in at least some important respects. See Barth, *Protestant Theology in the Nineteenth Century*, 425–661; Grenz and Olson, *20th Century Theology*, 39–62; Mackintosh, *Types of Modern Theology*, 60–100, 138–80; Welch, *Protestant Thought in the Nineteenth Century*, vol. 2, 1–30, especially 8–10.

References

Aquinas, Thomas. *Summa Theologica*. Translated by the Fathers of the English Dominican Province. New York: Benziger Bros., 1947.

Athanasius of Alexandria. *Against the Heathen*. Vol. 4. Edited by Philip Schaff and Henry Wace, translated by Archibald Robertson. From Nicene and Post-Nicene Fathers, Second Series. Buffalo, NY: Christian Literature Publishing Co., 1892.

———. *On the Incarnation of the Word*. Vol. 4. Edited by Philip Schaff and Henry Wace, translated by Archibald Robertson. From Nicene and Post-Nicene Fathers, Second Series. Buffalo, NY: Christian Literature Publishing Co., 1892

Augustine of Hippo. *The City of God*. The Works of Saint Augustine, Part I, Vol. 7. Translated by William Babcock. New York: New City Press, 2013.

———. "The Literal Meaning of Genesis." In *On Genesis*. The Works of Saint Augustine Part I. Vol. 13. Translated by Edmund Hill, O.P. New York: New City Press, 2002.

Bader, Günter. "Sünde und Bewußtsein der Sünde: Zu Schleiermachers Lehre von der Sünde." *Zeitschrift für Theologie und Kirche* 79, no. 1 (1982): 60–79.

Barth, Karl. *Protestant Theology in the Nineteenth Century*. Translated by Brian Cozens and John Bowden. London: SCM Press, 1972.

———. *The Theology of Schleiermacher*. Edited by Dietrich Ritschl, translated by Geoffrey W. Bromiley. Grand Rapids, MI: Eerdmans, 1982.

Calvin, John. *Institutes of the Christian Religion*. Vol. 1. Edited by John T. McNeill, translated by Ford Lewis Battles. Louisville: Westminster John Knox, 1960.

Christian, C. W. *Friedrich Schleiermacher*. Peabody, MA: Hendrickson, 1979.

Clayton, Philip. *In Quest of Freedom: The Emergence of Spirit in the Natural World*. Göttingen: Vandenhoeck & Ruprecht, 2009.

Deane-Drummond, Celia. "In Adam All Die? Questions at the Boundary of Niche Construction, Community Evolution, and Original Sin." In *Evolution and the Fall*, edited by William T. Cavanaugh and James K. A. Smith. Grand Rapids, MI: Eerdmans, 2017.

Dole, Andrew. *Schleiermacher on Religion and the Natural Order*. Oxford: Oxford University Press, 2010.

Dolhinow, Phyllis. "Review of *Demonic Males* by Wrangham and Peterson." *American Anthropologist* 101, no. 2 (1999): 445–46.

Dupré, Louis. *Passage to Modernity: An Essay in the Hermeneutics of Nature and Culture*. New Haven: Yale University Press, 1993.

Flöel, Ernst. *Der Entwicklungsgedanke in Schleiermachers Lehre von der Sünde*. Dissertation. Ludwigs-Universität Gießen, 1913.

Grenz, Stanley J., and Roger E. Olson. *20th Century Theology: God and the World in a Transitional Age*. Downer's Grove, IL: Intervarsity Press, 1992.

Hick, John. *Evil and the God of Love*. Third edition. London: Macmillan, 1977.

Hrdy, Sarah Blaffer. *The Langurs of Abu: Female and Male Strategies of Reproduction*. Cambridge, MA: Harvard University Press, [1977] 1980.

Insole, Christopher J. *Kant and the Creation of Freedom: A Theological Problem*. Oxford: Oxford University Press, 2013.

Irenaeus of Lyons. *Against Heresies*. Vol. 1. Edited by Alexander Roberts, James Donaldson, and A. Cleveland Coxe, translated by Alexander Roberts and William Rambaut. From Ante-Nicene Fathers, Buffalo. NY: Christian Literature Publishing Co., 1885.

Kane, Robert. "Libertarianism." In *Four Views on Free Will.* Oxford: Blackwell, 2007.

———. *The Significance of Free Will.* New York: Oxford University Press, [1996] 1998.

Kant, Immanuel. *Critique of Judgement.* Translated by Werner S. Pluhar. Indianapolis: Hackett, [1790] 1987.

———. *Critique of Practical Reason.* Revised edition. Translated by Mary Gregor. Cambridge: Cambridge University Press, 2015.

———. *Religion Within the Boundaries of Mere Reason And Other Writings.* Translated and edited by Allen Wood and George Di Giovanni. Cambridge: Cambridge University Press, 1993.

Kierkegaard, Søren. *The Concept of Anxiety: A Simple Psychologically Orienting Deliberation of the Dogmatic Issue of Hereditary Sin.* Edited and translated by Reidar Thomte and Albert B. Anderson. Princeton, NJ: Princeton University Press, 1980.

Lamm, Julia A. *The Living God: Schleiermacher's Theological Appropriation of Spinoza.* University Park, PA: Pennsylvania State University Press, 1996.

MacIntyre, Alasdair. *After Virtue: A Study in Moral Theory.* London: Bloomsbury Academic, [1981] 2007.

Mackintosh, Hugh R. *Types of Modern Theology: Schleiermacher to Barth.* New York: Charles Scribner's Sons, 1939.

Mariña, Jacqueline. "Where Have All the Monads Gone? Substance and Transcendental Freedom in Schleiermacher." *The Journal of Religion* 95, no. 4 (2015): 477–505.

Marks, Jonathan. "Review of *Demonic Males* by Wrangham and Peterson." *Human Biology* 71, no. 1 (1999): 143–46.

McCormack, Bruce L. "Introduction: On Modernity as a Theological Concept." In *Mapping Modern Theology: A Thematic and Historical Introduction,* edited by Kelly M. Kapic and Bruce L. McCormack. Grand Rapids, MI: Baker Academic, 2012.

McFarland, Ian A. "The Fall and Sin." In *The Oxford Handbook of Systematic Theology,* edited by Kathryn Tanner, John Webster, and Iain Torrance. Oxford: Oxford University Press, 2007.

———. *In Adam's Fall: A Meditation on the Christian Doctrine of Original Sin.* Oxford: Wiley-Blackwell, 2010.

Messer, Neil. *Selfish Genes and Christian Ethics: Theological and Ethical Reflections on Evolutionary Biology.* London: SCM Press, 2007.

Nelson, Derek R. *What's Wrong with Sin? Sin in Individual and Social Perspective from Schleiermacher to Theologies of Liberation.* London: T&T Clark, 2009.

Niebuhr, Reinhold. *The Nature and Destiny of Man: A Christian Interpretation.* Vol. I. London: Nisbet, 1941.

Pannenberg, Wolfhart. *Systematic Theology.* Vol. 2. Translated by Geoffrey W. Bromiley. Edinburgh: T&T Clark, 1994.

Pedersen, Daniel J. *The Eternal Covenant: Schleiermacher on God and Natural Science.* Berlin: De Gruyter, 2017.

Peterson, Gregory. "Falling Up: Evolution and Original Sin." In *Evolution and Ethics: Human Morality in Biological and Religious Perspective,* edited by Phillip Clayton and Jeffrey Schloss. Grand Rapids, MI: Eerdmans, 2004.

Porter, Jean. *Nature as Reason: A Thomistic Theory of the Natural Law.* Grand Rapids, MI: Eerdmans, 2005.

Schleiermacher, Friedrich D. E. *Introductions to the Dialogues of Plato*. Translated by William Dobson. London, 1836.

——. *Lectures on Philosophical Ethics*. Edited by Robert B. Louden, translated by Louise Adey Huish. Cambridge: Cambridge University Press, 2002.

Smith, James K. A. "What Stands on the Fall? A Philosophical Exploration." In *Evolution and the Fall*, edited by William T. Cavanaugh and James K. A. Smith. Grand Rapids, MI: Eerdmans, 2017.

Suchocki, Marjorie. *The Fall to Violence: Original Sin in Relational Theology*. New York: Continuum, 1994.

Tillich, Paul. *Systematic Theology*. Vol. 2. Chicago: University of Chicago Press, 1957.

Vance, Robert. *Sin and Self-Consciousness in the Thought of Friedrich Schleiermacher*. Lewiston, NY: Edwin Mellen, 1994.

Vander Schel, Kevin M. "Friedrich Schleiermacher." In *T&T Clark Companion to the Doctrine of Sin*, edited by Keith L. Johnson and David Lauber. London: Bloomsbury T&T Clark, 2016.

Vial, Theodore. *Schleiermacher: A Guide for the Perplexed*. London: Bloomsbury T&T Clark, 2013.

Welch, Claude. *Protestant Thought in the Nineteenth Century*. Vol. 1. Eugene, OR: Wipf and Stock, [1972] 2004.

——. *Protestant Thought in the Nineteenth Century*. Vol. 2. New Haven: Yale University Press, 1985.

Wenz, Gunther. "Sünde und Schuldbewusstsein: Zur Hamartiologie in Schleiermachers Glaubenslehre." *International Journal of Orthodox Theology* 8, no. 2 (2017): 9–56.

Westhelle, Vítor. "Original Sin Revisited: Schleiermacher's Contribution to the Hefnerian Project." *Currents in Theology and Mission* 28, no. 3–4 (2001): 385–93.

Wilson, John E. *Introduction to Modern Theology: Trajectories in the German Tradition*. Louisville: Westminster John Knox, 2007.

Wilson, Michael L., et al. "Lethal Aggression in *Pan* Is Better Explained by Adaptive Strategies Than Human Impacts." *Nature* 513 (2014): 414–17.

Wrangham, Richard, and Dale Peterson. *Demonic Males: Apes and the Origins of Human Violence*. New York: Houghton Mifflin, 1996.

Wyman Jr., Walter E. "Rethinking the Christian Doctrine of Sin: Friedrich Schleiermacher and Hick's 'Irenaean Type'." *The Journal of Religion* 74, no. 2 (1994): 199–217.

——. "Sin and Redemption." In *The Cambridge Companion to Friedrich Schleiermacher*, edited by Jaqueline Mariña. Cambridge: Cambridge University Press, 2005.

——. "Testing Liberalism's Conceptuality: The Relation of Sin and Evil in Schleiermacher's Theology." In *Ethical Monotheism, Past and Present: Essays in Honor of Wendell S. Dietrich*, edited by Theodore M. Vial and Mark A. Hadley. Providence, RI: Brown University Press, 2001.

Zwingli, Ulrich. "On Original Sin." In *On Providence and Other Essays*, edited by William John Hinke. Durham, NC: The Labyrinth Press, [1922] 1983.

2   Schleiermacher on the fall of the Devil

> The ridiculous is in short the specific name which is used to describe the vicious form of a certain habit; and of vice in general it is that kind which is most at variance with the inscription at Delphi.
>
> – Plato, *Philebus*

Traditional accounts of the origins of sin, accounts that explain sin as due to the creature's fault, often do not rest content with explaining *human* sin solely in terms of *human* fault. Instead, the tradition often also includes the Devil in its accounts, and often for a combination of two reasons. First, the Devil is an actor in scripture, the historical confessions of the church, and the history of doctrine. He is simply among the standard cast of characters and, in consequence, many feel obliged to give the Devil some part. Second, and more importantly, the Devil is often given a specific role: the role of tempter. In this role, the Devil joins traditional accounts of the origins of sin as not only an actor but also an explainer. That is, the temptation by the Devil at least partially explains the rebellion and sin of Adam. The Devil's bad influence serves to make Adam's sin more plausible, more understandable if not more reasonable.

The usefulness of the Devil is, however, not so clear. The fall of Adam is supposed to account for why there is sin and evil while *denying* that anything is sinful or evil by nature. In order to do this, the tradition relies on Adam's willed rebellion. In telling a story of this rebellion the Devil, perhaps, offers some help. But with that help a further problem arises: the origins of *the Devil's* sin. Any account of the Devil's sin that terminates in the Devil's wicked nature will not do, for then evil does, after all, have its origins in an evil nature. Therefore, the Devil must, like Adam, have been created good, but must also, like Adam, have fallen. The story of the Devil's change from good angel to enemy of God and tempter of Adam is what the fall of the Devil tradition, in turn, seeks to explain.

This chapter explores Schleiermacher's arguments against the necessity, usefulness, and even coherence of the fall of the Devil tradition. These arguments are not, however, significant only in providing reasons to reject traditional accounts of the Devil and his fall. They are also parts of, and precursors to, Schleiermacher's criticisms of the traditional accounts of the origins of human sin. Historically, the fall of the Devil has often served as not only an account of the events that led to human sin but also a thought experiment on the conditions of sin in a clear case. Schleiermacher's criticism of the fall of the Devil likewise serves as just such a thought experiment – only in reverse. Schleiermacher aims to show that the fall of the Devil can be ignored in Christian dogmatics, or even actively eliminated, *and* that explanations, including but not limited to the fall of the Devil, for human or any other sin will always end in absurdity, infinite regress, or such triviality that they can simply be excised. His argument against the fall of the Devil thus begins a series of arguments against a whole *class* of potential explanations.

Finally, in the case he makes, we begin to see one of the most important yet overlooked patterns in Schleiermacher's argument – namely, that Schleiermacher's case relies on decidedly traditional (especially Aristotelian) accounts of agency and action for its force – accounts which also begin to fill out the equally ancient account of value he champions. Schleiermacher's argument against the fall of the Devil tradition is an anti-traditional account on remarkably traditional premises.

The Devil reduced

Schleiermacher's regard for traditional accounts of the Devil, and its related use in explaining the fall of humanity, is unambiguously negative. "The idea of the Devil as developed among us," he says, "is so unstable that we cannot expect anyone to be convinced of its truth; but besides, our Church has never made doctrinal use of the idea."[1] In the sections that follow, Schleiermacher aims to vindicate this claim. And, leaving the historical point aside – it is not at all obvious that the church has made no doctrinal use of the idea of the Devil[2] – Schleiermacher advances a powerful reductive argument.

That argument has as its target the following view: "The principal points in this idea are these: that spiritual beings of a higher perfection [*hoher Vollkommenheit*], who lived in close relationship with God, voluntarily [*freiwillig*] changed from this state to a state of antagonism and rebellion against God."[3] The idea of the Devil Schleiermacher has in mind, therefore, is assumed to include a range of traditional claims and assumptions, not merely reflective of one thinker.[4] First, the idea of the Devil includes the *origin* of the evil within the Devil. That is, the very idea of the Devil includes the transition, the change, the fall, from good to evil angel. Second, the idea of the Devil implies that this transition is one for which the Devil, and the evil angels more generally, must be culpable – hence the emphasis on their *voluntary* antagonism and rebellion. And finally, the idea of the Devil implies that the Devil enjoyed a high degree of perfection prior to this rebellion.

"Now," Schleiermacher warns, "we cannot ask anyone to accept this [account] unless we are first able to help them over a great number of difficulties."[5] What are these difficulties? He outlines several.

Schleiermacher's first line of criticism is one that strikes against the account of motivation and judgment the fall of the angels supposes:

> First, as to the so-called fall of the good angels: the more perfect these good angels are supposed to have been, the less plausible it is to find any motive [*Motive*] but those presupposing a fall already, e.g. pride and envy. Now also, if, after the Fall, the natural powers of the Devil remained undiminished, it is impossible to conceive how persistent wickedness could exist side by side with superlative insight [*Einsicht*].[6]

That is, the plausibility of the fall of the good angels depends on telling a story about how something went wrong. The good angels, after all, took an extraordinary turn for the worse. But in order for this story to make sense as a story of the good angels' own action, they have to act with a motive, an aim.[7] Otherwise, it is not an intentional action that can be ascribed *to the angels*. Their fall might have happened by accident, or they might have even been victims.[8] But the whole point of the story of the fall of the angels is to secure the origins of evil in voluntary, and hence culpable, action which can be ascribed to some agent, but not to God. Here, according to Schleiermacher, is where things start to unravel.

The account of the fall of the good angels depends for its explanatory power on the angels falling from perfection. But, Schleiermacher claims, any account of *motivation* which suffices to explain their wicked voluntary act necessarily *presupposes* some imperfection on the part of the agent. Otherwise there should be no reason for their fault in the first place; and without such a reason the good angels would have endured in their perfection. In this case, Schleiermacher offers arrogance and envy as candidate imperfections that might be invoked to explain the fall of the good angels, though any other fault could be substituted in this particular argument. Such faults would so explain. But the vices of arrogance and envy are themselves moral imperfections. Clearly, something is already defective on the part of an agent whose motivation is formed by them. Yet that very imperfection is what the fall, so motivated, is supposed to explain. To explain the fall by appeal to the vice of the fallen is not an explanation at all, but, rather, that which demands explanation.

The result, Schleiermacher thinks, is a deep incoherence in the account. Either the perfection of the good angels was not actually so, in which case there is no *change* to explain or be explained; or the good angels' perfection was genuine, but their fall was not, and could not, be rationally motivated – their intelligence could not have informed their wicked motives, for such insight would have prevented it. The angels might, of course, have still fallen, and even still willed to fall, but because no motive can be offered for their fall which is compatible with their "superlative insight" – because no good reason can be offered for their willing on the part of the thing willed – their fall cannot be properly voluntary.[9]

This last point is crucial. Notice that Schleiermacher's case is against the *motive* offered for a *voluntary* fall – the only account of the origins of sin that secures the culpability the traditional account requires. If the perfection of the good angels is maintained, and if a change occurred (i.e., if they fell), that change cannot have been voluntary because, on the supposition of their perfection, no angel could have been sufficiently motivated by such faults. Why? Because, to be truly voluntary, the aptness of the angels' judgment must be at least roughly indexed to the good of the thing willed. They must have acted in accordance with their judgment, and their judgment must at least somewhat accurately appraise the relative merits of various goods to be pursued.[10] In order for the angels to will to reject *God*, the supreme good who they were created to worship, something has to go very wrong. Either they: (1) somehow don't know that the good they reject is the supreme good; (2) or they do know the good they reject is supreme and reject it anyway. If, in the first place, they will what they will because they don't know how truly good the good they reject is, they act on the basis of ignorance. But the tradition denies this, and in any case, it does not generate the culpability the traditional account demands.[11] Yet, on the other hand, if they will what they will *knowing that the good they reject is best*, they still will for no *good* reason, and so irrationally. Because a voluntary action is one in which the good that is willed plays an essential role in determining action, to will with no good motive – that is, to be determined to action by a motive wholly inadequate to one's subsequent ends (distant or proximate) – is not properly voluntary.[12]

This last point deserves reiterating. Schleiermacher's reduction of the traditional account of the fall of the good angels relies on a specific, if implicit, notion of voluntary action. Actions are explained by motivations, by goods to be pursued. Voluntary actions, specifically, consist in self-conscious motivations and judgments. They are actions we could in principle give an answer to if asked, "Why did you do that?"[13] Given this account of voluntary action, the conditions for Schleiermacher's reduction are already included in his summary of the position he intends to attack, especially the condition that the fall of the good angels was, in fact, voluntary.

Now, alone this proves little. But as Schleiermacher cycles through the difficulties with his theory, each turns again and again on the plausibility of a *motive* correlated with questions about "insight" (or "understanding") – terms relating to judgment. Alternative accounts of voluntary action might not appeal to judgment to explain motive, motive to explain the determination of the will, but rather would simply appeal to the will itself as self-motivating. With his extensive appeals to the intellectual basis of motivation, Schleiermacher rejects this alternative, an alternative which will be considered further in the following chapters.

On Schleiermacher's grounds, therefore, any account of the fall of the angels which seeks to avoid the problem of a preexistent defect must appeal to ignorance (which is itself a preexistent, though non-culpable defect), or to irrational, and therefore, involuntary, action on the part of the angels. No truly uncorrupted angel could have *voluntarily* willed to rebel against God; and angels which already suffer corruption and defect fail to explain the origins of sin and evil. They are effect, not cause.

The same problems inherent in the account of the good angels' motivation also undermine the traditional account of the Devil post-fall. If the change that occurs in the fall diminishes the Devil's perfection, it must diminish his power, and vice versa. But the Devil's *insight* is a function of power and perfection alike since the Devil's insight is a power of judgment. That is, the *power* of judgment and its goodness are mutually implicative: to judge *well* is to have greater power of judgment, and vice versa. Diminish one and you diminish the other. Thus, the Devil, whatever power he enjoys post-fall, cannot enjoy that power with the same degree of perfection. And so, no account of the Devil, Schleiermacher argues, can simultaneously maintain the Devil's originally perfect power and his moral debasement at the same time. When the Devil is corrupted, his power is necessarily impoverished.

What is more, in the very act of rebelling the good angels show themselves to be already lacking in insight from the start. Schleiermacher explains:

> For such insight must, in the first place, have shown every conflict with God to be a completely useless enterprise. It can only be thought to afford a momentary satisfaction even to one lacking true insight, whereas the insightful, to undertake such a conflict and persist in it, must of necessity will to be and remain unblessed [*unselig sein und bleiben wollen*].[14]

Any being *truly* possessing insight would recognize rebellion against God to be in error.[15] Even a being enjoying only very poor understanding, let alone a properly intelligent being, could grasp the futility and evanescence of such conflict with the *Whence* upon which we depend absolutely. If the angels are, indeed, beings of a high degree of perfection, they must be intelligent. And if they were not, it is not clear that they were either very great beings in the first place, or rational agents who could act voluntarily.

For this reason nothing about Aquinas's influential argument[16] that the Devil's motivation consisted in a desire to be like God in a more modest sense satisfies Schleiermacher's objection – for the Devil should have known that rebellion, however modest, would lead to alienation, and if he couldn't have known better, he can't be culpable – hence Schleiermacher's wording of "*any* conflict with God" (emphasis added). Explanations like Aquinas' that the Devil's inordinate desire was with respect to the means of acquiring the divine likeness suffers from the same problem. If anything, it makes matters worse, for the wild disparity between the Devil's ends and means emphasizes the insanity of the whole act: *no* means used by the Devil could possibly accomplish what the Devil was after, and yet the Devil supposedly acted anyway – which serves only to reiterate the basic explanatory problems with which Schleiermacher began his criticism.

Further evidence for these commitments is found in Schleiermacher's elaboration on the conditions of the foregoing description of an intelligent being willing to remain unblessed. His regard of this notion as absurd is plain from the foregoing paragraph where Schleiermacher uses the idea as an argument-ender. But he also continues the thought in yet another reduction of the traditional account of the fall of the good angels.

Schleiermacher argues that should an intelligent being "will to be and remain unblessed," we should, again, have grave doubts about that being's agency. As he explains,

> This is precisely what is explained in someone as "possession," because no explanation of their attitude can be derived from the subject themself. Is it not, then, still more impossible to find an explanation in the most perfect condition of the angels – by whom would *they* be possessed?[17]

The introduction of the idea of "possession" [*Besessenheit*] is clever, but not tricky. In the context of the Devil it is literarily fitting to use this term over others. But the criticism is not limited to possession, in a strict sense, alone. Rather, the idea of possession stands for any number of conditions in which a rational being might not act voluntarily. We might substitute "insanity" very aptly. What these conditions hold in common is essential: that "no explanation of their [a possessed person's] attitude can be derived from the subject themself." If no explanation of the agent's attitude can be derived from the agent, their actions are not only not voluntary but also not even *their own* actions.

Plainly, should an agent be possessed, their actions would not be voluntary.[18] But to argue *from* the conclusion that, because the Devil was acting nonvoluntarily, he was, therefore, possessed, begs the question. So how can we make sense of Schleiermacher's move from a description of judgment and will to a conclusion that the agent in question is no longer acting voluntarily? To do this we need to supply more premises than Schleiermacher outlines explicitly, premises that Schleiermacher simply assumes.

Once more the key transition in this argument is from an absurd motivation to non-voluntary action. Importantly, it is the absurdity of the motivation which suffices to *make* the action non-voluntary. But why? The answer is, once more, that Schleiermacher is using an account of motivation and judgment in which motivation regards the relative merits of goods to be pursued. That is, what is being judged is the best thing to do; and agents pursue what they judge best. That does not mean their judgment is infallible. Agents often err in their judgments about the best. But it does mean that, in order to act voluntarily, agents must at least have good reason to *think* that the goods they pursue are best, not merely arbitrary reasons, but good reasons on the part of the thing under consideration – regardless of whether those things, in fact, turn out to be best. Agents' judgments about, and inclinations toward, the relative goodness of things to be pursued amount to motives. And a crucial test of irrationality, and hence involuntariness, is whether agents respond in appropriate sorts of ways to plausible reasons.

The decision the good angels supposedly make in their rebellion is a kind of insanity (or non-culpable ignorance) on this account because it is a voluntary action willed on the basis of a supposedly intelligent, insightful judgment about the best which is not merely in error but the *very worst* judgment possible, one devoid of *all* merit and *utterly* contrary to the angels' good: that the best course to pursue is one of permanent alienation from God. Indeed, the judgment is so inept that it is impossible to explain why any agent would even think it *could* be a good to pursue. Such a motive would have to be based on judgment devoid of all intelligence and insight. It would be the self-conscious pursuit of an extreme ill with *no* adequate basis in the agent's assessment of the merits of what was willed. That is *why* "no explanation of their attitude can be derived from the subject himself." Any explanation of the Devil's attitude would be in terms of the goods pursued; but *there are no goods* to adequately explain that attitude. The Devil's rebellion is, instead, either the result of ignorance or a kind of insanity, like eating rocks or yelling at the sun. As insanity, it cannot, at the same time, be rational; and as irrational, it cannot be voluntary.[19]

The criticism of the fall of the Devil as amounting to "possession" does two things. First, it shows the incoherence of the idea of a voluntary rebellion from God from the side of its motivation, apart from the vexing questions about how motivation connects to the perfection of the agent. The agent's perfection is not germane in cases of possession or insanity because, since the agent does not act voluntarily, the agent no longer properly *acts* in the relevant sense. Second, as possession shows more clearly than insanity (though not more truly), in order to explain the fall of the good angels, we would have to look to at least some *extrinsic* cause. And not only does this, too, contradict the traditional account of the angel's rebellion as voluntary, but it also begins an infinite regress. We would then have to ask, "by whom would they be possessed," and so on, *ad infinitum*. Any account with any agent, or set of agents, as the root cause of rebellion against God will face the same formal problems. On the version of will, motivation, and judgment Schleiermacher holds, such explanations will always terminate in non-culpable ignorance, insanity, or other non-voluntary conditions.

If the Devil did fall, it was not voluntary, and not even clear that the Devil's fall was the Devil's own doing – that is, an *action*, even if non-voluntary, ascribable *to the Devil*. That is, if *no* explanation of an agent's actions can be derived from the agent themselves (see earlier) such an action not only fails the test of reasonableness necessary to generate its voluntary status but also fails the more basic criterion of *control* also necessary for an action to be ascribed to an agent. Absent all control, supposed actions are at most suffered by an agent. The exception is *indirect* control agents can have over their passions, and so forth, through care, planning, habit cultivation, and so forth. But in the case of the Devil, any culpability-generating indirect control for which the Devil could be held responsible would then need to be explained by prior failure and so on, thus beginning an infinite regress. In consequence, the only kind of control that can apply in this situation is *direct* control, which possession or insanity rules out.[20]

Schleiermacher's next criticism strikes against the explanatory power that the fall of the Devil is supposed to provide. On the traditional account, the fall of the original humans is at least partly explained by their temptation by an already-fallen Satan. The efficacy of this temptation is, in turn, explained by the Devil's supremely dangerous power. But, according to Schleiermacher, the necessary conditions for the fall of Satan undermine his power. "Again," he argues,

> if the Devil at the time of his fall lost the finest and purest intelligence [*Verstand*] (and it is indeed the greatest derangement [*Zerrüttung*] to become the bitterest and most obdurate enemy of God after being God's friend), then it is inconceivable, on the one hand, how through one aberration of the will [*Verirrung des Willens*] the intelligence [*Verstand*] could be forever lost, unless the error was already due to a lack of intelligence [*Mangel an Verstand*]; and on the other hand, how could the Devil, after such a loss of intelligence, be so dangerous an enemy? For nothing is easier than to contend with senseless wickedness.[21]

Beginning with the identity of power and goodness united under the concept of perfection, as well as with the argument that any moral fault presupposes a lack on the part of the agent, Schleiermacher deflates the fall of the Devil, if there was such a fall, into an ineffectual one. The result would be a being of mere "senseless wickedness": senseless because it could be due only to utter lack of intelligence and insight, "the worst possible derangement," that one would will to become God's enemy. Because this ignorance is an imperfection of both goodness and power – the two are treated as one under the "high degree of perfection" – to explain the fall of the Devil in this way is to degrade his power in proportion to his wickedness. The greater the fall, the greater the Devil's impotence. And as the Devil's power diminishes, so too does the explanatory power of the theory. If the Devil is supremely wicked, theories of his fall are, then, supremely useless.

Schleiermacher's attack does not end there, though. On the traditional account of the fall of the Devil, it was not the Devil alone who fell but a host of angels, the Devil among them. This, according to Schleiermacher, causes yet more trouble for the traditional account.

Even if it is possible to articulate a coherent account of the fall of a good angel, a further problem arises for the theory of angelic rebellion: explaining the fall of one group of angels in distinction from those who did not fall. That is, explaining why *only some* angels fell. "For if they were all alike," Schleiermacher says, "and in that case no special personal motive [*besondere persönliche Motive*] could be felt by the group, how is it to be explained that one group sinned and the other did not?"[22] On the one hand, besides the idea that angels are distinguished only according to number,[23] the traditional account of the fall of the angels depends on the idea that there is no *prior* reason for their fall.[24] Otherwise, the complete explanation for their fall must at least partially depend on something extrinsic to the angels' wills, such as their differing natures or circumstances or some other condition. But in order to rule out the fall by reason of prior disposition or circumstance, the angels must all be identical in the relevant respects. They must be equal in perfection, alike in circumstance, and so on. Yet, on the supposition of their equality, it is impossible, Schleiermacher argues, to offer a reason sufficient to generate voluntary action as to why some angels fell but others did not because explanations of the eventual difference of the condition of good and bad angels begins in their intrinsic identity in all the relevant respects. This relevant sameness makes all difference in their actions utterly arbitrary. Because explanations that begin and end with the angels' equality are arbitrary, they are, in the final analysis, no explanation at all. Such explanations do not, and cannot, by their own admission, offer reasons on the part of the angels for why some, but not all, of those angels fell. In order to explain the differing actions of identical beings, we would need to have recourse to extrinsic conditions, but this is exactly the kind of explanation the fall of the angels denies – and is meant to exclude in principle.

Appeals to the instability of the angels' wills do not make this account more intelligible. And any hope of making sense of the angels' initial actions in light of their effects simply magnifies the explanatory lack of the account. *Why* the bad angels did what they did and the good angels did otherwise is, instead, all the more puzzling when one considers the extreme circumstances they cast themselves into, the permanence of those circumstances, and so on – circumstances which, again, the intelligence and insight of beings of a high degree of perfection would have been able to anticipate. As Schleiermacher says,

> It is certainly no less difficult if we assume that, prior to the fall of one group, all the angels may have been in a partially unstable state of innocence, but that one group because of one deed [*That*] have been forever judged and condemned while the other groups, because of their resistance have been for ever confirmed and established, so that henceforth they cannot fall.[25]

The notion of a will, equally unstable among all the angels, makes the division of angels into fallen and not fallen arbitrary and inexplicable, or else natural and inevitable. In consequence, the theory of the fall of the good

angels turns out to demand far more in explanation than it offers in explanatory help.

Beyond explaining the initial actions that led to the fall of the good angels
lies the problem of explaining the *present* actions of the wicked angels. This
argument is from the futility of the angels' opposition to God.

> [W]ith regard to the condition of the angels after the fall, it is difficult
> to see how the two following ideas can be held consistently: The fallen
> angels, already oppressed by great ills and expecting still greater, at the
> same time out of hatred to God and to relieve their feeling of distress,
> engage in active opposition to God, while yet they are unable to effect
> anything except by God's will and permission, and thus would find
> far greater alleviation for their distress as well as satisfaction for their
> hatred of God in absolute inactivity.[26]

That is, motivated by hatred and suffering, the evil angels oppose God in
an effort to better their condition. This is both unhelpful in offering relief
and ineffective in principle, for nothing – including the opposition of the
evil angels – falls outside the will of God. The angels are thus said to pursue
an aim which is both useless and impossible and this supposedly suffices to
explain their ongoing rebellious activity.

At least two things are going on here. First, the coherence of the account
of angelic opposition is attacked, once again, on the basis of the wicked
angels' motivation. Their actions are supposedly motivated by hatred to
oppose God, from which, perhaps, a certain satisfaction arises. But the consequences of their rebellion are, in fact, distress and suffering. Their continued rebellion yields only more of the same – or worse. According to the
notion of their continued rebellion they pursue opposition to God as a good,
but according to that same theory, they derive, and could derive, only ills
from their pursuit. Once again, the supposed good the wicked angels pursue
is good in no way; and so their pursuit of it – now not the initial pursuit,
but their *continued* pursuit – is a kind of insanity, or other deep irrationality,
which utterly undermines their agency.

Schleiermacher's second point is against the very idea of a creature, however great, *actually* opposing God: the sole omnipotent being and that upon
which all depend absolutely. Since everything exists and acts only by virtue
of the divine preservation, even the rebellion of the wicked angels could
proceed only with divine permission. The alternative portrays God and the
wicked angels as univocal, competitive, causes and thus destroys the fundamental feeling of absolute dependence at the heart of Christian faith.[27] Thus
the opposition of the wicked angels is necessarily futile, and futile at every
step. They can never, in principle, oppose God. Therefore, not only is the
plausibility of their motivation once more called into question, but also the
only reasonable thing they *could* be motivated to do under such hopeless
conditions is *literally nothing*. Their only recourse is "absolute inactivity"

which, if even possible,[28] would exclude them from the mischief of subjecting humans to temptation.

Finally, Schleiermacher attacks the idea of a political unity of fallen angels, the basis of the teaching that the wicked angels comprise a community of opposition to God and temptation to humans of which Satan is prince. He asks,

> Finally, should the Devil and his angels be thought of as a kingdom [*Reich*], and thus working in a coordinated way, although only outwardly and mostly in human affairs, now, with the limitations already outlined and generally acknowledged, such a kingdom is inconceivable [*nicht zu denken*] unless the overlord [*Oberherr*] is omniscient [*allwissend*] and foreknows what God will permit; and besides, not only does the evil in one person mostly hinder the same evil in another, but in each person one evil hinders another.[29]

Though Schleiermacher does not say so, it is clear from context that he believes it is impossible, or at least false, that the Devil enjoys omniscience; therefore, the idea of a kingdom of fallen angels is inconceivable. However, even if it is plain what he thinks, this last claim of Schleiermacher's is not obviously a good argument. How might the foregoing passage – which is all Schleiermacher devotes to this specific question – be considered persuasive?

The first sub-argument is simply another appeal to the futility of opposing God. Because all action, including opposition to God, can proceed only as compatible with the divine determination, the only way to succeed in the efforts to tempt ascribed to the evil angels would be if those angels knew which of their efforts God would allow to succeed, and to pursue them accordingly. In order to know this, the argument goes, the leader of said kingdom must be omniscient. The manner in which this ends the argument suggests that Schleiermacher finds such notion absurd, as indeed he should, since he argues in §55 that the full conditions of omniscience can be satisfied only by God, as the one being on whom everything depends absolutely.[30]

The second argument is less obscure and more to the point. Here Schleiermacher claims that "not only does the evil in one person mostly hinder the same evil in another, but in each person one evil hinders another." This argument is against the possibility of a political union or commonwealth of truly evil beings, as well as against the efficacy of their common pursuits. The (again tacit) premise at work here is that kingdoms, or political unions, depend on cooperation. The Devil and his angels are, in contrast, always necessarily hindering both one another and even themselves. Because their wickedness necessarily hinders their individual, and especially their collective, pursuits, they could not successfully constitute a kingdom.

Now, the plausibility of this last claim is not obvious. History supplies ample examples of humans engaged in wicked cooperative endeavors. Some of these evil kingdoms might even appear to have been unhindered or even empowered by their wickedness. In order to sustain this argument, Schleiermacher would have to deny that these evil kingdoms were, in fact, empowered, or even unhindered, *by their wickedness*. He would have to claim something like the following: that, for example, the power of the Soviet Union under Stalin was due not to Stalin's bloodlust or the state's cruelty and capriciousness but to the unrelated virtues of the Russian people or the better side of communism. What wickedness there was in Stalin's regime did not enhance Soviet power, but diminished it. Moreover, in the case of the kingdom of evil angels, evil is amplified beyond the worst human wickedness. Stalin did many evil things, but he fought for at least some genuine goods, told some genuine truths, and so on. But, according to Schleiermacher, the extreme derangement of the fallen angels deprives them of more and more of these powers the greater their descent. Cooperative endeavors, like individual actions, depend on the power of their contributors. If Schleiermacher is right – and many will want to contest this sort of account – then because the loss of the angels' perfection entails the loss of their power (as earlier), the loss of their perfection likewise entails the loss of their power to cooperate. Indeed, in denying the evil angels power and insight, and so the ability to recognize and attain individual goods, Schleiermacher has already denied them the ability to act effectively in pursuit of common goods.

All told, Schleiermacher has given powerful reductive arguments directed at several of the most important aspects of the traditional teaching regarding the fall of the Devil. Schleiermacher's arguments aim to undermine the internal plausibility of that fall itself as well as the explanatory work it is supposed to do in accounting for the origins of evil generally and human sin in particular. But what are Schleiermacher's aims in so doing?

The Devil in dogmatics

In the section following his arguments against the fall of the Devil, Schleiermacher says more about the purpose of these arguments and their relevance for Christian dogmatics. Yet the significance of what he claims goes beyond his particular dogmatics and the rules he sets himself.

> "There are two ways, in particular," he says, "in which a doctrinal use might be made of this conception. The evil in man may be traced back to the prior evil in Satan and explained by it; and the Devil may be represented as active in the punishment of sin."[31]

That is, the two distinct doctrinal uses are: one, that the Devil may be used to explain human sin; or two, that the Devil may be seen as the agent punishing sin. "Our confessions, however, are too cautious to base anything concerning this doctrine on so hazardous an idea," Schleiermacher claims.

> As regards the former, they [the confessions] only group the Devil with the wicked by making him their leader, in which case the presence of evil

in Satan does not clarify the explanation [*Erklärung*] of evil in humanity, and the latter requires just as much explanation as the former. In
other passages, moreover, if evil is traced back to the temptation of
Satan, the purpose is less to provide an explanation than a modification
of the opinion that the Devil was instrumental in putting quite another
creature in place of the original human.[32]

That is, Schleiermacher claims that the authority of the confessions is not
touched by either use of the Devil in doctrine because those confessions do
not, themselves, advance the relevant sorts of explanations. Whether this is
true is open to debate. Nevertheless, what Schleiermacher means to say is
clear enough: appeals to the authority of the confessions can be dismissed
because they are not *about* the same thing.

Schleiermacher makes the same case for minimizing the role of the Devil
in scripture,[33] though I will not repeat his arguments passage by passage
here. Suffice it to say, he regards every mention of the Devil in scripture as
explicable in a way that does not require either that the Devil explains the
origins of sin or that the Devil punishes sin. This section follows the same
pattern as those passages dealing with the confessions: scripture, like the
confessions, is underdetermined with respect to the traditional account of
the fall of the Devil. Because scripture does not require the accounts Schleiermacher aims to dismiss, it cannot, he thinks, be used as leverage against
his arguments. These claims are, again, highly contestable.

Interestingly, however, Schleiermacher advances another, different set of
claims regarding the Devil as instrument of divine punishment.

> If, again, here and there the power and might [*Macht und Gewalt*] of
> the Devil is included under the punishment of sin, on the one hand we
> find that this does not have any special bearing on the deliverance of
> man from sin and its punishment, and we might as well speak simply
> of the influence of evil apart from a personal overlord of evil; on the
> other hand, if the power [*Macht*] of the Devil (and his greatest power
> lies in tempting to sin) were a result of sin [*eine Folge der Sünde*], then
> when he accomplished his greatest act of temptation he must have been
> powerless [*ohnmächtig*] – which is also inconsistent. Elsewhere, how-
> ever, punishment too is represented as something that the devil and the
> wicked have in common. And again, the fairly frequent idea that the
> Devil is the instrument of God in the punishment of the wicked is incon-
> sistent with his antagonism to the divine purpose.[34]

Unlike the cases regarding the origins of sin and evil, Schleiermacher freely
admits that the confessions have something to say about the Devil as the
instrument of punishment. Even so, he does not admit the doctrine, and that
difference is worth noting. In this case, the doctrine is either deemed sub-
sidiary to more important concerns, reduced to uselessness, or reduced to
incoherence *despite* Schleiermacher's admission that the confessions make

use of the idea. In this case at least, argumentative considerations *override* confessional authority.

This difference becomes still more noteworthy in the context of Schleiermacher's parting line from the section regarding the first use of the doctrine of the Devil: that of explaining the origins of sin and evil in humanity. "But, indeed," he says, "Letting oneself be tempted presupposes aberration and evil, so that the explanation [by satanic temptation] appears to be no explanation at all."[35] It is not *merely* that we may be free to ignore the doctrine. It is, rather, a doctrine that explains *nothing*, a doctrine without a reason for being. And the obvious implication is that a doctrine with no explanatory use is one which *should* be excised.

So, which position is Schleiermacher advancing overall? Is the Devil simply a non-necessary postulate for Christian dogmatics? Or is the Devil actively explained away in virtue of the *reductio ad absurdum*, infinite regress, and Ockham's razor arguments that Schleiermacher makes? The weight of Schleiermacher scholarship has emphasized the former: that Schleiermacher's dogmatic decisions are explicable exclusively, or at least mainly, in light of the methodological constraints he proposes for Christian dogmatics.[36] In this case, that means that the absence of such theories of the Devil in the confessions would be the most relevant factor. And this interpretation has merit. Schleiermacher clearly appeals to the lack of a "doctrinal use of the idea" by the Church.[37] On this interpretation, Schleiermacher's reductive arguments could be read as arguments against the narrow and specific claim that these theories of the Devil are necessarily included in Christian dogmatics because they are certainly and necessarily features of the Church's confessions, and so on. If they are not necessary, they may be discarded.

Nevertheless, the second option, that Schleiermacher is advancing a case against theories of the Devil *in spite of* what the confessions may say, also has its virtues. Indeed, very few of Schleiermacher's foregoing arguments conclude *only* that x or y part of the Satan tradition can be dismissed because the relevant authorities, like the confessions, don't appeal to them. Instead, the bulk of Schleiermacher's case opposes the teachings of the Satan tradition on the basis of their internal inconsistency or by eliminating those teachings by showing that they, in fact, do not do worthwhile explanatory work.

The best view is probably a combination of the two options. That is, Schleiermacher advances some arguments independently of worries about authorities, relying only on incoherence and infinite regress arguments. These arguments do not fall outside the methods of dogmatics he has laid out for himself, but neither are they reducible to those methods. In other cases, however, he also does rely in part on appeals to things like the confessions to support his arguments – only not quite in the way scholars have usually thought.

Rather, Schleiermacher's minimalist approach to authorities does important work in his arguments from the principle of economy. Because economy is a virtue only if all things are equal, we might, for instance, feel *obliged* to include an account of the Devil should the confessions or scripture clearly teach it – even if it is not necessary to account for human sin and evil. What I take Schleiermacher to be doing by playing down the role of the Devil in the confessions and scripture is minimizing our explanatory obligations to those authorities. The less the confessions and scripture require an account of the fall of the Devil, the more powerful the arguments from economy become. In service of his overall case, method and argumentation are, therefore, organically related. The prolegomena of *The Christian Faith* set favorable conditions for *some*, but not all, of his arguments which otherwise might not be as persuasive.

On the whole then, Schleiermacher advances a two-pronged attack against the traditional account of Satan's fall – especially against the use of the Devil to explain human evil and sin. It is, Schleiermacher argues, an incoherent account, an insufficient account, and, besides, nothing about scripture or the confessions requires it. It cannot or at least does not work, and even if it could, it need not. Yet crucially, these are *two different* arguments against two different things, not two arguments against the same thing, because the things they are supposed to explain are different. Schleiermacher's Ockhamistic reduction is actually a double reduction: the Devil does not do the explanatory work he is supposed to do (and so can be eliminated), *and* there is no need to posit the existence of such a creature in the first place. This explains a puzzle in Schleiermacher's presentation – namely, that Schleiermacher argues his stronger claim first, and his weaker claim second. This is a very odd rhetorical structure. One would normally reverse this order of argumentation, ending on the strongest claim. However, the oddness of this structure disappears when it becomes clear what is happening: that these are two distinct arguments. What initially might look like a rhetorically weak follow-through to the incoherence of the fall of Satan tradition is, actually, the deliberate and methodical elimination of Satan as, first, *explanans*, and then as *explanandum*.

What, then, is the place of the Devil in Christian dogmatics? Schleiermacher's response is both subtle and striking. "Since," he explains,

> that from which we are to be redeemed remains the same (as does also the manner of our redemption) whether there be a Devil or no, the question as to his existence is not one for Christian Theology, but a cosmological question [*kosmologische*], in the widest sense of the word.[38]

The Devil is not properly a topic for *theology* at all. The question of the Devil is irrelevant; and not only that but also it is merely an object of curiosity discoverable by such means as curiosity provides. No, as Schleiermacher claims,

> [The question of the Devil] *is exactly like that of the nature of the firmament and the heavenly bodies* [*ganz gleich der über die Natur*

des Firmamentes und der Himmelskörper]. In Christian dogmatics [*Glaubenslehre*] we have nothing either to affirm or deny on such subjects; and so we are just as little concerned to dispute the conception of the Devil as to establish it.[39]

This second question, the *existence* of the Devil, is simply not a question for Christian theology. It can be left to those who study the nature and contents of the universe, only as relevant for Christian theology as the bare stuff of which the stars and planets are made.

Explaining the fall without a Devil

Schleiermacher's reckoning with the fall of the Devil is not included in the section of *The Christian Faith* treating of the origins of sin more generally, but it is not unconnected. In fact, in his compact discussion of the fall of the Devil he includes variations of arguments he will repeat in his treatment of the fall of Adam. Moreover, by reducing the fall of the Devil to incoherence, or at least uselessness, Schleiermacher has eliminated a potential explainer of Adam's fall. Because the fall of the Devil can't be explained, and itself explains nothing, appeal to the fall of the Devil makes the fall of Adam no more intelligible.

Indeed, as the tradition's most plausible source for the temptation of Adam, Schleiermacher's case against the fall of the Devil is an *a fortiori* argument against *any* attempt to explain human sin by appeal to some prior sin of some other creature. That is, it is a case against the whole class of *partially regressive* explanations of the origins of sin: accounts of the origins of sin that explain sin by what came before it, by some earlier cause, and yet which do not simply terminate in some created state. As we will see, whether the creatures under examination are angels or humans, Schleiermacher regards these sorts of explanations as unstable. They tend to point us backwards, to some earlier fall, some prior state or cause. And yet, at the same time, they require that we not proceed *all* the way back lest God become the author of sin. Schleiermacher's case against the fall of the Devil is, by extension, an argument against all such partially regressive explanations, accounts that point us back from Adam but do not point us back far enough.

Schleiermacher's reduction of the fall of the Devil also sets the stage for his attacks on the culpability that traditional accounts of sin generate from the fall. Again, by beginning with the Devil, Schleiermacher shows that even this most wicked of creatures' rebellion was not properly voluntary. The greater the good from which the evil angels rebelled and the greater their power to recognize it, the more severe the rebellion. Therefore, on the face of things, a greater punishment is deserved. But, as Schleiermacher argues, the truth is actually the reverse: the more severe the rebellion, the more irrational; but the more irrational the rebellion, the *less* voluntary. And an involuntary action is not one for which we are culpable. And if even *the Devil* is not culpable for his fall, it seems that Adam cannot be culpable either.

Finally, the fall of the Devil is not only part of the explanation of the origins of human sin. It is also, as we have seen, an account that shares important formal similarities. Most importantly, both the fall of the Devil and the fall of Adam attempt to explain evil in terms of sin, sin in terms of fault. Neither the Devil nor Adam was born a sinner. Their sin is, rather, in both cases, a work of the will. And both Adam and the Devil will to turn from the supreme good to lesser goods with profound consequences. Because of these formal similarities, the fall of the Devil functions as a clean canvas to think through the problems related to the fall of Adam. Just as the tradition has looked to the fall of the Devil for the conceptual structure that supports the fall of Adam, so when Schleiermacher seeks to dismantle traditional accounts of the fall of the Devil, he is already at work undermining traditional accounts of the origins of human sin.

Notes

1 *GL* §44; *The Christian Faith*, 161. Presumably the 'Church' Schleiermacher has in mind is the Evangelical (i.e., Protestant) Church, although, as we will see, his argument does not depend on a strict confessional limit.
2 See *GL* §45 for Schleiermacher's reply to this concern.
3 *GL* §44.1; *The Christian Faith*, 161. Translation revised.
4 See, for example, Anselm, *On the Fall of the Devil*, §4.; Aquinas, *Summa Theologica*, Ia, Q. 63, a. 5.
5 *GL* §44.1; *The Christian Faith*, 161. Translation revised.
6 *GL* §44.1; *The Christian Faith*, 161. Translation revised.
7 Schleiermacher's account tends to conflate motives, aims, and intentions as amounting to, or at least partially constituting, sufficient reasons for acting. Cf. Anscombe, *Intention*, 18–24. For a contemporary view more akin to Schleiermacher's in this respect, see Davidson, "Actions, Reasons, and Causes."
8 See the following chapter, "Schleiermacher on the Fall of Adam" for more on the correlation between acting on the basis of determining reasons and act ascription.
9 Or so Schleiermacher seems to imply. If not, it is not clear how his criticism of the fall of the Devil tradition, playing the good reasons for the evil angels' motivation off their voluntariness, is supposed to amount to an argument against the coherence of that tradition. But Schleiermacher clearly intends his arguments to expose incoherence. Therefore, this is most plausibly what he has in mind.
10 That is to say, Schleiermacher is appealing to what contemporary theorists characterize as appropriate responsiveness to reasons as a necessary condition of control and, therefore, of responsible agency. See Fischer and Ravizza, *Responsibility and Control*.
11 Culpable ignorance does no good here either since it, in turn, would need to be explained either by some prior *voluntary* negligence or else further ignorance, and so merely begin a regress to the true cause, or else be infinite and so no explanation at all. In any case, the kind of ignorance clearly presupposed is antecedent ignorance, which renders an act involuntary. See Aquinas, *Summa Theologica*, I–II, Q. 6, a. 8, resp.

12 For a developed version of this argument on Augustine's grounds applied to the fall of Adam, see Bowlin, "Hell and the Dilemmas of Intractable Alienation."

13 See Anscombe, *Intention*, 9–13; Aquinas, *Summa*, I–II, Q. 6, a. 1, resp; Audi, "Acting for Reasons."

14 *GL* §44.1; *The Christian Faith*, 161. Translation revised.

15 See Anselm, *On the Fall of the Devil*, §§22–24.

16 See Aquinas, *Summa Theologica*, Ia, Q. 63, a. 3, resp.

17 *GL* §44.1; *The Christian Faith*, 161. Translation revised.

18 For an important recent defense of this claim see Wolf, "Sanity and the Metaphysics of Responsibility."

19 See Bowlin, "Hell and the Dilemmas of Intractable Alienation," 198–200.

20 For an explanation of the account of agency this argument supposes see Jorati, *Leibniz on Causation and Agency*, 149–62. For a criticism of the control criteria and an argument that we can be justly blamed for involuntary sins see Adams, "Involuntary Sins."

21 *GL* §44.1; *The Christian Faith*, 161. Translation revised.

22 *GL* §44.1; *The Christian Faith*, 162.

23 For a refutation of this assumption see Aquinas, *Summa Theologica*, Ia, Q. 50, a. 4.

24 Aquinas's explanation that the rest of the fallen angels, besides the Devil, were moved to rebel by the exhortation of the Devil still presupposes a susceptibility to that exhortation, which implies the same ignorance or fault that we saw earlier in regard to the Devil's fall. Moreover, it is not at all clear why, supposing the Devil's encouragement, only some angels fell and not others. What *specifically* motivated given angel *A* to fall remains unexplained. See Aquinas, *Summa Theologica*, Ia, Q. 63, a. 8, resp.

25 *GL* §44.1; *The Christian Faith*, 162.

26 *GL* §44.1; *The Christian Faith*, 162.

27 *GL* §§51–54; *The Christian Faith*, 200–19.

28 Schleiermacher identifies the *being* of a thing with its *powers* and *activities*. Therefore, if something were to cease to act in every respect whatsoever, it would cease to exist. See *GL* §46 postscript; *The Christian Faith*, 176. See Chapter 4 for another important application of this claim.

29 *GL* §44.1; *The Christian Faith*, 162. Translation revised.

30 *GL* §55; *The Christian Faith*, 219–28.

31 *GL* §44.2; *The Christian Faith*, 162.

32 *GL* §44.2; *The Christian Faith*, 162. Translation revised.

33 *GL* §45; *The Christian Faith*, 163–70.

34 *GL* §44.2; *The Christian Faith*, 163. Translation revised.

35 *GL* §44.2; *The Christian Faith*, 163. Translation revised.

36 See Wyman, "The Role of the Protestant Confessions in Schleiermacher's The Christian Faith."

37 *GL* §44; *The Christian Faith*, 161.

38 *GL* §45.2; *The Christian Faith*, 167

39 *GL* §45.2; *The Christian Faith*, 167. Translation revised.

References

Adams, Robert Merrihew. "Involuntary Sins." *The Philosophical Review* 94, no. 1 (1985): 3–31.

Anscombe, Elizabeth. *Intention*. Oxford: Basil Blackwell, 1958.

Anselm of Canterbury. *On the Fall of the Devil*. From *Anselm: Basic Writings* Translated by Thomas Williams. Indianapolis: Hackett, 2007.

Aquinas, Thomas. *Summa Theologica*. Translated by the Fathers of the English Dominican Province. New York: Benziger Bros., 1947.

Audi, Robert. "Acting for Reasons." *Philosophical Review* 95, no. 4 (1986): 511–46.

Bowlin, John. "Hell and the Dilemmas of Intractable Alienation." In *Augustine's City of God: A Critical Guide*, edited by James Wetzel. Cambridge: Cambridge University Press, 2012.

Davidson, Donald. "Actions, Reasons, and Causes." In *The Essential Davidson*. Oxford: Clarendon, 2006.

Fischer, John Martin, and Mark Ravizza, S. J. *Responsibility and Control: A Theory of Moral Responsibility*. Cambridge: Cambridge University Press, 1998.

Jorati, Julia. *Leibniz on Causation and Agency*. Cambridge: Cambridge University Press, 2017.

Schleiermacher, Friedrich D. E. *The Christian Faith*. Edited by H. R. Mackintosh and J. S. Stewart, translated by D. M. Baillie, et al. Berkeley: Apocryphile, [1928] 2011.

———. *Der christliche Glaube nach den Grundsätzen der evangelischen Kirche im Zusammenhange dargestellt*. Second edition. Edited by Rolf Schäfer. Berlin: Walter de Gruyter, [1830/31] 2008.

Wolf, Susan. "Sanity and the Metaphysics of Responsibility." In *Free Will*, edited by Gary Watson. Second edition. New York: Oxford University Press, 2003.

Wyman Jr., Walter E. "The Role of the Protestant Confessions in Schleiermacher's *The Christian Faith*." *The Journal of Religion* 87, no. 3 (2007): 355–85.

3 Schleiermacher on the fall of Adam

Protarchus: The consequence is, that two out of the three lives which have been proposed are neither sufficient nor eligible for man or for animal.

Socrates: Then now there can be no doubt that neither of them has the good, for the one which had would certainly have been sufficient and perfect and eligible for every living creature or thing that was able to live such a life; and if any of us had chosen any other, he would have chosen contrary to the nature of the truly eligible, and not of his own free will, but either through ignorance or from some unhappy necessity.

– Plato, *Philebus*

The fall of the Devil has historically, among other things, functioned as a testing ground for the basic conceptual apparatus that accounts for Adam's fall, which in turn accounts for all humans' sin. Schleiermacher's critical treatment follows this same pattern. In his examination of the fall of Adam, Schleiermacher repeats and amplifies many of his arguments against the fall of the Devil. But he doesn't *merely* repeat these arguments. He also builds on them, adding a number of conceptual layers to his treatment.

Continuing his arguments from motivation, Schleiermacher presses on the tradition the problem of explaining why Adam willed what he willed. As with the fall of the Devil, he argues that every possible story of motivation either exonerates Adam from culpability on the basis of ignorance, compulsion, and so on, or makes Adam's sin innate, and so eliminates the idea of a *fall* of Adam altogether.

In a different, but complementary, line of argument, Schleiermacher attacks the consistency of the supposed change in human nature brought about by Adam's first sin. Even if we could offer an adequate account of motivation, Schleiermacher argues, the fallen Adam could not be the same individual as the Adam who fell, because they would not have the same human nature. The traditional account of Adam's fall fails on this second basis also. Moreover, because any account of a change in nature runs into basic conceptual difficulties, the Christian faith cannot credibly oblige us to offer a story of the beginnings of death and desire that presupposes that change in nature.

Together with his dismissal of the fall of the Devil, Schleiermacher's case against the fall of Adam amounts not only to a criticism of particular theories of their respective falls but also to a cumulative case against the *newness* of sin – in principle. Yet, once again, as with his argument against the fall of the Devil tradition, we come to discover that Schleiermacher's argument against the fall of Adam is premised on deeply traditional assumptions about agency, culpability, change, and identity – premises which he aims to preserve despite, or perhaps through, his denial of the fall of Adam.

Adam's inclination to sin

Schleiermacher subjects the traditional account of Adam's fall to much the same treatment as the tradition's account of the fall of the Devil, charging it with both explanatory lack and incoherence. As with the fall of the Devil he announces his verdict unambiguously: "But whether we take the narrative of the first sin literally or ascribe to it a universal significance, the attempt seems doomed to failure."[1]

Indeed, his first move is to link the Devil's temptation to the question of Adam's fall. Satanic temptation is a traditional feature of this account, but it is not without further difficulties – even on the assumption that there is a Devil to tempt Adam.

> The prevalent interpretations are that humanity sinned through the seductions of Satan and by a misuse of his free will. In the present instance these two factors cannot well be separated completely, for sin is always a misuse of free will. On the other hand, the more we ascribe to the action of Satan, the more nearly the temptation approximates to sorcery or violence, and so the [human] act, and therefore also the sin, are correspondingly less.[2]

Sin *must* involve a misuse of free will, since it is that by definition. But relating this misuse and so this sin to the Devil's temptation is not straightforward. The more Adam's sin is explained by Satan's temptation, the more Adam's action is really ascribed to Satan. That is, the more Adam does what he does because of Satan's temptation, the more it is actually *Satan's* doing. Adam's part becomes that of a patient, not an agent, victim, not perpetrator. Whatever the manner in which it is accomplished, *Adam's act* is diminished proportionally to its ascription to the Devil's temptation.[3]

The solution to that problem might seem straightforward: the fall of Adam should not rely so heavily on the temptation of Satan for its explanatory help. "But again," says Schleiermacher,

> the less the temptation of Satan, the less it is possible to make do apart from an already existing sinfulness, since misuse of free will is not, in itself, an explanation [*Erklärungsgrund*], but something must be assumed that drives it to misuse [*was zum Mißbrauch hintrieb*].[4]

What might seem like an easy solution, to simply abandon recourse to the Devil's temptation, is actually no solution at all. It suggests that a sinfulness preceded Adam's fall – which undermines the point of the doctrine. The tradition would, however, answer that the misuse of free will is exactly what is supposed to explain the fall. Schleiermacher anticipates this reply, and rejects it. No, Adam's will is not *explanans* but *explanandum*, that which itself stands in need of explanation – specifically *why, exactly, was Adam's will thus prompted?*

Schleiermacher is not denying that Adam misused his free will, and so sinned. Schleiermacher is, instead, denying that Adam's free will provides a sufficient answer to his question. He is not only asking why Adam sinned *in general*, so any answer that ends with something like "because Adam willed to" is no answer at all. Rather, Schleiermacher is asking why Adam *willed* what he *willed*, and when put this way we can plainly see how insufficient the reply "because he willed it" is. Schleiermacher wants to know more, to have an explanation not just in terms of Adam's will but *of* Adam's will. This marks an important distinction with traditional accounts of sin and the fall, but the distinction is not a simple contradiction of the tradition, say, by flatly denying the role of the will. No, what Schleiermacher is doing is pushing the series of *why* questions back into Adam's will itself, and it is because the question is a different question that the traditional answer won't do.

Now one major theological tradition holds that the will simply *is* the terminus of explanation of its own acts, that when we explain someone's actions by saying, "because she willed it," we have reached the end of all possible explanation and can go no further.[5] Schleiermacher will consider that alternative ahead (and we will consider it further in the next chapter). But there is a different account of the will that holds that the will is susceptible of further explanation. For instance, if I determined to eat an apple (whether in lieu of forgoing food, or instead of, say, an orange) I will to eat the apple *because* of certain reasons or causes:[6] I think it is tasty or healthy, it is closer to me, I already had an orange today, or whatever. It is to this second account of how the will works that Schleiermacher addresses this line of criticism. If, according to this tradition, the will is not the terminus of explanation, such further *why* questions are admissible.[7] And if they are, in principle, admissible, they are only arbitrarily *not* admitted regarding Adam's will in particular. A sufficient answer to this question, or a series of these questions, *explains* the determination of Adam's will. And so, we are back to Schleiermacher's initial point: that there will always be some prior cause that explains Adam's will which, in turn, explains Adam's sin, and that it is for such determining causes that we should search.

Given that counter, the tradition might answer that this is exactly the work the temptations of Satan are supposed to do; that is, to give an account of what prompted Adam to freely will as he did. Schleiermacher has still further doubts about this appeal.

Then if we fall back directly upon the suggestions of Satan, these again could not have taken effect unless there was already something present in the soul which implied a certain readiness to pass into sensuous appetite; and any such inclination toward sin must therefore have been present in the first pair before the first sin, else they would not have been liable to seduction.[8]

If we need to identify what prompted Adam to will as he did, an obvious place to look is to the seductive suggestions of Satan, for, once seduced, Satan's subsequent suggestions to Adam explain why Adam willed what he willed.[9] But Schleiermacher's doubts in this case are cast on the effectiveness of Satan's seduction in the first place. As Schleiermacher suggests, in order for Adam to be genuinely seduced by Satan, he must have been *susceptible* to seduction already. There must have been some part of him which was already inclined to find the Devil's suggestions appealing, something in him which was already disposed to have his will prompted to action by such thoughts. In order to explain Adam's temptation, this inclination must have *preceded* the temptation itself. But in that case, it is not the Devil's temptation nor Adam's free will but the *prior disposition to sin* that is the basis of the explanation.

To see Schleiermacher's point clearly, consider this example. In the midst of a weight-loss program I attend a party. At this party, there are lots of sweet treats, greasy snacks, and caloric drinks. I succumb to temptation and eat and drink merrily – despite my best interest and initial intent. Now, there are a few ways of making sense of my being tempted.

The first is probably the most familiar to most of us: I simply found that the desirability of the food outweighed my determination to eat well. We could explain this in more detail by appeal to ignorance or forgetfulness,[10] by a story about the weakness of the will,[11] or my being overtaken by passion for cookies and chips.[12] But notice: whichever specific story we offer along these lines is going to involve an explanation in terms of failure of one kind or another. And failure of this sort is supposed to be the kind of thing that Adam's condition in paradise, unlike mine at the party, does not permit. If not, Adam's failure, like ours, becomes ordinary, even inevitable. If you invite Adam to enough parties, he will eventually succumb to temptation and gorge himself. In that case, however, Adam was already, in some sense, no matter how minutely, like me, *predisposed to find the snacks tempting*. But if Adam is that, he is that by nature, not by choice. And God, not Adam, made Adam's nature.

The second way to make sense of my temptation is to appeal to external causes. Maybe the snacks were *particularly* appealing because, say, the host knew my favorite foods. That case would certainly help explain why I found those exact foods tempting, but it would not explain my failure to maintain my dietary goals in spite of the temptation, or indeed why I was seriously *tempted* at all. At least, it would do so with no more clarity than our first option earlier.

To make this plainer, let's say I enjoyed supreme fortitude in pursuit of my weight-loss goals (if not, I suffer a preexistent lack – see earlier). In order to give an account that makes sense of my falling into temptation despite my utter determination to the contrary, the story would have to get more extreme. Say the host provided only unhealthy food. I could simply abstain. No simple dilemma like that could suffice because, given my sufficient determination, neither the presence of bad food nor the temporary threat of no food could sway me.

But say the host was actually *out to tempt me*. In order to get me to eat the unhealthy food despite my larger aims, the hosts would have to do things like mislabel and disguise the food, or else, restrain me at their party (now effectively their prison) for long enough – days even – that my health was jeopardized more by my not eating than my eating poorly. I could surely be made to eat junk food under such circumstances. However, whether by trickery, compulsion, or some other necessity, my eating the unhealthy food would be less and less something I could be fully at fault for.[13] In extreme cases, my falling to "temptation" would even cease to be *bad* under the circumstances – if, for instance, I ate junk food to fend off starvation. So too with Adam's temptation by the Devil. Adam would, in the end, have to be *made* to sin.

This argument has remarkable consequences for Adam's supposed culpability. Even if Adam was somehow said to *choose* to sin under these circumstances of overwhelming temptation, we could not ascribe this sin to him as the sort of choice for which he was fully culpable. It would be a classic example of an action, which though intentionally willed, is also compelled, and so is at least *partially* involuntary.[14]

What makes Schleiermacher's particular application of this argument most interesting is that, because of the supposed perfection of Adam's initial state, this argument eliminates not only full-scale culpability but also even remote complicity. In some cases, we can be compelled to act, say, by threat, but we are still limitedly culpable in what we do. We might, after all, have chosen not to cooperate with, say, the hostage taker, and instead chose to suffer an extreme loss in order to avoid aiding another in evil.[15] And so, when we nevertheless cooperate under duress, depending on the severity of the threat, our options, and other details of circumstance, we *might* at least be held at fault for our actions.[16] Maybe Adam should be held accountable in just this way even if he cannot be held *fully* culpable? But Schleiermacher anticipates this objection. Indeed, he counts on it, for his position is that *some* disposition to sin must have preexisted Adam's sin. In order to deny his claim, an opponent must be committed to the notion that *no disposition whatsoever* preexists Adam's sin. But such a position eliminates *any* recourse to the source of Adam's sin *in Adam*, for if no disposition to sin could be found in him, nothing – *literally nothing* – could tempt him to sin apart from deception or compulsion. In consequence, Adam's state of sin is something for which Adam cannot even be partly complicit.

When Schleiermacher argues that "the more we ascribe to the action of Satan, the more nearly the temptation approximates to sorcery or violence, and so the [human] act, and therefore also the sin, are correspondingly less,"[17] he is setting up the first horn of his dilemma. The second horn follows:

> But, again, the less the temptation of Satan, the less it is possible to explain the facts apart from a sinfulness already present, since misuse of free will by itself is no explanation, but forces us to assume something else as prompting it.[18]

Schleiermacher's overall argument then amounts to this: either Adam enjoyed a sinless state in which only temptation amounting to compulsion could prompt him to sin, or Adam never enjoyed such a sinless state. Because the sinlessness of the initial state and the temptation required to get Adam sinning are proportional with one another, the traditional account is forced either to concede Adam's compulsion and so deny his culpability, or to deny his compulsion and so concede that there never was such a sinless state.

Yet perhaps the *locus* of the sin, the temptation or even the disposition, has been misidentified, or identified too generally? Schleiermacher denies this as well. "Nor does it avail," he says,

> to break up the first sin into a number of elements with a view to finding some infinitesimal part as its germ; for when what we have to deal with is a definite act, we must seek for something that will explain the act as a whole.[19]

What Schleiermacher has in mind here are views, apparently like one suggestion of Luther's,[20] that the true explanation of sin lies in some part or feature of the act that explains how sin gets into the whole act, but that exempts the act as a whole from explanation as sinful. Instead, Schleiermacher denies the basis of this atomistic action description. When an act is definite, when it is one thing and not another, any complete explanation will be an explanation of the act as a whole. "And this we can never find," Schleiermacher continues,

> as long as we assume an inner state in which there was no spontaneous activity of the flesh, and the God-consciousness alone held sway; for in that case no sinful appetite could ever have arisen in the pair themselves, nor could Satan have made them believe that God had forbidden something out of jealousy, but their trust in God must already have been extinguished.[21]

Had there not been something amiss on the part of the first humans themselves, they could not have been liable to sin or suggestion, unless they had *already* ceased to trust God. "But if such a trust had died out," Schlei-ermacher says, "they must already have lost the image of God, and sin-fulness must already have been present, whether in the form of pride or otherwise."[22] Whatever the locus of sin in the act, it always forms part of a complete act. And that complete act in turn presses us back upon Schleier-macher's previous dilemma.

But maybe there is still another way to explain why Adam willed what he willed and so why he sinned. "Our last resource," Schleiermacher says,

> would then be to explain the first sin as due to such a misuse of free will [*Mißbrauch des freien Willens*] which had no ground [*Grund*] in the first man's inward being, that is, to say that he chose the evil without determining reasons [*ohne Bestimmungsgründe*].[23]

With this "last resource" Schleiermacher hits closer to the mark of the tradi-tion, following Augustine, of explaining the misuse of the will by appealing to *the will itself*, apart from the object willed, as the reason for why the will willed as it did (the specifics of which we will take up in greater detail in the following chapter). The remainder of Schleiermacher's treatment of the idea deserves quoting.

> But either this must have taken place prior to his having had any exercise in the good at all, since even the briefest exercise would have induced a facility which, in the absence of conflicting determining rea-sons [*Bestimmungsgründe*], must have proved active [*thätig*], in which case his sin must have been his first free act [*erste freie That*] – which can be admitted least of all. Or else there was an impossibility that rep-etition of actions should produce any facility in the first pair, and this again would imply that no confirmation in good and no increase in the power of the God-consciousness was possible for them – an idea that conflicts with every view of humanity's original perfection.[24]

A great deal is going on here, though the overall point is clear: the notion that Adam chose as he did without motive will not work. Let us look more closely to each point in turn.

In the first option, Adam's choice of evil "must have taken place prior to his having had any exercise in the good at all." That is, Adam could not have had prior acquaintance with the good and his direction of the will toward it. Why? Because had he been so acquainted, the will would have been inclined, however minutely, by such practice to the good. And, apart from reasons *not* to act – "in the absence of conflicting determining reasons" – that this account demands, Adam would, in fact, have inclined to the good. Therefore, Adam could neither be acquainted with the good nor be practiced in it. And that requires that this first sin was Adam's first act. This will, it turns out, just sins straightaway, at its earliest opportunity, and apart from consideration about the good. What happens so immediately and so surely looks an awful lot like it happens naturally and necessarily. In other words, the will, on this account, seems purpose-built to sin. And that makes for poor advertising for this account of freedom.

Like a frictionless bearing, the will on this hypothetical account possesses an indifference, and a certain *sort* of indifference at that. On the account Schleiermacher aims to deny, the will enjoys an *indifference of equipoise* – that is, an indifference to the judgments the intellect makes about the relative merits of goods to be pursued. It can equally will one thing over another apart from (or in addition to) the intellect's judgments, and this equality of inclination *constitutes* its freedom – an alternative position we will continue to explore in the following chapter.

Schleiermacher's reply is most interesting in framing his objection to this account of freedom and the will's indifference in terms of indifference to *the good*. It is the perceived relative merits of things to be pursued, as both to their utility and to their intrinsic worth, that gives motive. But Schleiermacher does not only rest on this point. He also combines it with the utter unacquaintance with exercise in the good – namely, virtue – that indifference to the good demands. In order for the will to truly enjoy the indifference of equipoise that this account requires, it must not be sufficiently inclined by either judgments about the goods to be pursued *or* habits and practice. Because Schleiermacher is committed to the view that *any* practice creates a facility, however minute, for the thing practiced, an indifference of equipoise, according to him, cannot be sustained.[25]

This is where Schleiermacher's second option becomes important. Perhaps it was not, in fact, possible for the first pair to gain facility in the good, even if they exercised it; that no habits and practices that inclined in this way could be developed by repetition. This view, while not the least admissible position,[26] is nevertheless faulty. It clearly implies that, if no actions could produce a facility of the relevant sort, then it was *impossible* for the first pair to become better, either by securing the blessedness they had or through increase in their God-consciousness. Do not, however, let the God-consciousness distract. Schleiermacher's claim is that this is "an idea that conflicts with *every* view of humanity's original perfection,"[27] not only his own. No, the exact way this blessedness is explained is beside the point. Whether we accept Schleiermacher's account of the God-consciousness or some other notion of piety, righteousness, or otherwise, the problem will be the same: that the supposed paradise of the first humans was one in which it was, for whatever reason, impossible for them to get better and impossible for them to stay good – hardly favorable conditions for their preservation in righteousness. And this position, Schleiermacher argues, is the only way out of the problems posed by the first notion, the idea that no good practice could influence the first pair in their indifference of equipoise.

By this point the reader has likely noticed that Schleiermacher's account of Adam's willing is dependent on an attack on the lack of motive or inclination that determines the will. And champions of the contrary view, of the picture of the will as free when undetermined by motives, will reasonably object that this account of the will begs the question.[28] That is, Schleiermacher's reduction of accounts of Adam's (or Satan's) will which attempt to show the incoherence or insufficiency of the will do not so much argue *to* as argue *from* his preferred account of motive determining will. We will take up this question at length in the following chapter, but for now it is worth noting that while this is certainly an argument *from* principles, and indeed, principles which others might reasonably dispute, Schleiermacher might provide support for those principles from other resources, and in turn uses these to support his account of willing. In the worst case, his argument can still be viewed as an attempt to force those who disagree to *commit* themselves, on pain of inconsistency, to the more radical notion of an undetermined will, an idea which might have unexpected and unsavory consequences.

Given his account of the will's dependence on a sufficient motive, Schleiermacher continues his attack on the traditional account of the fall when paired with the biblical narrative. "This difficulty of representing to ourselves the emergence of the first sin without assuming a foundation for it in a prior sinfulness is immensely aggravated if we consider the circumstances in which the Mosaic narrative exhibits the first pair."[29] He explains,

> For one thing, it is almost impossible to conceive of temptation, or the abuse of free will, amid such simplicity of life, and where the natural wants were so easily satisfied; since in such a condition of things no single object could offer an exceptionally strong allurement.[30]

The conditions the original pair enjoys in the biblical narrative make their temptation all the more implausible. They have no wants or needs. Without wants or needs they can have no unaddressed desires. And without such desires, they could not be tempted to satisfy them. "And again," Schleiermacher presses, "it is quite impossible to imagine a direct intercourse with God without an intensified love to God and an increased knowledge of Him which must have preserved our parents from the influence of foolish illusions."[31] The original couple could not even have desired something greater, because they already enjoyed fellowship with God – a fellowship necessarily attended by love and knowledge, thus guarding against "foolish illusions." This last phrase is noteworthy. In it Schleiermacher has included *both* the possibility of insanity or perversity *and* the possibility of ignorance. In so doing, he denies recourse to either explanatory strategy. If it was as genuine, complete, and persistent as claimed, the direct relationship with God enjoyed by the first pair in the biblical narrative contradicts both possible traditional explanations of the fall of Adam.

As with his other arguments, Schleiermacher's target with this reduction is a specific account not merely of the origins of sin but of the notion that the first humans *began* to be sinners at all. It is an argument against any account of the fall whatsoever. "And indeed," he says, "in view of the ease with which sin might have been avoided, the more literally we accept the narrative, the greater is the propensity to sin which must be assumed as already present."[32] Or, as he says shortly thereafter, "[N]othing of a peculiar or novel nature took place in our first parents as a result of the first sin; and what is represented in our symbolical books as such a result must be assumed to have preceded the sin."[33] As Schleiermacher explains at length,

> The understanding must have been involved in an utterly heathen darkness before it could have credited a falsehood to the effect that God grudged humanity the knowledge of good, and the will must have lacked the energy to resist even the weakest enticement if the mere sight of the forbidden fruit could exert such power over it. In fact, *Adam must have been sundered from God before his first sin*; for when Eve handed him the fruit he ate it without even recalling the divine interdict; and this presupposes a like condition of his nature; for surely incorrupt nature could not have indulged appetite in express disobedience to the divine command. Nor can it fairly be maintained that this reading hangs entirely on a literal interpretation of the Mosaic narrative, for, whatever idea we have of the first sin, we must always assume the priority of some sinful element; and if we seek to understand that sin genetically, we must follow a method akin to that adopted here.[34]

Schleiermacher argues, in no uncertain terms, that the first sin must, of necessity, be explained by a prior sinful condition; that this *condition* preceded the first *act*; and so the traditional explanation that Adam's (and, therefore our) sinful condition is explained by Adam's sinful act should be reversed. Adam's corruption *preceded* his sinful act, "for surely incorrupt nature could not have indulged appetite in express disobedience to the divine command."[35]

Importantly, Schleiermacher's argument does not only apply to the Genesis narrative, let alone to only one reading of it. No, his claim is – crucially – that regardless of the particulars of the story we offer, "if we seek to understand sin genetically"[36] – that is, according to its causal antecedents – we will *necessarily* be committed to the conclusion that some sinful element *preceded* the first sin. Any account of the origins of sin which explains the origins of a sinful element in a sinful act is unworkable, and cannot work *in principle*.

This is a truly remarkable claim. Perhaps Schleiermacher is right *in fact*. Or perhaps his is even the better overall account, the more plausible. But why does he think an account of sin's origins *must* (i.e., of necessity) work the way he thinks it does? The answer to this is one of the most distinctive, interesting, revealing, and important features of his theology.

In order to generate the necessity he claims to generate, Schleiermacher must argue *from* higher principles, not *to* them. And this is exactly what he does. We can see this in both his arguments for the insufficiency of motive and for his arguments that a sinful act must be explained by a sinful nature. In both cases the argument assumes: (1) that a sufficient explanation *can* be given; (2) that a sufficient explanation *must* be given; and (3) that a sufficient explanation is a *complete* explanation – that is, one for which no facts remain unexplainable in principle. In short, Schleiermacher's case is based on the *principle of sufficient reason,* applied to efficient and final causes alike. Once this principle is deployed, any account that does not satisfy it is *necessarily* inadequate.

We saw, both in his criticism of the fall of the Devil and in his foregoing criticism of the fall of Adam, Schleiermacher applies this principle to the stories of the different agents' motivations. Inadequate accounts were those which were not able to give a sufficient reason for *why* the Devil and Adam willed what they willed. We will return to this theme at length in the following chapter, Chapter 4, where we look at the traditional alternative, that the cause of the fall was *deficient.* There we will consider reasons Schleiermacher might have for discarding this notion, or at least certain senses of it. Before we do, however, we need a yet more complete picture of how Schleiermacher deploys the principle in other contexts. The next section of this chapter, however, deals at length with a second, related application of the principle of sufficient reason: the grounding of acts in natures.

Nature and act

As we just saw in Schleiermacher's argument against the traditional account of the fall of Adam, Schleiermacher repeatedly argues that the sinful act of Adam presupposes his sinful condition, his sinful nature. This line of argument assumes that the acts of things are explained by their natures; that what things *do* are explained in terms of what things *are.* And, as I claimed earlier, Schleiermacher's case depends on a strong version of this account of things: that what things do can be *sufficiently* (i.e., completely) explained by what they are – under particular conditions, of course. Put differently, Schleiermacher holds to the view that nothing can actually do more than it can potentially do; and nothing can potentially do more than is in some sense natural to it. In this section we examine this strong principle more closely and look at what work it does in Schleiermacher's arguments.

Before we turn to the application of this principle, however, I want to present another important piece of evidence for Schleiermacher's subscription to it. The foregoing arguments imply that Schleiermacher subscribes to a strong account of how natures sufficiently explain actions. Indeed, the explanatory role of natures is the only premise that completes his arguments. In the same section, though, and only a few lines later, Schleiermacher also makes this premise perfectly explicit. "Still less," he says,

> is it possible to suppose that such a transformation of nature should have resulted from an act of the individual in question, *since the individual*

can only act in accordance with the nature of the species, but never can act upon that nature.[37]

An individual can act *only* in accordance with their nature, *never* upon it. What we see in the following argument is this principle applied to the supposed transformation of human nature caused by Adam's first sin.

Along with the idea that any act of an agent with a certain nature is necessarily an act in accordance with the agent's nature, this formulation adds yet another dimension to Schleiermacher's account: a limited anti-reflexivity principle. That is, not only is human action necessarily in accordance with human nature, but also humans "can never act *upon* that nature."[38] But why this second clause? Surely even if humans can act only in accordance with human nature they might *also* act upon that nature? This objection is understandable. However, there is good reason to think that, on a version of the principle of sufficient reason applied to natures as the *sufficient* explanation for a creature's actions, this anti-reflexivity principle is simply a corollary.[39] That is, these are two ways to say the same thing or to cash out the same idea. I will say more about both in turn.

Natures ground acts. That is, they explain *why* some particular thing is *able* to do what it does. Natures do not explain this generically, but specifically. That is, they not only explain why all things or only individual things do the things they do; rather, they also explain why things *of a kind* do the things that are characteristic of their kind.[40] For instance, crows do some very different things than horses. One sort of thing can fly, the other cannot. One sort of thing can gallop, the other cannot. The ability of crows to fly and horses to gallop *as individuals of a species* is alike explained by their natures. They can do the things they can do *because* they are the sort of things they are. Because their natures are what determine crows and horses as the sorts of things they are, and because what they are enables them to do the sorts of things they do, if an act is beyond their nature, they are strictly unable to do it. It is impossible. Individuals can act only in accordance with the nature of their species, whether crows, or horses, or humans.

If an individual can act *only* in accordance with the nature of their species, the individual cannot act upon that nature. This holds for a simple reason. Since a nature is the sufficient ground for *all* the potential actions of an individual of a kind, there is nothing that an individual *can* do that is not *already included* in the potential of that nature.[41]

Importantly, this claim allows for a wide variety of self-change while denying the self-reflexivity of individuals acting upon their own *natures*. And so counterexamples of self-change are generally no objection at all. Self-change is, largely, a perfectly admissible category, with the caveat – and this is key – that the change involved is *natural* (rather than unnatural) change.[42] For instance, I can move my hand with my foot. Or I can grow from a child to an adult. Both of these are instances of self-change. But these instances of self-change, and all similar instances, are strictly natural.

I never cease to be a human being, or to do more than a human being can do, when I move or alter my own body, or when I develop unconsciously. As natural, these changes are not modifications *of* my nature, even though they are instances of self-change, but are rather acts *by* and *in accordance with* my nature, just as Schleiermacher's principle states.[43]

Schleiermacher brings this principle, with its twin aspects, to bear on the origins of sin. If humans *did* sin, they must have been *able* to; and if humans were able to sin, it must have been a feature of human nature all along. "If, however," Schleiermacher explains,

> human nature in the first pair was the same before the first sin as it appears subsequently alike in them and in their posterity, we cannot say that human nature was changed as a result of the first sin, and the statement of our symbolical books to that effect is one we must depart from.[44]

The difficulties for the traditional account do not end there – for if an action did allegedly change the nature of an individual, they would then not be creatures of the same nature. For example, say that Sally the seahorse somehow acts upon her nature and changes it. Whatever thing she is now – and if she exists she will necessarily be some specific sort of thing – she will not be a seahorse any longer. Even if she could maintain her substantial identity – that is, even if she could remain *Sally* (which is itself doubtful in the extreme; see ahead) – she could not be the same *kind* of thing as before. And if we nevertheless want to say that Sally did indeed remain a seahorse, we would have to concede that she did not change her seahorse *nature*. She might have changed coincidentally or otherwise, but not essentially.

Likewise, Adam's sin could not have changed human nature because anything that Adam *can* do is already something a *human* can do. Schleiermacher's argument proceeds in the same way. As he explains,

> No one could be asked to believe that in a single individual the nature of the species could be changed and yet that individual remain the same; for the terms "individual" and "species" lose their meaning unless everything met with in the individual, whether successively or simultaneously, can be understood from and explained by the nature of the species. If an individual manifests some attribute incompatible with the definition of the species, then either the definition of the species has been wrong from the start and needs to be corrected, or we were misled as to the identity of the individual.[45]

Because of the grounding work "individual" and "species" do, nothing attributable to an individual of a certain species can fail to be comprehended by each. And if something *is* attributable to an individual which cannot be understood and explained by the definition of the species, then there are only two possibilities: either the definition of the species needs to be revised, in which case the given individual's attributes fall under the new definition, or the individual in question has simply been misidentified, in which case their attributes will fall under the definition of the species to which the individual properly belongs. But in no case can anything attributable to an individual *genuinely* fail to be understood and explained by the nature of the species.[46]

To shed light on Schleiermacher's argument, consider this example. Jeff is a crab. And as a crab, anything that is true of Jeff must be true of crabs as a species – not necessarily true of every single crab, but at least attributable to crabs in general. Nothing that is true of a particular crab can fail to be true of crabs as a whole. What is true of crabs must be something which is *potentially* attributable *to crabs* because crabs are the sorts of things they are. But one day we begin to notice that Jeff is doing some extraordinary things for a crab. Jeff is running around, swishing his tail, gathering acorns, and storing them in holes in the ground and in trees. Of course, we are stunned because we have never seen another crab do this. To make sense of Jeff's very odd behavior we can explain it in one of two ways: either that Jeff is indeed a crab, but crabs are very different animals than previously thought and our new understanding of what it means to be a crab must include a whole range of new bodily structures and behaviors; or that we were simply mistaken from the start. Jeff isn't a crab, but a squirrel, and his behaviors fall under the definition of his true species quite well.

What holds for Jeff the crab holds for Adam the human. There cannot be a human being, Adam, who was unable, according to his nature, to do certain things and then became able to do so according to his same human nature. Neither could there be a human being, Adam, who was able to do certain things according to his nature, and then became unable. No, either Adam was able or unable to be or do certain things from the start, in which case there was no change in human nature, or Adam was wrongly described as "human," in the same sense, in one or both instances. The account of the fall in which Adam's *nature* is changed depends, Schleiermacher argues, on a subtle homonymy: on two words like duck (the animal) and duck (the action of lowering one's head) that sound the same *but actually mean two different things*.[47] In this case the traditional account trades on two different meanings of "human nature" – "human nature" and "*human nature*" – which sound the same to say, but actually describe two different animal kinds: Human$_1$ and Human$_2$. Once the distinction is clarified, we will notice that at least one of the notions of "human" applied to Adam can't hold, or else there cannot have actually been a change in the first place.

If the two sorts of "human" described by Adam before the fall and Adam after the fall are really two different animal kinds, explained by very different natures, then there is, of course, a deep confusion in the animal nature under question. But that is not all, for if the natural kind under question changes, then so too does the individual. That is, because a given individual is always a determinate individual, and so an individual *of a kind*, when that

kind changes, so too does that individual's identity. Consider Jeff the crab
once again. Let us say Jeff is, in fact, a normal crab who lives under water
and on the shore pinching and scuttling and doing typical crab-like things.
Then say we manage to give Jeff an entirely new nature, one that is now not
a crab but, say, that of a human. In what meaningful sense is Jeff *the same
Jeff* any longer? We could, of course, still *call* this new creature, this human,
"Jeff," but there is no substantial identity between the old "Jeff" and the
new "Jeff." This is simply another instance of homonymy, only this time
with regard to the individual's identity, not with regard to the nature of the
individual – though the change in nature *necessitates* the change in substantial identity. We can see this most clearly with a less science-fiction-like case
of the transformation of natures: the normal way Jeff the crab is transformed
into a human named Jeff is when a human whose name happens to be Jeff
catches, kills, cooks, and eats Jeff the crab. In such an instance, we would
never think the crab now *is*, in a genuine substantial sense, Jeff the human.
The fact that we use the same sounds to name both is purely coincidental.

The same problem holds for Adam pre- and post-fall if human nature was
altered in the event. In fact, with the change of his nature, the first Adam is
not just transformed but destroyed. He, *this* Adam of *this* nature, ceases to
exist and in his place lives another individual of another nature, an individual who just happens to be named "Adam" in the same way Jeff the human
and Jeff the crab were only coincidentally signified by the same sounds.

Yet say there *was*, somehow, nevertheless, a change in human nature. In
that case, Adam, Schleiermacher argues, could not have been the agent of
that change. "Hence we cannot well hold to the idea under discussion without cónceding a share in the matter to the Devil."[48] This view has important
consequences:

> For if it is quite certain that an alternation in a determinate nature can-
> not be effected by that nature itself, the actual alteration can be appor-
> tioned between the man and the Devil only in this way, that the element
> of action is ascribed to the latter, and mere passivity, or receptivity, to the
> former. But in that case, it must be further admitted that, if the individu-
> als are to remain the same, it is a mere confusion of speech to describe
> the outcome as merely an alteration of their nature, and that it is more
> correct to say that the human nature which God originally created was
> destroyed by the Devil through the first sin, when the nature acquired
> was the work of the Devil in the same degree as was the first sin, because
> the nature created by God so remained purely passive as to allow itself
> to be completely permeated by the alteration wrought by the Devil.[49]

If, as Schleiermacher insists, the anti-reflexivity principle holds, then any
alteration of Adam's nature can be only the unnatural work of an extrinsic
cause; and since this alteration was for the worse, the work is, as per the
tradition, best ascribed to the Devil. And because an individual can, *in no*

way, alter their own *nature*, the agency in this change must lie *entirely* with this extrinsic cause (in this case Satan).

The only admissible self-change is natural. But *any* alteration *of* a nature is, by definition, unnatural. Therefore, the alteration of Adam's human nature cannot be self-change in any respect. But such change has a cause: the Devil. And so the Devil is, it turns out, the whole and entire extrinsic cause of the unnatural change of Adam's human nature. Adam is, and must be, *completely* passive with respect to the Devil's doings. Once again, Adam cannot be responsible, or even remotely complicit, in his fall.[50] His only part is to suffer his fate. Just as the cause of the first sin should be really ascribed to the Devil's temptation, so too the change in Adam's nature should really be ascribed to the Devil in the same way. If so, this change in human nature was purely tragic for Adam. He was in no way active in this transformation, but simply suffered what the Devil wrought. Because he was not active, he could not be an agent; and because he was not an agent, he could not be responsible. He was simply a victim of the Devil's designs – a difficulty which is greatly magnified both by God's ineptness in creating Adam unable to resist the Devil and by God's neglect in aiding him.

If the individual under question is the same person whose nature was altered by the Devil so thoroughly then, as earlier, "it is a mere confusion of speech [*Sprachverwirrung*] to describe the outcome as *merely* [*nur*] an alteration of their nature."[51] That is, if we are keeping our thoughts and words in order, this will not be the same person slightly changed, but a new person with a new nature, a true *transformation*. In that case, the human nature originally created by God was not so much altered as *destroyed*. By the power of the Devil, human nature$_1$ ceased to exist. In its place was a new nature, as before, only now a nature of the Devil's creation. Like the crab, the old, original human nature was not, then, merely modified but consumed.

Schleiermacher intends this series of arguments to amount to an absurd reduction of the transformation of Adam's nature. The alarming consequences of this hypothetical passive destruction of human nature are meant to count so greatly against its plausibility that we are left with one choice: Adam's human nature was not, and could not have been, changed by either Adam or anything else, on pain of incoherence and impiety. Human nature was thus unaltered by the first sin. Indeed, because natures ground acts, our original created natures explain human beings' possibility and disposition to sin. Sin, as it turns out, is inevitable and, in one sense, inherent in human nature – though, nevertheless, not *natural* in the normative sense, as we will see in the following chapters.

Human nature, explanatory requirements, and their limits

In traditional accounts of the fall, Adam's will explains his fall, his fall explains his transformed state, and his transformed state explains a number of common features of ordinary life that are, despite their universality, unnatural and bad. According to the tradition, things like lust and death are disorders of the original nature of things, distortions of life as it was before the fall. In the traditional reckoning, whatever one's account of the origins of human sin, it must, at the same time, explain this natural disorder. Schleiermacher, in contrast, prefaces his treatment of the fall with arguments for limits on what one can require the fall to explain correlated with his denial of a change in human nature. In short, if human nature was not, and could not have been, changed by the first sin, death and sexual desire could not be a disorder of that nature.

Death is likewise, according to Schleiermacher, an inevitable and natural phenomenon. Indeed, to be the sort of thing that dies is so basic to humans' animal life that the notion of a human that doesn't die is to think of a different sort of creature. As Schleiermacher explains,

> If we think away the gradual decay of organic powers, the possibility that the organism may be destroyed by external forces of nature, and disappearance through death, what we are thinking of is no longer beings of our kind, while yet real human history would only begin when all these things were present.[52]

The necessity of death is conditional, but its conditions are necessary. To be a human is to be an animal with a life marked by development and decay. To be an organism in the world is to be the sort of thing that is not invincible, which can be and so eventually will be destroyed by external forces of nature.[53] By virtue of the basic conditions of our existence as finite organisms, death is a necessary consequence.

To imagine a human that does not die is to think away basic conditions of actual humans. To then describe an animal that does not die is then not to describe humans, in the ordinary sense, at all whether that animal is called "human" or otherwise. The issue is, once again, one of homonymy. The name of the animal that does not die, Human$_1$, only superficially and coincidentally shares the same sounds as humans as they are now, Human$_2$. Schleiermacher's point, therefore, is not limited to historical claims of matters of fact. He does not think people began to die; but even if this could be contested, his point remains that any supposed human which did not die, no matter how similar in other respects, would actually be a different species. Humans, in the same sense, cannot have *begun* to die as a result of a change in their nature. If there was an animal that did not die, when it began to die, it became a different sort of animal.[54]

The same applies to sexual desire – albeit in a more qualified sense. Recall that, according to Augustine, the first humans would have reproduced (had they gotten around to it before sinning) not only without disordered desire but also really without sexual desire in the broadest sense because sexual desire is, for Augustine, disordered desire *tout court*. It is against this notion that Schleiermacher directs his criticism. Of course there is such a thing as disordered sexual desire,

> But when Augustine understands by the expression "desire" [*con-cupiscentia*] simply the proper life-process of these functions, and at the same time holds that it cannot be thought of as co-existing with original righteousness, he seems to be at least as much open to blame as the Pelagians, if they considered the opposition between the lower and higher faculties as humanity's original condition, and included all acquired perfection under the removal of that opposition. For Augustine's opinion presupposes also an original contradiction between the spirit in humanity and that which is necessary for humans' animal life.[55]

Unlike death, which, as a necessary consequence of our organic life, cannot in itself be a disorder, sexual desire can be, and sometimes is, disordered. But, when Augustine extends this disorder to cover virtually the whole of humans' sexual activities, he goes too far. In consequence, he includes under the umbrella of disorder much of what is natural and necessary to humans' animal life. Now, Schleiermacher does not include any more details than this. But it is clear that at least some of what Augustine reckoned concupiscence Schleiermacher deems a "*proper* life-process"[56] – that is, a natural and normal animal function proper to human beings.

If, in an effort to deny Schleiermacher's premise that some of what Augustine deems disordered is actually natural and necessary, one claims that such desire is nevertheless disordered because human nature is disordered, the old problem of homonymy rears its head once again. Sexual desire is "necessary for humans' animal life"[57] *as we are now*. To then describe a "human" for whom sexual desire is unnecessary is to describe a different species, only coincidentally known by the same name. Like an animal that does not die, an animal that does not include sexual desire and its attendant functions is a different sort of animal altogether.

As with death, the problem of a change in human nature vis-à-vis sexual desire is magnified by the very basic fact that sexual desire extends to many other species besides human beings. The traditional solution is as dramatic as it is elegant: to affirm that the whole of nature was transformed by the first sin. The same desire on the part of other animals can then be explained by one and the same disorder. But notice: this is only a thing to be explained on the supposition that human nature was changed by the first sin. If one denies an alteration of human nature, there is no need to extend that change to the world as a whole. Indeed, as Schleiermacher explains, no authority can be summoned to the contrary:

> In view of all this, no reason can well remain for doubting that the original perfection of the world relatively to humanity was at the beginning no other than what we have here described, and that neither the Old

Testament story nor the relevant indications in the writings of the New Testament compel us to hold that humanity was created immortal, or that, with alteration in his nature, the whole arrangement of the earth relatively to him was altered as well.[58]

The scriptures can be variously interpreted; the tradition can be contested. There are serious reasons to doubt the necessity of the teaching in regard to either the doctrine of a change of human nature or its amplification to a change in the world at large.

But, moreover, and most importantly, the alteration of the world relative to human nature yet again brings the same burden as every attempt at explaining apparent disorder by a change in the nature of a thing: coincidental homonymy. Just as with the human nature supposedly lost with Adam's fall, so the world as a whole suffers the same transformation, and so the same loss of identity. And so in calling it the "same world" we suffer the same confusion. That is, just as human nature before and after the fall is only coincidentally, not really, "human nature," but a mere coincidence and accident of speech, so too the *world*, if wrapped up in this transformation, is also only called the *same* world confusedly. No, if the first sin did not only bring about a change in human nature but also change the world as a whole, then, like Adam's transformation by the Devil, the world was not really modified but destroyed. With its transformation the very nature of the world was altered, and so lost; and so the world as it was created by God was not merely disordered but longer exists.

Schleiermacher, thankfully, denies that the world was so altered. Indeed, he thinks the Christian faith is obligated to propose no such theory regarding a change of nature of the world or the things in it. Accordingly, many traditional *explananda* can simply be ignored. His argument is, in the final analysis, not only that one account or the other of the fall of Adam fails but also that any attempt fails *in principle*; and, at the same time, that the Christian faith is no worse off for this fact. Reason does not allow it, and piety does not demand it. "[T]here is," Schleiermacher says, "no reason why we should lay down any special doctrines concerning the first humans."[59]

Sufficient reason and the fall

Schleiermacher's reduction of the traditional account of the fall of Adam repeats, amplifies, and extends his reduction of the fall of the Devil. Adam's first sin, Schleiermacher argues, could not have brought about his sinful nature. No, the causal story must proceed in exactly the opposite direction. It is Adam's nature which, according to Schleiermacher, is the only thing that could explain Adam's acts, sinful or otherwise.

As we saw, Schleiermacher's case is supported by a twin application of the principle of sufficient reason. The first application of that principle was directed against Adam's motivation. That is, it is an application of the principle of sufficient reason directed against the insufficiency of final causes in the traditional account. Motives determine actions; and every action has a motive sufficient to explain the action. Of course, things like ignorance, insanity, and compulsion can be part of such a sufficient explanation. But the traditional account of Adam's fall is largely denied recourse to such explainers on the condition that it seeks Adam's (and his posterity's) culpability. More important still, any such explanation implies defect that precedes the act. In consequence, even if culpability is abandoned in favor of tragedy, one is still forced to admit that the conditions of sin preceded the first sin. Since, as we saw with the fall of the Devil, any regress either terminates in such conditions or turns infinite, there is no way to explain Adam's sinful state by appeal to his act of sin, and no need to explain his sinful state as a corruption of his nature by the Devil or any other means. Because there is a sufficient reason for why Adam sinned, such sin will always be explicable (in principle) through a series of *why* questions which eventually and necessarily terminate in Adam's condition or the conditions of his existence.

Schleiermacher's second application of the principle of sufficient reason regards Adam's nature, its grounding of his acts, and, as a result, the incoherence of the very idea of a persistent subject with different natures. In this application, natures, as the sufficient reasons for the act of a thing of a kind, are always sufficient to explain how a thing is able to do the things it does.[60] Because nothing does more than it *can* do, everything Adam does is natural (in this sense). To avoid this problem, one must propose, as the traditional account of Adam's fall does, a change in human nature. This Schleiermacher denies. The very idea of a change in nature paired with persistent identity is, he argues, chimerical. If Adam's nature changed, the new and the old "Adam" would not be the same person; if human nature changed, the new and the old "human" would not be the same species; and if, because of sin, nature itself was altered, the world before the first sin and our world would be different worlds entirely. No, because of the role natures play in grounding acts and individuals, no act can fall outside of a nature and any change in nature destroys identity. Due to these difficulties, and given the modest explanatory demands of piety, Christians need offer no such account of the transformation human nature, or accounts of the traditional corollaries to a change in human nature, such as the supposed advent of death and desire.

Overall, Schleiermacher's case is a powerful argument against the coherence of traditional accounts of the origins of sin. If these origin stories fail, or even if only their burdens exceed their benefits, they can be eliminated without loss. This is ultimately what Schleiermacher aims to do. In their place he offers his own developmental account of sin and its relation to human nature, which we will examine in the coming chapters.

Before we do, however, a final, all-important objection to Schleiermacher's account must be noted. Much of the tradition would recognize all these points on the condition that there was, in fact, a sufficient reason for sin. Indeed, it is remarkable how traditional Schleiermacher's premises are. But, at the same time, the tradition would *deny that there is such a sufficient reason for sin*. That is, Schleiermacher's case works well on his terms. But the tradition denies (or qualifies) those terms. Therefore, in order for Schleiermacher's case to be persuasive, advocates of his view must be prepared to offer a reply to the traditional notion that sin has no efficient cause, but only a *deficient* one. In the following chapter we examine the notion of deficient causes. There we will see what reasons Schleiermacher might have to qualify or reject the idea, and what good reasons one might still hold to think that, strictly speaking, there *is never* a deficient cause.

Notes

1 *GL* §72.2; *The Christian Faith*, 293.
2 *GL* §72.2; *The Christian Faith*, 293. Translation revised.
3 See Aristotle, *Nicomachean Ethics*, III.1.
4 *GL* §72.2; *The Christian Faith*, 293. Translation revised.
5 As mentioned in Chapter 1, a range of historical and contemporary examples of this view in theology include: Barth, *Church Dogmatics*, IV.1, 478–513; Hick, *Evil and the God of Love*, 262–91; Kant, *Religion within the Boundaries of Mere Reason*; Bishop Tempier, *Condemnation of 1277*, §151.
6 See Davidson, "Actions, Reasons, and Causes."
7 Once again, for a seminal account of the connection of *why* questions to the ascription of intentional acts see Anscombe, *Intention*, 9–13.
8 *GL* §72.2; *The Christian Faith*, 293.
9 It might be objected that this principle would require us to say that every genuine temptation issues in sin. But Christ was genuinely tempted, and yet was without sin (Hebrews 4:15), which is against the hypothesis. This is an interesting point of dispute, but Schleiermacher's solution is revealing: he heavily qualifies the sense in which Christ was *seriously* tempted: his sinlessness ruled out the *possibility* that pleasure and pain, while being truly present to him, could *ever* truly determine his state of mind. See *GL* §98.1; *The Christian Faith*, 415.
10 See Aristotle, *Nicomachean Ethics*, III.1.
11 See Aristotle, *Nicomachean Ethics*, I.13.
12 See Aristotle, *Nicomachean Ethics*, III.1, 11.
13 See Aristotle, *Nicomachean Ethics*, III.1.
14 See Aristotle, *Nicomachean Ethics*, III.1.
15 See Aristotle, *Nicomachean Ethics*, III.1.
16 See Aristotle, *Nicomachean Ethics*, III.1, 10.
17 *GL* §72.2; *The Christian Faith*, 293. Translation revised.
18 *GL* §72.2; *The Christian Faith*, 293.
19 *GL* §72.2; *The Christian Faith*, 294.
20 *GL* §72.2; *The Christian Faith*, 294, n. 1.
21 *GL* §72.2; *The Christian Faith*, 294.
22 *GL* §72.2; *The Christian Faith*, 294.
23 *GL* §72.2; *The Christian Faith*, 294. Translation revised.
24 *GL* §72.2; *The Christian Faith*, 294. Translation revised.
25 See earlier, *GL* §72.2; *The Christian Faith*, 294. Translation revised.
26 *GL* §72.2; *The Christian Faith*, 294.
27 *GL* §72.2; *The Christian Faith*, 294. Translation revised, emphasis added.
28 For an argument that rejecting the causal account of reasons is insufficient to escape the necessity of appeal to such reasons in a complete account, see Strawson, *Freedom and Belief*, 29–35.
29 *GL* §72.2; *The Christian Faith*, 294.

30 *GL* §72.2; *The Christian Faith*, 295.
31 *GL* §72.2; *The Christian Faith*, 295.
32 *GL* §72.2; *The Christian Faith*, 295.
33 *GL* §72.2; *The Christian Faith*, 295.
34 *GL* §72.3; *The Christian Faith*, 295–96. Translation revised, emphasis added.
35 *GL* §72.3; *The Christian Faith*, 295–96.
36 *GL* §72.3; *The Christian Faith*, 296.
37 "*Und noch weniger läßt sich denken, daß eine solche Umwandlung der Natur solle die Wirkung einer That des fraglichen Einzelwesens selbst gewesen sein, da es ja immer nur mit der Natur seiner Gattung handeln kann, niemals aber auf dieselbe.*" *GL* §72.3; *The Christian Faith*, 296. Translation revised, emphasis added.
38 *GL* §72.3; *The Christian Faith*, 296. Emphasis added.
39 See Aristotle, *Metaphysics*, IX, 1.
40 The likely source of this strong view of natures is classical. See Aristotle, *Physics*, II.1.
41 This follows the basic Aristotelian premise that the motion (i.e., change) of a thing presupposes a thing capable of such motion. See Aristotle, *Physics*, VIII.1.
42 For the crucial distinction between natural and unnatural, see Aristotle, *Physics*, VIII.4. Schleiermacher, following Aristotle, denies that agents are capable of self-reflexively producing *unnatural* change.
43 The same anti-reflexivity principle applies to habits as well as individual acts. See Aristotle, *Nicomachean Ethics*, II.1.3–4.
44 *GL* §72.3; *The Christian Faith*, 296.
45 *GL* §72.3; *The Christian Faith*, 296.
46 See Aristotle, *Parts of Animals*, I.4; *Posterior Analytics*, II.13.
47 For the classic discussion of homonymy, see Aristotle, *Categories*, I.1.
48 *GL* §72.3; *The Christian Faith*, 296.
49 *GL* §72.3; *The Christian Faith*, 296.
50 See Aristotle, *Nicomachean Ethics*, III.1.
51 *GL* §72.3; *The Christian Faith*, 296. Emphasis added.
52 *GL* §50, postscript; *The Christian Faith*, 243.
53 See Aquinas, *Summa Theologica*, Ia, Q. 49. a. 2. resp.
54 Aquinas very cleverly avoids this issue by supposing that, though Adam was immortal before his fall, he was not *naturally* immortal, but immortal by a supernatural gift. Although this eliminates the possibility of a change in nature, it exacerbates issues of agency and culpability given the extent to which God was active in preserving Adam in this immortal state. See Aquinas, *Summa Theologica*, Ia, Q. 97. a. 1. resp.
55 *GL* §61.5; *The Christian Faith*, 255. Translation revised.
56 *GL* §61.5; *The Christian Faith*, 255. Emphasis added.
57 *GL* §61.5; *The Christian Faith*, 255.
58 *GL* §59, postscript; *The Christian Faith*, 244 Translation revised.
59 *GL* §61.4; *The Christian Faith*, 251–52. Translation revised.
60 It might be objected that this too quickly moves from the nature of a thing to its *acts*, whereas natures need only explain a thing's *powers*. But recall that Schleiermacher identifies the *being* of a thing with its *powers and activities*. Natures, therefore, explain not only why a thing *can* do something but also why a thing *does* (under specific circumstances). See *GL* §46, postscript; *The Christian Faith*, 176.

References

Anscombe, Elizabeth. *Intention*. Oxford: Basil Blackwell, 1958.
Aquinas, Thomas. *Summa Theologica*. Translated by the Fathers of the English Dominican Province. New York: Benziger Bros., 1947.

Aristotle. *Categories*. Vol. 1. Edited by Jonathan Barnes. Princeton: Princeton University Press, 1984.

———. *Metaphysics*. Vol. 2. Edited by Jonathan Barnes. Princeton: Princeton University Press, 1984.

———. *Nicomachean Ethics*. Vol. 2. Edited by Jonathan Barnes. Princeton: Princeton University Press, 1984.

———. *Parts of Animals*. Vol. 1. Edited by Jonathan Barnes. Princeton: Princeton University Press, 1984.

———. *Physics*. Vol. 1. Edited by Jonathan Barnes. Princeton: Princeton University Press, 1984.

———. *Posterior Analytics*. Vol. 1. Edited by Jonathan Barnes. Princeton: Princeton University Press, 1984.

Barth, Karl. *Church Dogmatics*, IV.1. Translated by Geoffrey W. Bromiley. Edinburgh: T&T Clark, 1956.

Bishop Tempier. "Condemnation of 1277". In *Chartularium Universitatis Parisiensis*, edited by Denifle, H. and E. Châtelain, vol. 1, pp. 543–558, Paris, 1889.

Davidson, Donald. "Actions, Reasons, and Causes." In *The Essential Davidson*. Oxford: Clarendon, 2006.

Hick, John. *Evil and the God of Love*. Third edition. London: Macmillan, 1977.

Kant, Immanuel. *Religion Within the Boundaries of Mere Reason and Other Writings*. Translated and edited by Allen Wood and George Di Giovanni. Cambridge: Cambridge University Press, 1993.

Schleiermacher, Friedrich D. E. *The Christian Faith*. Edited by H. R. Mackintosh and J. S. Stewart, translated by D. M. Baillie, et al. Berkeley: Apocryphile, [1928] 2011.

———. *Der christliche Glaube nach den Grundsätzen der evangelischen Kirche im Zusammenhange dargestellt*. Second edition. Edited by Rolf Schäfer. Berlin: Walter de Gruyter, [1830/31] 2008.

Strawson, Galen. *Freedom and Belief*. Second edition. Oxford: Oxford University Press, 2010.

4   Schleiermacher on the fate of deficient causes

Socrates: Still there was, as we said, a fourth class to be investigated, and you must assist in the investigation; for does not everything which comes into being, of necessity come into being through a cause?

Protarchus: Yes, certainly; for how can there be anything which has no cause?

– Plato, Philebus

As we saw in the previous chapter, important arguments of Schleiermacher's depend on the application of a version of the principle of sufficient reason for their completeness.[1] Indeed, Schleiermacher's reduction of the fall of the Devil, too, depends on the principle of sufficient reason as a tacit premise. It was the principle of sufficient reason that not only authorized but also required Schleiermacher to ask what motivated Adam's and the Devil's willing. And it was the principle of sufficient reason that demanded that all of Adam's acts be explicable by Adam's nature.

Given the distinctiveness of his account, especially in relation to the tradition going back to Augustine, a reader would be more than justified in wondering how much work this principle does, how exactly it works, and to what use Schleiermacher puts it. This chapter aims to answer these questions by showing that, in each and every case, Schleiermacher's position implies, or his arguments for his position depend on, a version of the principle of sufficient reason. Only when his tacit use is made explicit are Schleiermacher's arguments truly appreciable, both with respect to their depth and originality and with respect to their persuasive power. It is only in the light of the principle of sufficient reason that Schleiermacher's account is illuminated, the points of debate and disagreement are specified clearly, and, finally, the foundation is laid for Schleiermacher's alternative account of sin and its origins – including sin's relation to God's causality.

The great alternative to Schleiermacher's account, and the traditional theological substitute for a full-fledged principle of sufficient reason, is the account of sin's explanation by *deficient* causes originating with Augustine. Because Augustine's account is venerable and sophisticated, and solves so many problems at once, and because it is the inspiration for so many other accounts that come after him, we will spend some time looking at it in detail. What will become clear is that Augustine's account is not easy to dismiss, both because of its internal resources and because of the difficult consequences that follow from its denial. In addition, we will see that, despite Schleiermacher's important differences with Augustine and the appeal to deficient causes, Schleiermacher nevertheless maintains an account of determined deficiency. That is, Schleiermacher's disagreements with the deficient cause tradition turn out to be specific, not general. And this matters greatly both with regard to relating his account to the tradition's and with regard to the virtues of his own account, which we will examine in later chapters.

Even so, differences remain. Therefore, one further aim of this chapter is to offer an explanation of *why* Schleiermacher felt able, and even obliged, to hold to the principle of sufficient reason with respect to sin and sin's origins knowing that this would create an impasse with many, if not all, of the theologians who came before him. The explanation I offer points to two of Schleiermacher's well-known influences, Leibniz and Spinoza. I look at how their uses of that principle explain major moves Schleiermacher made in the two previous chapters and look ahead to important claims in subsequent chapters as he gives his own, alternative, account of sin and sin's origins.[2] Because Leibniz and Spinoza faced objections to their use of the principle of sufficient reason (or something like it),[3] their explanations and replies to objections help us understand why Schleiermacher found that principle defensible, even compelling, despite its limited contradiction of the tradition.

After that, we turn to Schleiermacher's most important grounds for why the Christian faith requires the application of the principle of sufficient reason with respect to sin, and why it might even be desirable. It is, Schleiermacher tells us, our absolute dependence on God, including our free acts, that implies that there is, in principle, a causally complete explanation for everything – including sin. The difficulties attending this view will be considered as well.

Finally, a disclaimer is in order. Because deficiency regards a lack of *perfection*, some might worry that Schleiermacher's argument, even should it succeed, could do so only at the price of a disastrous account of *value*. This is an important concern that motivated traditional accounts of deficient causality. This topic will be addressed more fully in the following chapters. For now, however, it should be reiterated that Schleiermacher does not discard every notion of deficiency. Rather, Schleiermacher is concerned to deny only certain notions, or applications of, deficiency: namely, the specific theory that holds that defects are, in principle, incompletely explicable, that there *is* no complete explanation for some acts because there is no efficient cause, only a deficient one. For Schleiermacher's own account of value, however, the reader must await his account of sin and its connection to the teleological perfection of the world.

Deficient causes

When Augustine rejected the Manichaeism of his youth, he was forced to reckon with the problem of accounting for the fact of sin in light of God's good creation without merely appealing to the material or created world as intrinsically bad, as in itself evil. In its place, Augustine required an account of how a good world could go bad, an account that did not terminate in a second, evil principle, and one that did not make the good God the cause of evil. Because Augustine recognized that any efficient causal chain could eventually be traced back to God as First Cause, his ingenious solution was to deny that sin and evil had an efficient cause at all; that the cause of sin and evil was, rather, deficient.

Augustine put the idea of a deficient cause to extensive use not only by accounting for the imperfection that sinners suffer by virtue of their sinful condition, or the failure to attain perfection that this condition implies, but also in telling a story of how *any* humans *became* sinners in the first place. If Augustine had merely given such an account, that alone would be impressive. Yet he did more still. If Augustine is right, and if his account works, then his account not only explains how humans became sinners but also does so in such a way as to both secure their full culpability and, at the same time, deny any culpability of God.

In order to secure Adam's culpability, Augustine must be able to attribute Adam's first sin to Adam as a voluntary act. Moreover, on his grounds, Augustine must do so in a way that relieves God of responsibility for Adam's sin. Otherwise, Adam's punishment, his damnation in particular, would be unjust. But God is Adam's creator. It is God who made Adam's nature, and Adam's nature that now enables and disposes him to act as he does. Therefore, Augustine must find a way to attribute Adam's sin to Adam as a voluntary act while, at the same time, denying that this act is natural and, therefore, that God shares any blame for it. This is not as easy as it might sound. Many acts are *both* natural *and* voluntary. And so Augustine's account *must* divide Adam's willing from his nature such that his nature does not sufficiently explain why he willed what he willed. Sin, for Augustine, must be unnatural.

As we saw in previous chapters, Schleiermacher contests this account, and accounts like it. But notice: if Augustine's account succeeds, it solves a host of problems at once. Therefore, there are powerful motivating reasons to maintain Augustine's account, or something like it, and to maintain it with enough fidelity to the original account that it solves the same problems and solves them similarly well.[4]

Deficient causes are the tool that does the bulk of this work for Augustine, specifically a deficient *will*. It is this special kind of cause, a deficient cause, which precludes any causal connection between Adam's nature and his will because the cause of his will was not a *reality* at all, and so could not have its basis in a nature. Instead, as Augustine tells us, a deficient cause is a lack, an absence, a nonentity.[5] Any attempt "To want to discover such causes is like wanting to see darkness or hear silence."[6]

Accordingly, when Schleiermacher asks *why did Adam will thus?* Augustine can reply that there is no sufficient answer to this question *in principle* when what Adam willed was sinful, and his will itself evil. In the first place, Augustine might defend an account of the will as substantially more independent from the intellect than Schleiermacher would.[7] More importantly, however, even should Augustine agree that the will follows the intellect's judgments, these judgments themselves would be faulty, their fault would be a lack, a kind of nothingness, and so the cause of the sin would be similarly deficient. Since there is no cause of something that does not exist, it is senseless, according to the deficient will tradition, to expect a cause for the sinful act of an evil will. It is a mistaken question and a false problem. And, importantly, it is confused in the same formal way that the Manicheans were confused: by supposing evil to be a sort of *thing* – because, again, only things can have efficient causes. No, "there is no cause of such a will except the defection by which God is abandoned, and even the cause of this defection is altogether lacking."[8]

It is this latter aspect of Augustine's account which is of greatest importance to the larger theological tradition and which poses the most important challenge. It is, in short, *this* aspect, Augustine's account of deficiency as such, that any critic of this classic account must reply to if an alternative is to be proposed. And it is this latter aspect which links the array of broadly Augustinian accounts of sin and sin's origins from Augustine to Thomas to the Reformers to twentieth-century theologians. Schleiermacher's criticism is no exception to this rule. If he is to advance his criticism of the traditional account on the grounds he does, by demanding a complete causal account within which even an evil will can be sufficiently explained, he must have countervailing reasons to reject Augustine's account – at least in part.

Sufficient reasons and deficient causes

Schleiermacher's defense of the principle of sufficient reason against deficient causes is not direct. He *assumes* the principle of sufficient reason – he does not argue for it. In that sense it is a true first principle. As we will see, however, Schleiermacher is not utterly silent on the matter, but supports a causal completeness thesis as an implication of our absolute dependence on God. But that is not, in itself, a defense, or even a full explanation of his application of the principle of sufficient reason to wills and natures. Therefore, in what follows I will fill in the gaps between what Schleiermacher has clearly, and necessarily, implied (see Chapters 2 and 3, and ahead, for evidence of these implications) and the "principle of monotheism" – that is, the principle that all depend absolutely on a single *Whence*.

Consider Augustine again on the will in his account of evil:

> But if we look for the efficient cause of this evil will, we will find none.
> For what is it that makes the will evil, when it is the will itself that
> makes the act evil? Accordingly, an evil will is the efficient cause of an
> evil act, but nothing is the efficient cause of an evil will.[9]

Because of the nature of evil, as a deficiency, it can be only to a deficiency
that its lack can be attributed. But that lack is, then, traceable only as far
as the thing lacking: the will. And therefore, there *is no* efficient cause of a
deficient will. It is the deficiency of the deficient will alone that terminates
the explanation.

Notice that this is precisely the kind of account that Schleiermacher
described in Chapter 3 as explaining "sin as due to such a misuse of free
will which had no ground in the first man's inward being, that is to say that
he chose the evil without determining reasons,"[10] for such reasons, however poor, would at least continue the explanation. And also notice that
Schleiermacher has, once more, already buried his criticism of the position
within his description. Whereas, for Augustine, the will itself can, at least
sometimes, be the end of all *why* questions regarding the will, for Schleiermacher, as for subscribers to the principle of sufficient reason in general, a
full account of the determination of the will *must* include reasons – that is,
causes sufficient to explain why the will inclined as it did. And while this
does not eliminate the notion of deficiency entirely, it does lie contrary to
Augustine's insistence that the will is the terminus of explanation.

But why would anyone, particularly a Christian theologian, feel persuaded
to reject the idea that the will is, at least sometimes, a sufficient explanation
for its own willing and so give up this powerful account of the origins of sin
and evil? To begin to see to what important assumptions underlie this discussion, consider this passage of Augustine's, where he provides an example
of why his account of the will makes sense, and why an account of the will
that demands a motive falls short:

> Suppose that two people who are of precisely the same disposition in
> mind and body [*aequaliter affecti animo et corpore*] see the beauty of
> one and the same body. The sight stirs one of them to illicit enjoyment,
> while the other stands firm in his chastity of will. What do we suppose
> is the cause that gives rise to an evil will in one and not in the other?
> What caused it in the one in whom it was caused? Not the beauty of
> the body, for that did not cause an evil will in both of them, although
> both had precisely the same view of it. Was it the flesh of the beholder?
> Then why did not the other's flesh do the same? Or was it the mind?
> Then why not the mind of both? For we presumed that they both had
> the same disposition of mind and body.[11]

Although Augustine goes on to entertain more explanatory options in this stunning passage, his reduction is already set to unfold from his premises. Indeed, it is these premises that are the key, and we will come back to them in a moment. But notice how, on Augustine's grounds, this argument inevitably leads to his conclusion that there is no sufficient reason for why one man willed one way and the other another way apart from the will itself. There is no other reason because we have tried all the options in principle. And yet one *did* will one way, while the other *did* will another way. If they *in fact* willed differently, there must be some difference accounting for their willing. But the only difference there *could* be is the will itself. So the will must be the cause of its own willing. On Augustine's grounds, then, the will *must* be the terminus of the explanation, because nothing else about the two men explains, or could possibly explain, their differing choices.

The possibility of this inference is due to the completeness of the explanatory options Augustine proposes. The different choices of the two men *might* be explained by differing dispositions of mind; or, perhaps, by differing dispositions of body. In either case, their different initial dispositions in either body or mind or both *could* explain their different choices. Or, alternatively, it might be a different object that promoted the two men to act: say, two different bodies beheld. Or it might have been the same body seen two ways. That, too, *might* explain why the one man succumbed and the other did not. But these were identical as well: the same person was seen in the same way in both cases. Therefore, it could neither be anything external (the object or its perception or the same thing under different circumstances) or any internal disposition (of either the body or the mind) which explains why the two men chose differently. And dispositions and circumstances are the only things that *can* explain this difference apart from the will since, crucially, Augustine includes the two men's minds in those dispositions and circumstances.

The strength of Augustine's argument, its insistence on the complete sameness of the two men and their circumstances, as well as their objects of perception, is also its weakness. Because Augustine's case depends not only on a strict identity between the two people willing but also on that identity holding in every relevant respect, then in order to deny his conclusion one might simply deny that such identity is possible. Note that this objection is not merely to the identity of the two men and their circumstances *in fact*. That would make only this one example unfeasible. We could change the example to, say, the slightly different medieval thought experiment of a donkey presented with two identical piles of food – Buridan's ass. No, however it is framed, the objection to the identity of things must be an *in principle* objection to the basic possibility of such identity. When Schleiermacher contrasts his position with the idea that no ground in the person willing, including a motive, can be found, he is clearly and necessarily denying that such cases exist, and, therefore, committing himself to the contrary view that indeed something on the part of the person willing must ground their willing. And so, if he is to avoid Augustine's conclusion and maintain that wills have some ground, he must be committed to the denial of such cases of two identical things in principle as well.

Perhaps the most thoughtful refutation of the possibility of the identity of any two (or more) things and circumstances in the history of thought comes from one of Schleiermacher's well-known influences: Leibniz. For Leibniz, this takes the form of a powerful and universal principle: *the principle of the identity of indiscernibles*.[12] Though it can be variously formulated, it is most broadly the principle that there are no two things that are entirely the same. It is this principle, or a version of it, to which Schleiermacher must hold if he is to successfully deny Augustine's account of the will as the terminus of explanation. If there are no two things that are entirely the same, there can be no two "men who are of precisely the same disposition in mind and body,"[13] for if they were *precisely* the same, they would not be two men, but one. And if they really were two, they could not be precisely the same. Therefore, the whole notion of *two* men, precisely the same, willing two different things is a non-starter. There simply never is such a case. Augustine's hypothetical is impossible.

The notion of *indiscernibility* might, however, mislead. It might suggest that two things are the same if we cannot *tell* them apart. Leibniz's principle denies this. The indiscernibility of two things is not merely conditional on *our* knowledge, but in principle. Were we to know everything that *could* be known about two things, which is to say, *everything* predicable of them, that would amount to saying that everything about them was, in fact and at every level, the same. We could not *tell* them apart because they would *be* one thing, not two.[14] It is, despite its apparent couching as an epistemic principle, a fundamentally ontological one.

But still someone might object that it is at least *conceivable* that we have two entirely alike things, distinguished only by number, and that *number alone suffices*, so that we could at least say there were *two* people, that one was first, the other second, or the like. This might take the form of a science-fiction thought experiment where a device that scans a person, body and mind, and replicates them in every way on the spot was used to create two of the same people at the same time on the same day: not merely a clone but an instant and complete replica. How would the principle of the identity of indiscernibles be defended in such cases? Surely, two of the *same* person would count as a counterexample in principle, even if such devices do not exist.

This is where the power and extent of the principle of the identity of indiscernibles become truly apparent. For Leibniz, the principle is primarily couched in terms of predication (to correlate with his doctrine of conceptual containment).[15] What comprises an individual's identity is not a distinct individuator, like Scotus's *haecceity*, but the totality of an individual's predicates. And these turn out to be vast – infinite, in fact – because these predicates include all relations, and an individual has *some* relation to everything else in the universe. That is, say we managed to replicate a person, Kate, and make a simultaneous and apparently identical copy of Kate in one moment so that the Kate copied and the Kate produced were exactly alike in age and appearance and so on. Assuming we did all this, $Kate_1$ and her copy, $Kate_2$, would still not be *identical* and never could be, in principle, in many respects. In the first place, $Kate_1$ existed *before* $Kate_2$. That logical and temporal priority would be a relational predicate grounded in the respective Kates, so that being before and after are things that are actually different *about* $Kate_1$ and $Kate_2$ – that is, predicates, like all predicates for Leibniz, which have a basis on the part of things. Indeed, everything that ever happened to $Kate_1$, everything she did, everything that was ever true of her, could be summoned to differentiate her from $Kate_2$, and we only ever need a single differing predicate to distinguish an individual in principle.

In the same vein, Augustine's two men, in order to be *exactly* alike, would strictly have to have been born at the same moment in the same place to the same mother, had all the same thoughts, shared the same body, and stood in the same relation to *everything else in the world*, including standing at the same spot at the moment of their willing. But the *sameness* of these things must be so strict in order to be truly and completely the same that the two must have stood inside each other's bodies and other absurdities – or else be one and the same person. And such strict indiscernibility is impossible to maintain, even as a hypothetical.

The payoff to all this is that, if not in the absolute strictest sense *identical* (i.e., actually one and only one man), Augustine's two men not only could be but also *must* be different in *some* way, however small, in mind or body or both. And that minute difference would be sufficient to explain any difference in their willing. What this reveals is that, despite its very commonsense framing, Augustine's argument that *the will alone* could explain the difference in what the two men willed depends on a metaphysically fantastic premise: that the *two* men were *exactly* alike. In order to defeat Augustine's reduction, we need only to doubt his setup.

The identity of indiscernibles provides powerful reasons to doubt not only Augustine's specific example but also every similar example, in principle. The two or more things in question could be people or plants or angels. The principle still holds that, if they are truly *different* – that is, not strictly one and the same thing – there must be something on the part of the thing that differentiates them. If two or more things are never *exactly* the same, there is then always, in principle, some distinct explanation on the part of the thing and its circumstances for a thing's determinate actions. If so, there never can be, in principle, "such a misuse of freedom as had no ground whatever in the first man's inward being"[16] because the effort to *guarantee* such ungrounded freedom depends on exactly those sorts of circumstances the identity of indiscernibles shows to be impossible.

Schleiermacher not only disavows the general idea of an ungrounded explanation an action but also specifically denies the notion of a *will* without *determining reasons*. This is the exact "indifference of equipoise" that Leibniz dismisses in his theodicy and which I briefly mentioned in the previous chapter. It is the possibility of reasons which are insufficient to determine the will that are a necessary condition of such indifference of equipoise. As Leibniz explains,

> It is not to be imagined, however, that our freedom consists in an indetermination or an indifference of equipoise [*une indifférence d'equilibre*], as if one needs to be inclined equally to the side of yes and of no and in the direction of different course, when there are several of them to take. This equipoise in all directions is impossible: for if we were equally inclined towards courses A, B, and C, we could be equally inclined towards A and towards not A. This equipoise is also absolutely contrary to experience, and in scrutinizing oneself one will find that there has always been some cause or reason [*cause ou raison*] inclining us towards the course taken, although very often we be not aware of that which prompts us: just in the same way one is hardly aware why, on issuing from a door, one has placed the right foot before the left or the left before the right.[17]

That is, if, contrary to Leibniz and Schleiermacher, freedom *might* consist in an indifference of equipoise, it must *ex hypoethesi*, in such cases, not be inclined by reasons sufficient to determine it. On the contrary, Schleiermacher's view on the matter is Leibniz's view: that, without exception, we will what we will *because* of reasons – that is, because reasons are, in and of themselves, sufficient (and necessary) to determine the will. Therefore, questions about *why* we willed what we willed can always be answered in principle for voluntary actions.[18] Of course, as Leibniz points out, we are often unconscious of the causes or reasons of our being inclined one way or the other, and it seems we are rarely, if ever, aware of *all* our motives. Therefore Schleiermacher, with Leibniz, must be committed to the view that *why* questions about why we willed what we willed are at the very least answerable *in principle*, if not always in fact.

If correct, such an account of the will counts very heavily against any reading that interprets Schleiermacher's account of freedom as undetermined, because *reasons determine* in and of themselves.[19] Moreover, on Schleiermacher's account, there is no possibility of *insufficient* determining reasons, preserving some remaining role for an indeterminate will. In the first place, all of Schleiermacher's criticisms depend on there being no such insufficiency; and in the second place, since reasons determine, there are always, in principle, sufficient determining reasons if we have any reasons to act whatsoever.

Recall how this contrasts with Augustine's account. "But if we look for the efficient cause of this evil will," he says, "we find none."[20] But the rejection of the indifference of equipoise claims the opposite: there *must* be a reason sufficient to determine the will to this evil choice, a motive which inclines the will to evil, a motive which *explains* why the will inclined as it does. And that, of course, then warrants all of the difficult follow-up questions Schleiermacher offered in the previous two chapters about motive and agency.

Importantly, however, Schleiermacher affirms, *with* Augustine, that "sin is always a misuse of free will."[21] It is *both* sufficiently causally determined *and* defective with respect to its ideal use. This is to say, it is not deficient with respect to its *efficient* cause, but it *is* defective with respect to its end or purpose. We will take up this theme in greater detail in the following chapters when we look at Schleiermacher's own account of sin. For now it is important to notice that his rejection of traditional accounts of the origins of sin depends on the principle of sufficient reason applied in such a way that, despite the "misuse" of free will that sin implies, no account of sin can merely terminate in the will and its deficiencies, but must be further grounded in the desires, perceptions, judgments, and inclinations that, together, provide a motive sufficient to determine a will to evil – a controversial claim that will require Schleiermacher to explain how his account of sin is compatible with God's benevolence and the goodness of the created world.

Nature and its determined failures

How is a good nature capable of going bad *at all*? Alongside his exploration of the terminus of explanation for an evil will in an evil choice, Augustine raises this broader question. The two are not, of course, unrelated. The former regards the specifics of how sin arose, the latter its general conditions. The puzzle Augustine faces is not merely with regard to creation's goodness, or its transition from good to evil, but also the possibility of evil arising from something that God, the supreme good, made. Augustine's reflections on this problem prove tremendously influential and potent:

> Thus, if anyone claims that the one who consented caused his own evil will, even though he was certainly good prior to his evil will, he should ask why he caused it. Was it because of his nature? Or was it because his nature was created out of nothing? It will then be found that the evil will has its origin not in the fact of his nature but in the fact that his nature was created out of nothing. For, if his nature is the cause of his evil will, how can we avoid the conclusion that evil comes from good and that good is the cause of evil (presuming that it is really true that an evil will stems from a good nature)? But how can this be? How can it be that a good nature, although mutable, should, before it comes to have an evil will, cause something evil, that is, should cause the evil will itself?[22]

Augustine's reply to his own question brings us back full circle, for it is to this question that he answers that *there is no efficient cause*, and that trying discover one "is like wanting to see darkness or hear silence."[23] But in putting the question again in this very general way, we see not only what is at stake for Augustine in giving the answer he gives, and how it central it is for solving the problem at hand, but also what other accounts of the origins of sin and evil have sought from Augustine's account beside merely his account of the will.

One inheritance of Augustine's line of argument is a question; the other is an answer. The question is how, if at all, evil can originate from good. The answer takes the form of the nature of creatures *as creatures* – that is, as mutable things. As Thomas Aquinas puts it,

> As, therefore, the perfection of the universe requires that there should be not only beings incorruptible, but also corruptible beings; so the perfection of the universe requires that there should be some which can fail in goodness, and thence it follows that they sometimes do fail.[24]

Schleiermacher's case against the fall of the Devil and the fall of Adam picks up where this account leaves off. Schleiermacher insists, beyond the limited extent which Thomas grants,[25] that evil has a cause sufficient to determine it *as* evil, which is to say that every failure has a cause, and that this cause is wholly sufficient to account for its effects. Evil, in short, is not exempt from the principle of sufficient reason. Despite having no independent existence – evil, for Schleiermacher, is still a privation, not a subsisting thing – the failures of created things which constitute evils *do* have causes and these causes can, in principle, sufficiently account for evil.

The reader will immediately recognize that one of the profound drawbacks of Schleiermacher's approach is that it seems to commit him to the view that, if the causes of evil can be traced back in principle, they can eventually be traced back to God. This is almost certainly the greatest difficulty with Schleiermacher's account, and any reader would be right to wonder about it. Importantly, this inference is not unsound, and Schleiermacher not only admits that God is the cause (even in a sense the "author") of evil but also eagerly affirms it, for otherwise evil and its causes would not depend on God and thus, in Schleiermacher's view, our absolute dependence on God, and with it our piety, would be destroyed. Of course, his account is much more sophisticated than that, and for a full explanation and defense the reader will have to wait until we take up the topic in Chapter 7. But now any reader should be assured that this is not slander. It actually is an implication of Schleiermacher's view, and one that he not only recognizes but also embraces.[26]

Schleiermacher is not, however, content to admit that traditional accounts of the origins of sin and evil fare better than his own account. The reason is, once again, that, on the basis of the principle of sufficient reason, the traditional account reduces to his own: for, if we believe Augustine that the mutability of creatures generates the *possibility* of them failing, and if we believe Thomas that if a thing *can* fail it *sometimes* will, we will then be entitled to press further and ask why a thing fails now and not then, some times and not others. In other words, what Augustine hinted at and Thomas makes explicit, that the conditions of existence *in general* make such failure not only possible but also inevitable, entitles us to ask about the *specific* conditions of *actual* failures. And these conditions will be causes that *determine* not only that things might fail but also that they do. And these causes will, in turn, have prior causes, and so on, back, ultimately, to God as the First Cause. Under the power of the principle of sufficient reason, once someone like Thomas puts Augustine's pregnant question into the form he does, it will amount to Schleiermacher's teaching on the matter, or else amount to incoherence.

However, not just any version of the principle of sufficient reason would require the deterministic conclusions explored here and in the previous two chapters. Historical sources for this strong version of the principle are rare. And of all the candidate accounts I know of, none are quite as complete a match as that advanced by Benedict Spinoza in his *Ethics*.

Accordingly, Schleiermacher's reductions that we explored in the previous two chapters are best explained by his following Spinoza on the matter, specifically by a subscription to something like Spinoza's axiom, A3, that "From a given determinate cause the effect follows necessarily; and conversely, if there is no determinate cause, it is impossible for an effect to follow."[27] The first clause of this axiom is common, going back to the ancients.[28] It is the second clause that is stronger and more interesting. This clause demands that for any effect, there must be a prior determining cause, and that without such a cause there can strictly be no such effect. This axiom, though uncommon, is still, in itself, not strictly unique.[29] But Spinoza amplifies this axiom through the combination of a few further moves. And it is Spinoza's amplification which makes it the most likely inspiration of Schleiermacher's equally strong claims on the matter.

Let us turn to Spinoza to see how this strong version of the principle of sufficient reason works. Spinoza infers from IP16C1 – that "God is the efficient cause of all things that can fall under an infinite intellect" – that "A thing which has been determined by God to produce an effect has necessarily been determined in this way by God; and one which has not been determined by God cannot determine itself to produce an effect."[30] This tells us two things: first, "that a thing which has been determined by God to produce an effect, cannot render itself undetermined,"[31] for, in that case, effect would not follow cause with the necessity that A3 demands; and second, that because "all things have been determined by the necessity of the divine nature to exist and produce an effect in a certain way,"[32] it follows from the divine necessity, and the necessity by which effects follow causes, that "There is nothing contingent."[33] That is, because of the necessity by which effects follow causes, and because the chain of causes goes all the way back to the absolutely necessary divine essence, it is absurd, a contradiction of a necessary truth, to think that any other effects *could* have been produced, even if these causes were "accidental" causes (in Aquinas's words earlier). And this is the basis of Schleiermacher's connection between the principle of sufficient reason and our absolute dependence on God, which we will look at more ahead.

Yet this is not the most jarring and controversial part of Spinoza's account, nor it is the only significant connection to Schleiermacher's view. Rather, extraordinary consequences follow from the pairing of this series of claims with IIP7, that "The order and connection of ideas is the same as the order and connection of things."[34] From the application of his causal completeness thesis to *thought* as well as to extended things, Spinoza can claim that thought, which includes the will (if there is a will), is as completely causally determined as other things are, such that if we were to think other than we do, it would imply a contradiction, *and* that such thoughts, again including the will, are so determined by the same causal chain that finds its source in the divine essence. As Spinoza says,

> It follows, secondly, that will and intellect are related to God's nature as motion and rest are, and as are all natural things, which (by P29) must be determined by God to exist and produce and effect in a certain way. For the will, like all other things, requires a cause by which it is determined to exist and produce an effect in a certain way.[35]

Because the will, like any other natural thing, follows necessarily from its causes, never follows without a determining cause, and cannot be rendered undetermined, not only does the will have sufficient determining causes in principle, but also these causes can be traced back to the absolute necessity of the divine essence. This is Schleiermacher's most unique and controversial move. It is implicit in his directing of the principle of sufficient reason over and over again to questions of the determination of the evil angels' and Adam's will to sin. Spinoza's strong account of the exhaustive determination of all things, *including the will*, explains the distinctiveness of Schleiermacher's account in this same respect.

It is the inclusion of the will in the determinate causal chain that sets Schleiermacher's account apart from so many major theological accounts before and after. Compare Aquinas once again. Though Aquinas agrees with Spinoza's strong causal axiom, A3, in respect to *natural* things, he does not agree in respect to *voluntary* things. As Aquinas explains,

> Evil has a deficient cause in voluntary things otherwise than in natural things. For the natural agent produces the same kind of effect as it is itself, unless it is impeded by some exterior thing; and this amounts to some defect belonging to it. [. . .] But in voluntary things the defect of the action comes from the will actually deficient, inasmuch as it does not actually subject itself to its proper rule.[36]

And so, according to Aquinas, the defect of the will cannot be attributed to a prior determining cause in the same way that Spinoza and Schleiermacher insist that it can. In consequence, "God is the author of evil which is penalty," says Aquinas, "but not of the evil which is fault."[37]

In contrast, Schleiermacher's account *necessitates* that the will is included, as Spinoza includes it, as a "natural thing" which, like everything else in nature, is sufficiently determined to produce the effect it does – which is to say as a thing that is not exempt from the causal completeness the principle of sufficient reason requires. If it were not, Schleiermacher's pressing questions regarding both the fall of the Devil and the fall of Adam could always be answered as the tradition has: by appeal to will as deficient cause in one form or another ranging from the will as utterly independent and undetermined to the will as a created thing naturally susceptible of failure, but not determined as such by God. The fact that Schleiermacher finds these traditional answers unsatisfactory in principle, and not merely in fact, reveals the extent to which a difference in first principles, even a subtle difference, matters.

To repeat, however, this does not commit Schleiermacher to the denial that things are deficient in every sense. Importantly, all that is required by the view that deficiencies are sufficiently determined is that deficiencies of the will be explained in the same way as any other natural deficiency. For example, if someone suffered from a disease we could *explain* their ill health by appeal to the way the infection harms the body, the sources of that infection, and so on. We could, in short, offer a complete causal account of why something is *specifically* wrong. But nothing about this account requires us to deny that something *is wrong* just because we can give a complete account of its origins. The causal completeness thesis holds in the same way with respect to the will. So, for example, if one were to ask why someone willed the evil they willed, say, to murder, we could explain that they were motivated by hatred to kill Person P, for instance.[38] And if we were to then ask why they were motivated by hatred we could keep offering reasons: they were taught to hate, they suffered at the hands of those they now hate, they think killing will satisfy their hate, Person P is particularly worthy of hatred, and so forth, and so expand the causal story in practice as far as it was useful or relevant, and, in principle, to the whole universe. For the ills of the will are, for Schleiermacher, as determined to failure as the ills of nature are for Aquinas – because both are, in fact, for Schleiermacher, *natural things*.

This returns us to the second use of the principle of sufficient reason that we explored in Chapter 3: the grounding of acts in natures. Recall Schleiermacher's important dictum that "the individual can only act in accordance with the nature of the species, but never can act upon that nature."[39] It should now be clear how crucial the principle of sufficient reason is for explaining this claim and making it work. It is because Adam's nature is a determinate cause that it can produce some, but not all, determinate effects. And under determinate circumstances this determinate nature *necessarily* produces determinate effects. Because, however, it is a determinate cause it cannot render itself undetermined (by Spinoza's IP27); hence it cannot change its own nature.

This last point might seem to mark the greatest difference between Schleiermacher's account and the traditional account of the fall involving a change in human nature. And in important ways it does: for Schleiermacher denies that Adam *could* have done anything which altered his own nature. But, despite this significant difference, Schleiermacher's position circles back around to Augustine's in an unexpected way. "How can it be," Augustine asks, "that a good nature, although mutable, should, before it comes to have an evil will, cause something evil, that is, should cause the evil will itself?"[40] Though Augustine and Schleiermacher give very different accounts of the deficient causes that Augustine thereafter leads into, they both agree – remarkably – that, strictly speaking, *no good nature can cause itself to become evil*: Augustine, because deficient wills are not properly causes, and certainly not causes grounded in natures; Schleiermacher, because no animal can in any way ever corrupt its own nature through a violent act (in the Aristotelian sense).

The nearness of Schleiermacher's claims to the tradition is as striking as their difference and neither should be emphasized at the expense of the other. What Schleiermacher has done is to modify, not abolish, traditional claims about the origins of sin, albeit with profound consequences. Yet neither are the results utterly alien to the tradition. What is anticipated and endorsed by the tradition in limited respects Schleiermacher endorses wholesale, while what is endorsed wholesale by the tradition Schleiermacher endorses with qualification. The differences that exist then are substantial yet specific.

Absolute dependence as the warrant for the principle of sufficient reason

The principle of sufficient reason is controversial, and the consequences Schleiermacher draws even more so. Throughout this chapter we have seen how this principle explains Schleiermacher's views and funds his arguments. In this section, we consider what justification he gave for holding to it.

Now an obvious disclaimer is in order: Schleiermacher never uses the phrase "principle of sufficient reason." What he does is use the principle itself. That is, he uses what is commonly called the principle of sufficient reason – or at least a *version* of the principle of sufficient reason.[41] What I have done in this chapter is to show *that* his claims and arguments depend on its (largely tacit) use, and that they do so *without exception*. That is, whether in regard to efficient, formal, or final causes – in the form of questions about the will, natures, and so forth – Schleiermacher's positions *require the principle of sufficient reason in each and every case* to sustain his conclusions. Without it, he could not claim the specificity or necessity that he does as anything more than matters of personal preference.

In this section, I transition from showing *that* Schleiermacher subscribed to some version of the principle of sufficient reason, and instead aim to show *why* he felt able and obliged to do so. In each case, Schleiermacher's reasons reduce to the claim that anything other than the principle of sufficient reason contradicts our absolute dependence on God. That is, any exception to the causal completeness implied by the principle of sufficient reason violates what Schleiermacher sometimes calls the principle of monotheism.[42]

According to Schleiermacher, we are conscious of being absolutely dependent on God. "For we recognize in our self-consciousness an awareness of the world," he says, "but it is different from the awareness of God in the same self-consciousness."[43] And, indeed, the "original expression, i.e. that the world exists only in absolute dependence upon God,"[44] is, for Schleiermacher, a *true* and adequate proposition: "The proposition that the totality of finite being exists only in dependence upon the Infinite is the complete description of that basis [*Grundlage*] of every religious feeling which is here to be set forth."[45] That is, we do not merely *feel* absolutely dependent upon God, we are so *in fact*, and it is this fact that is the basis, or foundation, of our feeling.[46]

Not only is the awareness (see earlier) of our absolute dependence on God constitutive of Christian (and, more generally, monotheistic) faith, but also it is the very *absoluteness* of this dependence that distinguishes God from the world. Absent this distinction, it could well be

> possible to give a non-religious explanation of this sense of absolute dependence; it might be said that it only means the dependence of finite particulars on the whole and on the system of all finite things, and that what is implied and made the center of reference is not God but the world.[47]

Should we want, as Christians do want, to resist this reductive explanation of the feeling of absolute dependence to a feeling of dependence on the world as a whole, we need some way to distinguish God from the world non-arbitrarily.

It is *this distinction*, the distinction between that upon which we are relatively dependent and that upon which we are absolutely dependent, that Schleiermacher secures with his account of the world as the totality of the mutually affectable: "a feeling of dependence, indeed, so far as the other parts act spontaneously upon it, but also a feeling of freedom in so far as it likewise reacts spontaneously on the other parts."[48] Crucially, however, in both respects the feelings are not absolute but relative. We never feel ourselves absolutely dependent on the world, only on God; and we simply never have a feeling of absolute freedom:

> One who asserts that he has such a feeling [of absolute freedom] is either deceiving themselves or separating things that essentially belong together. For if the feeling of freedom expresses a forthgoing activity,

this activity must have an object that has somehow been given to us, and this could not have taken place without an influence of the object upon our receptivity. Therefore, in every such case there is involved a feeling of dependence that goes along with the feeling of freedom, and thus limits it. The contrary could only be possible if the object altogether came into existence through our activity, which is never the case absolutely, but only relatively.[49]

No created thing is absolutely free because the activity, including its object, is something given to it, not something independently created. Moreover, in order for us to be *absolutely* free we would not only have to be the genuine and spontaneous source of our own actions, the source of our own existence, *and* the existence of the *objects of our action*.[50] And plainly none of these ever obtains absolutely because our existence, our actions, and their objects all have their sources outside ourselves in at least some respects. The idea of an absolutely free member *of the nature system* is incoherent. There is only the relatively free and relatively dependent whole of creation, comprising a *single, interrelated world – including us and our acts*, and the one *Whence* upon which the whole order depends absolutely.[51]

Our absolute dependence on God has, as its corollary, the notion of God's *absolute independence*. As Schleiermacher explains, "[I]f the simple expression 'everything depends on God' is further supplemented by the negative 'but God depends on nothing,' at once a fresh opening is given for a division into positive and negative attributes."[52] Importantly, however, the opportunity that accompanies its affirmation parallels the difficulties that attend its denial. If *everything* whatsoever did not depend upon God in every way whatsoever, then God could not truly be said to depend on nothing, for there would be something independent of God, and so something which, in fact, conditions God.[53] But unless *this thing* were then something upon which all depended – in which case, the issue would simply be one of misidentifying God – there would be no *one* thing upon which all depend. In short, the uniqueness of God, the claim that there is one and only one God, and God's independence are also corollaries. Therefore, to deny that *everything* depends on God absolutely is to deny that God is unique.[54]

In order to resist the reduction of absolute dependence to dependence on a finite whole, or worse, the denial that we are absolutely dependent on anything at all (because there simply is no one thing upon which *all* depend absolutely), Schleiermacher thinks that all Christians (and, in fact, all monotheists) are committed not only to distinguishing God and the world, such that dependence on one cannot be confused for dependence on another, but also to grounding this distinction in the *absoluteness*, or completeness, of God as that which is the cause of all else.[55]

Notice what this means. Because nothing in the world is absolutely free, the existence of everything is a particular existence – determined partly by its nature and actions, partly by its circumstances. Relatively free causes are no exception to this rule. Their natures, desires, judgments, and actions are *included in* the causal nexus. There is no causal remainder. Further, nothing in the world is absolutely free because nothing but God is wholly the reason for its existence.[56] And, of course, the latter, the utter independence of God, is the *basis* of the feeling of absolute dependence. Therefore, *causal completeness* is not only a thesis to which Schleiermacher holds of preference or convenience but also a necessary implication of that most fundamental Christian commitment to the uniqueness of God. If the thing-thing relations that comprise the world and the God-world relation are all causally complete, then there is *in principle* a cause or reason (the two are synonymous) for everything to be, and to be as it is – which is to say, the principle of sufficient reason holds. Conversely, to deny the principle of sufficient reason amounts to the denial that there is a world in Schleiermacher's sense and that it depends absolutely on God.[57]

What Schleiermacher has done, then, is to use the world's absolute dependence on God, with God's independence as its corollary, to put positions like Augustine's on the horns of a dilemma: they can, Schleiermacher thinks, maintain the causal *incompleteness* they need to secure their strong account of an undetermined will and/or deficient causes only *at the expense* of God's uniqueness. Because, according to Schleiermacher, everything whatsoever is *absolutely* – that is, wholly – dependent on God, to claim there is one thing, the will, which is not wholly dependent on God is to deny that God is that upon which all depend absolutely. And so, while Schleiermacher's position includes the burdensome claim that God is the author of sin, he trades that difficulty for the ability to maintain a coherent notion of God as that upon which *all* depend *absolutely*. Since, Schleiermacher argues, it is the affirmation of the absolute dependence of the world on God, not the denial that God is the author of sin, which is the basis of Christian piety, he is not only authorized but happy to deploy the causal completeness thesis that underwrites his use of the principle of sufficient reason.

Freedom and dependence

Despite Schleiermacher's apparent commitment to a causal completeness thesis, it might be objected that there is a glaring exception in his own words: humans as free agents. Despite the fact that, as we saw earlier, Schleiermacher's positions rely on a commitment to the principle of sufficient reason in order to secure them, it might be thought that Schleiermacher's explicit statements on the matter overrule these necessary inferences. In this section, I show that they do not, that Schleiermacher is *explicitly* committed to accounts of (1) human freedom, and (2) causal completeness, that do not exclude each other. No, for Schleiermacher our free actions – and they are free – are as completely determined as every other cause. Far from undermining my claim that the principle of sufficient reason explains Schleiermacher's positions and arguments, his treatment of freedom provides additional evidence.

Let there be no doubt: Schleiermacher thinks we are, at least sometimes, free.[58] "Let us now attribute to ourselves free causality along with absolute dependence," he says,

> and causality also to every living being as assuredly as we hold it to have being for itself; and let us see complete absence of freedom only where a thing does not move itself and moves other things only insofar as it is moved.[59]

We are free while we are, nevertheless, absolutely dependent; freedom comes in degrees; and freedom (partly) *consists in* spontaneity or self-motivated action.[60] Nevertheless, the relation between our freedom and absolute dependence on God must be specified "in order to prevent a not infrequent misunderstanding, namely, that consciousness of our free-will is in opposition to the feeling of absolute dependence."[61] Thus, it is a *misunderstanding*, according to Schleiermacher, to think that our freedom and absolute dependence on God are opposed.

In what sense, however, are we absolutely dependent on God despite our freedom? This might be explained in more than one way, yet Schleiermacher's own explanation is highly specific:

> [H]owever much freedom resides in determination of will and resolution, action, emerging as it does under influences beyond itself, is always so conditioned that it only becomes what it is because it belongs to the very same universal system which is the essential indivisible object of the feeling of absolute dependence; and this would lose its significance in the whole province of history if we should think of free causes as excluded from this system.[62]

This statement is remarkable. Schleiermacher could have explained the relation between dependence and freedom very broadly as, for instance, a kind of divine permission to exercise our freedom, allowing a kind of indeterminacy of free causes with respect to the world.[63] But it is exactly that which he denies. No, the causes or reasons for our actions, *even those arising from the will*, are traceable to "influences beyond itself [the will]," and are *always* conditioned by the world. Indeed, it is because free causes fall *within* the nature system that this system, including everything reckoned as *history*, broadly conceived, can be the object of the feeling of absolute dependence.

Yet there is a potential problem with this account, for in an extended passage, Schleiermacher seems to deny just this conditioning of the world on our free will in the context of sin:

> [W]e cannot truly regard ourselves as merely passive and extraneously determined in our acts of sin. The very phrase "freedom of the will" conveys a denial of all external compulsion [*äußeren Nöthigung*], and indicates the very essence of conscious life – the fact, namely, that no

external influence [*äußere Einwirkung*] determines our total condition in such a way that the reaction too is determined and given, but every excitation really receives its determinate quality from the inmost core of our own life, from which quality, again, proceeds the reaction, so that the sin proceeding from that core is in every case the act of the sinner and of no one else. In like manner, the expression "freedom of the will" negatives the idea that the individual is in all cases determined by the common nature of humanity.[64]

There is a natural reading of this passage that flatly and fully contradicts my claim that, according to Schleiermacher, our will and actions are determined, that this determination is compatible with our freedom, and that human nature plays an essential role in that determination.

But does this passage necessarily, or even most plausibly, imply such a contradiction? I do not think it does. The first clue to this is its context: it comes from a section where Schleiermacher is inquiring into the relation of sin to God's causality. And what Schleiermacher is denying in this passage is not that our actions are determined but that they are determined in such a way as to cease being *our* actions, and so actions for which we are responsible.

The second clue to this reading is Schleiermacher's repeated use of the word "external" and its variations. It is "external necessity" [*äußeren Nöthigung*] which free will denies, "external influence" [*äußere Einwirkung*] which is incompatible with the attributability of an action to *us* and appeals to "predetermined" human nature which cannot exonerate us from culpability. Indeed, these phrases show that this passage is not concerned with issues of determination *tout court*, but is specifically themed around issues of *action attribution*.[65] External necessity, a kind of compulsion, *does* contradict the attribution of an action to a person who acts because of it because said person is not the proximate source of their action. That is precisely what the word *external* picks out in this case; and the idea harmonizes well with Schleiermacher's attack on the attributability of sin to Adam when his acts were found to be compelled. Conversely, Schleiermacher's description of our actions as coming from "the inmost core of our own life" is precisely the language of attributability – attributability that guarantees that "the sin proceeding from that core is in every case the act of the sinner and no other."[66]

None of these claims entails a contradiction of the determined nature of all finite existence, including finite freedom. Rather Schleiermacher believes, as Leibniz and Spinoza both believe, our inmost core – "soul," "mind," or otherwise – is *partially constitutive* of the complete causal nexus. Although *external* necessity and determination are incompatible with our freedom according to Schleiermacher, conditioned freedom partially constitutive of an exhaustively determined world is not.

However, Schleiermacher is not merely saying that the feelings of absolute and relative dependence and our freedom are *compatible* (though he is also saying that) – he is further claiming that they *condition one another*. As he explains,

> *Precisely because free causes form a part of the general system [Eben*
> *deshalb aber weil die freien Ursachen den allgemeinen Zusammenhang*
> *mitbilden],* we must be able to assert the same of the moment of activity
> itself and of the accompanying self-consciousness. It was in this sense
> that in our first elucidations of the fundamental feeling we explained
> how the relative feeling of freedom and the absolute feeling of depend-
> ence each involves and pervades the other, so that the latter cannot exist
> apart from the former.[67]

The feelings of relative freedom and absolute dependence "each involve and
pervade the other" *because* our freedom is conditioned by the world. And
this is not only with respect to the determination of our will, or of our condition or circumstances, but also true "of the moment of activity itself." *Our*
very spontaneity, the heart of our freedom and that which, alone, might be
thought to remain undetermined, is equally part of the mutually determined
system of nature.

One way the nature system conditions free agents is by determining the
sorts of animals they are, and thus their powers and inclinations. Humans
are no exception. And so Schleiermacher warns that

> we must observe, with reference to absolute dependence, that we
> assume no sharp antithesis between freedom and natural necessity in
> finite being, since anything which actually has a being for itself moves
> itself in some sense or other, even if it has no part of spiritual life; but
> even in the most free cause its range is ordained by God.[68]

Natural necessity, the necessity by which a thing acts according to its nature,
does not stand in contrast to its freedom. For freedom, according to Schleiermacher, consists in spontaneity, self-movement;[69] but things frequently act
spontaneously in the way they do *necessarily* because of the kind of thing
they are. Squirrels gather nuts, birds build nests, flies swarm to carcasses,
animals of all kinds eat and reproduce, freely *and* by natural necessity. Animals *want* these things, and they are under no compulsion, though they
cannot not strive for them. "Even in the most free cause," claims Schleiermacher, "its range is ordained by God,"[70] and so humans, and any animal
free in the same sense, always will freely within natural limits proper to
their kind.

Indeed, Christians must, Schleiermacher thinks, be committed to denying
the antithesis between freedom and natural necessity if for no other reason
than to avoid dividing creation from preservation, which, in turn, results
in dividing the existence of things from their activities.[71] As Schleiermacher
explains, it is a problem

> if we oppose free causes to natural ones so strongly that the former in
> their activity appear to be less dependent on God; for then they must
> derive their effectiveness partly from elsewhere while their existence

itself they derive from God, and thus an inequality is introduced between creation and preservation.[72]

And so, while we might be tempted to divide the actions of creatures from their natures, such that God creates, say, free human beings, but does not ordain that they should do certain things under certain circumstances, we would be in error to do so. We would be committing ourselves accidentally to the denial that all things depend upon God, for, however we explain their "effectiveness" [*Wirksamkeit*], it must be derived *from elsewhere* – that is, from other than God.[73]

To see exactly how specifically and completely Schleiermacher means this account of determined willing to extend, let us turn last to a description of willing that parallels, but, in so doing, deeply contrasts with, that offered by Augustine earlier. Continuing on the theme that our relative freedom and absolute dependence *involve and pervade* each other, Schleiermacher explains,

> Let us consider now the moment of action [*den Moment des Handelns*], starting from the point that every other free agent in the same position would have acted differently than the one actually there, just as the same free agent would have acted differently in another position, and that this position, whatever it may be, is within the universal system. Then no one can doubt that the effects of free actions take place in virtue of absolute dependence.[74]

Exactly unlike Augustine, but perfectly in accord with Leibniz and Spinoza, Schleiermacher *premises* his account of free action in the nature system on the view that an agent's identity and relations (x person in y circumstances) are together sufficient to determine a person's actions such that if either the person was substituted or the place was changed, the action *would* have been different – that is, *necessarily* different. From this we can clearly infer that it is something about the individual, their nature, and/or the sum of their circumstances, which *causes* them to act as they do, and that nothing about this causal completeness undermines the fact that this is a free action attributable to a genuinely free agent.

Freedom, therefore, is no exception to the causal completeness thesis that underwrites Schleiermacher's use of the principle of sufficient reason and is, in fact, a *condition* of it. Anything less than sufficient reasons are deficient, and Schleiermacher has rejected deficient causes.[75] Free causes are part of the world, constitutive of the causal nexus. And like everything in the world, they are mutually conditioned and conditioning of each other and all other finite things, and absolutely dependent on God. There is no hint of indeterminate freedom. No, in regard to our natures, our condition, our circumstances, and even the determination of our wills, our freedom is a determined freedom. And, indeed, it must be so in order to maintain our absolute dependence on God. "Whether or not that which arouses our self-consciousness and consequently influences us, is to be traced back to the any part of the so-called nature-mechanism or the activity of free causes," Schleiermacher says, "the one is as completely ordained by God as the other."[76]

It is this strong account of divine determination, extending even to the determination of deficient causes, which makes Schleiermacher's account so distinctive. It solves many problems and yet creates new difficulties for him at the same time. For instance, we will see more in Chapter 7 how his account forces him to concede what Augustine would not: that God is the author of sin. But before we turn to that subject and Schleiermacher's account of how that view and the goodness of God comport, we turn to his own alternative account of the nature of sin and its origins.

Notes

1 For the most complete explanation and defense of the principle of sufficient reason currently available, see Pruss, *The Principle of Sufficient Reason*.
2 For more on Leibniz's influence on Schleiermacher see Mariña, *Transformation of the Self in the Thought of Friedrich Schleiermacher*. For Spinoza's influence on Schleiermacher see Lamm, *The Living God*. For more on both and my account of how they are synthesized in Schleiermacher's thought, see Pedersen, *The Eternal Covenant*.
3 Scholars disagree about whether Spinoza tacitly used the principle of sufficient reason. See Garber, "Superheroes in the History of Philosophy"; Della Rocca, "Interpreting Spinoza"; Melamed, "Sirens of Elea."
4 See Couenhoven, *Stricken by Sin, Cured by Christ*.
5 Augustine, *City of God*, XI.22.
6 Augustine, *City of God*, XII.7, 43.
7 See Augustine, *City of God*, XI.17.
8 Augustine, *City of God*, XII.9, 45.
9 Augustine, *City of God*, XII.6, 42.
10 GL §72.2; *The Christian Faith*, 294, translation revised.
11 Augustine, *City of God*, XII.6, 43.
12 See Leibniz, "On Nature Itself," §13; "Monadology," §8.
13 Augustine, *City of God*, XII.6, 43.
14 For an in-depth explanation of the grounding of predicates in things see Garber, *Leibniz*, especially Chapter 5: "Complete Individual Concepts, Non-Communication, and Causal Connection," 181–224.
15 Again, see Garber, *Leibniz*, 181–224.
16 GL §72.2; *The Christian Faith*, 294.
17 Leibniz, *Theodicy*, 143.
18 See previous discussion of this in Chapters 3 and 4; and once more see Anscombe, *Intention*; Davidson, "Actions, Reasons, and Causes."
19 I discuss freedom more ahead. See Mariña, "Where Have All the Monads Gone?"
20 Augustine, *City of God*, XII.6, 42.
21 GL §72.2; *The Christian Faith*, 293.
22 Augustine, *City of God*, XII.6, 43.
23 Augustine, *City of God*, XII.7, 43.
24 Aquinas, *Summa Theologica*, Ia, Q. 48, a. 2, resp.

25 See Aquinas, *Summa Theologica*, Ia, Q. 49, a. 1, resp.
26 See Adams, "Schleiermacher on Evil."
27 Spinoza, "Ethics," IA3, 410.
28 See Aristotle, *Physics*, VII.1.
29 Aquinas, for instance, insists that every evil has an accidental cause. Aquinas, *Summa Theologica*, Ia, Q. 39. a. 1.
30 Spinoza, "Ethics," IP26, 431.
31 Spinoza, "Ethics," IP27, 432.
32 Spinoza, "Ethics," IP29, 433.
33 Spinoza, "Ethics," IP29, 434.
34 Spinoza, "Ethics," IIP7, 451.
35 Spinoza, "Ethics," IP32C2, 435.
36 Aquinas, *Summa Theologica*, Ia, Q. 49, a. 1, r. o. 3.
37 Aquinas, *Summa Theologica*, Ia, Q. 49, a. 2, resp.
38 For an extended argument that culpability for evil acts requires that evil acts be rational in the minimal sense of being end-ordered, see Vogler, *Reasonably Vicious*. For an argument that even many apparently or supposedly irrational acts exhibit a reasons-as-causes structure, see Davidson, "Paradoxes of Irrationality."
39 *GL* §72.3; *The Christian Faith*, 296.
40 Augustine, *City of God*, XII.6, 43.
41 See Dasgupta, "Metaphysical Rationalism"; for an argument for the principle of sufficient reason's enduring plausibility see Della Rocca, "PSR."
42 See *GL* §8.2; *The Christian Faith*, 35.
43 *GL* §32.2; *The Christian Faith*, 132.
44 *GL* §36; *The Christian Faith*, 142.
45 *GL* §36; *The Christian Faith*, 142.
46 This is a controversial claim which I defend in "Schleiermacher and Reformed Scholastics on the Divine Attributes." For a range of different, though sometimes overlapping, views see Adams, "Faith and Religious Knowledge"; Dole, "Schleiermacher's Theological Anti-Realism"; Richards, "Schleiermacher's Divine Attributes."
47 *GL* §32.2; *The Christian Faith*, 132.
48 *GL* §32.2; *The Christian Faith*, 132.
49 *GL* §4.3; *The Christian Faith*, 15–16, translation revised.
50 It is important to note here that Schleiermacher is not denying that we are *truly* or *genuinely* free, only that we are *absolutely* free, which is to say, having the source of our action in no extrinsic determination whatsoever – a position perfectly consistent with Spinoza's teaching on the matter. See Spinoza, "Ethics," IP17C2.
51 I explain and defend Schleiermacher's notion of the world as a single unified whole of the mutually affecting and affectable – including free causes – in Pedersen, *The Eternal Covenant*, 69–97.
52 *GL* §50.3; *The Christian Faith*, 199, translation revised.
53 Schleiermacher subscribes to the view that, because to *be* is to *act*, everything that exists stands in some conditioning and/or conditioned relation to everything else (and even knowledge of a thing is conditioning). God's uniqueness *consists in* the fact that God alone completely conditions all else, while God is in no way conditioned by other things. Therefore, unless God wholly conditions everything *ad extra*, those things which God does not wholly condition partly condition God (and other things), which contradicts Schleiermacher's claim that God depends upon nothing. Such a view casts God under the definition of a finite cause, as mutually conditioning and conditioned, and thus makes God a member of the nature system, a creature. On the other hand, the idea of something

that exists but which neither conditions, nor is conditioned by, anything else is impossible on Schleiermacher's premises. Such a thing simply does not exist. See *GL* §46 postscript; *The Christian Faith*, 176.

54 I develop this argument in detail in Pedersen, *The Eternal Covenant*, 73–76. See also Anselm, *Monologion*, VII; Aquinas, *Summa Theologica*, Ia, Q. 11, a. 3, resp.; Spinoza, "Ethics," especially the buildup of propositions leading to IP14.

55 See *GL* §§51 and 54.

56 *GL* §4.4; *The Christian Faith*, 15–17.

57 This is a point I argue at length in Pedersen, *The Eternal Covenant*, 69–97.

58 I qualify this to avoid unnecessary disputes and confusions, not to qualify the sense or extent to which Schleiermacher thinks we are free.

59 *GL* §49.1; *The Christian Faith*, 191.

60 It should be noted that all freedom is not necessarily reducible to spontaneity alone since Schleiermacher is here speaking of all degrees of freedom which, he claims, accompanies life universally, and sometimes all action in nature. See *GL* §32.2, 49.1; *The Christian Faith*, 132, 191.

61 *GL* §49.1; *The Christian Faith*, 189.

62 *GL* §49.1; *The Christian Faith*, 189.

63 This seems to be what Mariña has in mind by attributing Kant's account of transcendental freedom to Schleiermacher. Despite her sophisticated treatment, I disagree and think, instead, that passages like this allow for a more natural reading of Schleiermacher as a species of compatibilist that does not admit transcendental freedom, following, for instance, Julia Jorati's reading of Leibniz. Of course, Mariña is right to point out the loss of signature Leibnizian elements (i.e., monads), but this is *more* evidence, not less, for the interpretation that Schleiermacher thinks of free agents as situated and determined in the causal nexus since the removal of monads eliminates a key barrier to the adoption of the later Leibniz's account: namely, Leibniz's non-interaction thesis. See Jorati, *Leibniz on Causation and Agency*, esp. 114–47; Mariña, "Where Have All the Monads Gone?" 477–505.

64 *GL* §81.2; *The Christian Faith*, 334, translation revised.

65 On this point I agree with Mariña that action attribution is a key concern of Schleiermacher's account of agency in *The Christian Faith*. However, I disagree that this implies transcendental freedom as Schleiermacher's only, or even most plausible, option. See Mariña, "Where Have All the Monads Gone?" esp. 479; For Leibniz's solutions to the problems of attributability, spontaneity, and control, again see Jorati, *Leibniz on Causation and Agency*.

66 *GL* §81.2; *The Christian Faith*, 334.

67 *GL* §49.1; *The Christian Faith*, 189–90, emphasis added.

68 *GL* §49.1; *The Christian Faith*, 191–92.

69 *GL* §4.1; *The Christian Faith*, 13–14.

70 *GL* §49.1; *The Christian Faith*, 192.

71 *GL* §46, postscript; *The Christian Faith*, 175–78.

72 *GL* §49, postscript; *The Christian Faith*, 192–93.

73 One of the virtues of Mariña's account of the compatibility of divine determination and transcendental human freedom is that she does not make herself vulnerable to this charge.

74 *GL* §49.1; *The Christian Faith*, 190, translation revised.

75 Rather, Schleiermacher has rejected deficient causes in the specific brute fact sense (i.e., as deficient causes not susceptible of further explanation by efficient causes). He will, however, defend deficient causes as deficient with respect to their ideal. We take up this topic in the following chapter.

76 *GL* §49; *The Christian Faith*, 189.

References

Adams, Robert Merrihew. "Faith and Religious Knowledge." In *The Cambridge Companion to Friedrich Schleiermacher*, edited by Jacqueline Mariña. Cambridge: Cambridge University Press, 2005.
———. "Schleiermacher on Evil." *Faith and Philosophy* 13, no. 4 (1996): 563–83.
Anscombe, Elizabeth. *Intention*. Oxford: Basil Blackwell, 1958.
Anselm of Canterbury. *Monologion and Proslogion: With the Replies of Gaunilo and Anslem*. Translated by Thomas Williams. Indianapolis: Hackett, 1995.
Aquinas, Thomas. *Summa Theologica*. Translated by the Fathers of the English Dominican Province. New York: Benziger Bros., 1947.
Aristotle. *Physics*. Vol. 1. Edited by Jonathan Barnes. Princeton: Princeton University Press, 1984.
Augustine of Hippo. *The City of God*. The Works of Saint Augustine. Part I, Vol. 7. Translated by William Babcock. Hyde Park, NY: New City Press, 2013.
Couenhoven, Jesse. *Stricken by Sin, Cured by Christ: Agency, Necessity, and Culpability in Augustinian Theology*. Oxford: Oxford University Press, 2013.
Dasgupta, Shamik. "Metaphysical Rationalism." *Noûs* 50, no. 2 (2016): 379–418.
Davidson, Donald. "Actions, Reasons, and Causes." In *The Essential Davidson*. Oxford: Oxford University Press, 2006.
———. "Paradoxes of Irrationality." In *The Essential Davidson*. Oxford: Oxford University Press, 2006.
Della Rocca, Michael. "Interpreting Spinoza: The Real Is the Rational." *Journal of the History of Philosophy* 53, no. 3 (2015): 507–35.
———. "PSR." *Philosopher's Imprint* 10, no. 7 (2010): 1–13.
Dole, Andrew. "Schleiermacher's Theological Anti-Realism." In *Analytic Theology*, edited by Oliver Crisp and Michael Rea. Oxford: Oxford University Press, 2009.
Garber, Daniel. *Leibniz: Body, Substance, Monad*. Oxford: Oxford University Press, 2009.
———. "Superheroes in the History of Philosophy: Spinoza, Super-rationalist." *Journal of the History of Philosophy* 53, no. 3 (2015): 507–35.
Jorati, Julia. *Leibniz on Causation and Agency*. Cambridge: Cambridge University Press, 2017.
Lamm, Julia A. *The Living God: Schleiermacher's Theological Appropriation of Spinoza*. University Park, PA: Pennsylvania State University Press, 1996.
Leibniz, Gottfried Wilhelm. *Philosophical Essays*. Edited and translated by Roger Ariew and Daniel Garber. Indianapolis: Hackett, 1989.
———. *Theodicy: Essays on the Goodness of God, the Freedom of Man, and the Origin of Evil*. Edited by Austin Farrer, translated by E. M. Huggard. La Salle, IL: Open Court, [1951] 1985.
Mariña, Jacqueline. *Transformation of the Self in the Thought of Friedrich Schleiermacher*. Oxford: Oxford University Press, 2008.
———. "Where Have All the Monads Gone? Substance and Transcendental Freedom in Schleiermacher." *The Journal of Religion* 95, no. 4 (2015): 477–505.
Melamed, Yitzhak. "Sirens of Elea: Rationalism, Monism and Idealism in Spinoza." In *The Key Debates of Modern Philosophy*, edited by Antonia LoLordo and Stewart Duncan. New York and London: Routledge, 2012.
Pedersen, Daniel J. *The Eternal Covenant: Schleiermacher on God and Natural Science*. Berlin: De Gruyter, 2017.

————. "Schleiermacher and Reformed Scholastics on the Divine Attributes." *International Journal of Systematic Theology* 17, no. 4 (2015): 1–19.

Pruss, Alexander R. *The Principle of Sufficient Reason: A Reassessment.* Cambridge: Cambridge University Press, 2006.

Richards, Jay. "Schleiermacher's Divine Attributes: Their Coherence and Reference." *Encounter* 52, no. 2 (1996): 149–70.

Schleiermacher, Friedrich D. E. *The Christian Faith.* Edited by H. R. Mackintosh and J. S. Stewart, translated by D. M. Baillie, et al. Berkeley: Apocryphile, [1928] 2011.

————. *Der christliche Glaube nach den Grundsätzen der evangelischen Kirche im Zusammenhange dargestellt.* Second edition. Edited by Rolf Schäfer. Berlin: Walter de Gruyter, [1830/31] 2008.

Spinoza, Benedict. "Ethics." In *The Collected Works of Spinoza*, Vol. 1. Edited and translated by Edwin Curley. Princeton, NJ: Princeton University Press, 1985.

Vogler, Candace. *Reasonably Vicious.* Cambridge, MA: Harvard University Press, 2002.

5 Schleiermacher on the origins of sin

Socrates: Have we not found a road which leads towards the good?
Protarchus: What road?
Socrates: Supposing that a man had to be found, and you could dis-
             cover in what house he lived, would not that be a great step
             towards the discovery of the man himself?
Protarchus: Certainly.
Socrates: And now reason intimates to us, as at our first beginning, that
             we should seek the good, not in the unmixed life but in the
             mixed.

– Plato, *Philebus*

For Augustine the origins of sin and his overall account of value are inextricably linked. His account of the origins of sin is purposed to sustaining the goodness of creation *as created*. Those who follow Augustine share this account of value. On accounts like Augustine's, *the good* is always prior to its defects in just the same way that creation precedes the fall of Adam, which is to say, they subscribe to the *principle of parallel priority* as discussed in Chapter 1. To throw doubt on the traditional story of the origins of sin, then, is to raise deep and troubling questions about the goodness of humans – and indeed the world – as created, and the broader relationship between nature and value. When Schleiermacher denies not only the chronology but also the logic of the traditional account, he risks committing himself to the denial of the priority of the good, the normativity of natures, and similar claims that are traditionally taken to be entailments of the world as created by God, who is goodness itself.

In the previous chapters we saw Schleiermacher's criticism of traditional accounts of the origins of sin, as well as looked in detail at what principles and commitments supported his arguments. In this chapter we turn to Schleiermacher's own alternative account of sin and sin's origins in which these same principles and commitments are maintained while Schleiermacher simultaneously navigates their relation to his other commitments, especially the priority of the good and what he takes to be the delimiting "natural heresies" of all Christian faith: namely, the vicious excesses of

Manichaeism on the one hand, and Pelagianism on the other. As we will see, more than one possible account of sin and sin's origins inspired by Schleiermacher are rendered impossible by the very premises with which he sought to argue against traditional accounts of the origins of sin. Schleiermacher's own claims about sin's origins make this even more evident.

At the same time, however, this emphasis on novelty might lead to the opposite error: of thinking that Schleiermacher's account of sin and sin's origins is flatly anti-traditional. As we will see, Schleiermacher readily adopts classic accounts of sin, or at least important features of classic accounts, in service of his own. Not only is the recognition of these traditional features necessary in order to get Schleiermacher right, but also the accurate delineations of innovation and tradition are each necessary in order to avoid the excesses of one-sided readings of his doctrine. Seeing what is new prevents us from simply collapsing Schleiermacher's account into traditional accounts, while seeing what is inherited in these accounts prevents us from simply unmooring Schleiermacher from his predecessors and viewing his description of sin as more of a departure than it really is.

Moreover, recognition of the traditional aspects of Schleiermacher's account indicates, beyond his explicit remarks, those authorities whom he feels obliged to engage. And yet, as we have seen, Schleiermacher does not take traditional authority to require his assent, only his attention. But what the continuity with traditional authorities, like Augustine, reveals is the extent to which Schleiermacher *agrees* with the tradition, despite his criticisms. Carefully distinguishing between Schleiermacher's different uses of, and interactions with, traditional authorities allow us to distinguish his reasons for adoption from his reasons for rejection. And those inform the sophisticated and nuanced view of nature and value to which he, himself, subscribes.

Finally, in this chapter we will begin to look not only at interpretive puzzles but also at problems and objections posed by interlocutors, real and imagined. If, as Schleiermacher argues, traditional accounts come with great burdens, then champions of the tradition might well accuse Schleiermacher of the same. In this chapter we will entertain some of these most important objections, consider Schleiermacher's replies (or possible replies on his grounds), and see how his overall account is designed to overcome, or at least ameliorate, the disadvantages that accompany his view.

As we saw in the previous chapters, Schleiermacher rejects traditional accounts of the fall, both of the Devil and the first human beings. We have not, however, seen what he offers in their stead. Misunderstanding beckons temptingly. The effect of that misunderstanding has been to attract some to Schleiermacher's so-called account of the origins of sin, while repelling others – but both for the wrong reasons. Over time that same misunderstanding has seeped into the historiography of theology of the last two centuries, which, by failing to understand Schleiermacher, misidentified the origin and continuity of some ideas supposedly advanced by him, and ascribed to him ideas which are not his, while failing to credit him with ideas which are.

However, Schleiermacher's account of the origins of sin, rightly under-stood, promises more than accuracy. It is an account designed to overcome objections that troubled traditional accounts, and it is an account designed to cohere, in principle, with an explanation of human origins that coheres with history and natural science. But most of all it is a revision of the doc-trine that does not merely aim to be more intellectually defensible, but actu-ally desirable, possessing a beauty and an allure which reveal themselves only when we resist the doctrine's domestication.

This chapter will examine only sin's *origins and status*. For the time being we will be setting aside, as much as possible, issues specifically related to sin and the God-consciousness until the following chapter, when the moral psychology of sin will be taken up in detail. This approach naturally comes with its own burdens, but I am convinced, and aim to show, that Schleier-macher's account is, in general, comparable to traditional accounts; and that, therefore, not only is this division (temporarily) possible but also clari-fies both the novelty of Schleiermacher's account and its deep continuity with theological tradition.

This chapter first begins by considering the "natural heresies" of Man-ichaeism and Pelagianism, which broadly bracket out non-Christian accounts of sin. Next, Schleiermacher's further shared commitment with Augustine that "good cannot corrupt good" is introduced as a guiding prin-ciple. Third, we examine evidence that Schleiermacher saw the origins of sin as, like human origins generally, in evolutionary continuity with its natu-ral antecedents. Fourth, we explore Schleiermacher's account of the origins and development of sin, especially as it relates to the priority of the good. And, finally, we turn to Schleiermacher's explanation of how the original perfection of the world coheres with sin as innate – a crucial juncture that will bring us full circle to the natural heresies. All told we see how Schlei-ermacher *maintains* the priority of the good and the normativity of natures but *declines* to do so through the principle of parallel priority – that prin-ciple which implies that it is possible to maintain the foregoing only on the supposition that there was a past state of affairs of which sin is a privation.

The natural heresies

If, following Schleiermacher, we reject the ancient church doctrine of the fall of Adam and the consequent communication of Adam's corruption to the whole human race, we face a question. Either the human race is not corrupted by sin, or it is. If it is corrupted, we face further questions as to *how* it is corrupted: did humans *become* sinners, or were the first humans born sinners? If human nature did not *become* corrupted, we must explain how sin is somehow endemic to human beings. But if we make sin *natural* in the sense that it is *constitutive* of human nature to sin, then we commit ourselves to the view that to be human *is* to be a sinner. And this commit-ment bodes ill for any account of the salvation of *human* beings, for in order to be redeemed *humans*, we would, on this view, have to carry our sinful natures with us into heaven. Therefore, if we reject the traditional account of the fall, it is tempting to either discard the ubiquity and severity of sin, or to make sin necessary to human being, but both options come with severe consequences for basic Christian claims about creation and redemption.

These are the delimiting extremes Schleiermacher considers under the heading of the "natural heresies" – that is, to those heresies that regard human nature, not the nature of Christ. In respect to sin in particular, we will be dealing with only two: the *Manichean* and the *Pelagian* heresies. Though not unconnected to their historical instantiations, these types are technical terms for Schleiermacher. Moreover, they are not intended to be accurate portrayals of the figures and teachings whose names they borrow.[1] Therefore, Schleiermacher's specific use requires unpacking.

Schleiermacher thinks heresies of all kinds appear in Christian communions only *covertly*. If they were overt beliefs, their subscribers would not be, or even want to be, considered Christians:

> [I]f the concept of redemption is simply denied, or another redeemer is set up, and thus it is simply asserted either that men are not in need of redemption or that there is no redeeming power in Jesus, then the claim is no longer heretical but anti-Christian [*antichristlich*].[2]

These heresies suppose that their subscribers *intend* to be Christian, but *inadvertently* commit themselves to beliefs that contradict the basic Christian conception of redemption, or commit themselves to other beliefs which imply that contradiction.[3]

The heresy in question consists in implicitly denying the possibility of redemption. Accordingly, "*either* human nature will be so determined that a redemption in the strict sense cannot be accomplished, *or* the Redeemer will be determined in such a way that he cannot accomplish redemption."[4] The Manichaean and Pelagian heresies contradict either one clause in this formula or the other, and with respect either to human nature or to the nature of the Redeemer.

For present purposes we are concerned solely with the former, human nature. And, "As regards the former," Schleiermacher explains, "if humans are to be redeemed, they must be both in need of redemption and be capable of receiving it [*fähig sie anzunehmen*]."[5] The (covert) denial of this claim takes two forms:

> If, then, in the first place, the need of redemption in human nature, i.e. its inability [*Unfähigkeit*] to bring the feeling of absolute dependence into all human states of consciousness, is posited in such an absolute way that the ability to receive redeeming influences is made to disappear in the act, so that human nature is not simultaneously in need of redemption and capable of receiving it, but only becomes capable of

receiving it after a complete transformation [*gänzlichen Umschaffung*], this is equivalent to annulling our fundamental formula.[6]

To think of redemption in this way is to commit oneself to the Manichean heresy. "But on the other hand," Schleiermacher says,

> suppose the ability to receive redemption is assumed so absolutely, and consequently any hindrance to the entry of the God-consciousness becomes so utterly infinitesimal [*unendlich klein*], that at each particular moment in each individual it can be satisfactorily counterbalanced by an infinitesimal overweight. Then the need of redemption is reduced to naught [*Null*], at least in the sense that it is no longer the need of one single Redeemer, [. . .] and this aberration we may with good reason call, as above, the Pelagian.[7]

The only acceptable formula is one that avoids both extremes. That is, human nature must be *capable* of *receiving* redemption, but *incapable* of bringing such redemption about, apart from Christ.

A good deal is going on here. First, however, notice that, although Schleiermacher's definitions are sometimes cast in terms of the God-consciousness, they do not depend on his account of the God-consciousness for their force.

The Manichean heresy can be cast more generically, in Schleiermacher's own words, in relation to human nature's "*ability* to *receive* redeeming influences."[8] Perhaps unexpectedly for a heresy that borrows its name from a kind of cosmic dualism, it is, for Schleiermacher, a heresy which principally regards human nature. Moreover, it is cast in terms of nature and potency, action and passion. And, indeed, it is a very specific account of how redemption relates to both. The *natural* ability or power to *receive* something is a standard and straightforward case of a *natural passive potency* – an Aristotelean category that Schleiermacher adopts toward theological ends.[9] Redemption, Schleiermacher thinks, *must* be like this, and any other account of the relation of redemption to human nature is heresy. This is a very ambitious claim, and some might not be persuaded. But consider the alternatives, as Schleiermacher does.

One alternative is that human nature is *naturally incapable* of *receiving* redemption. That is, there is something intrinsic to human nature that is incompatible with the reception of redemption – whatever we think that redemption consists in or how it is received. This alternative is not that humans are incapable of saving themselves. Schleiermacher insists that humans are not able to do so (see ahead). But the kind of incapacity Schleiermacher has in mind is more serious, for Schleiermacher supposes that grace is, and must be, given to us by Christ. The question is whether human nature is the kind of thing that can, by virtue of the thing it is, receive grace. If human nature cannot receive grace, yet humans are in need of it, then the only way grace can be appropriated is if human nature is transformed – in the sense that human nature itself ceases to be what it is and so the saved cease to be human. But to so transform is to *destroy* the thing in question (the individual of a specific nature). Therefore, far from an idiosyncratic definition, applicable only to those who subscribe to his account of the God-consciousness, Schleiermacher is posing the classic Scholastic question: does grace destroy nature, or perfect it? And on this point, Schleiermacher agrees with his scholastic forebears.[10] If human nature must be completely trans-formed (i.e., destroyed), that can be only because human nature itself is antithetical to redemption.[11] But what God makes for redemption cannot fail in its purpose. So if God had created human nature, God would have necessarily made it well – namely, capable of receiving redemption. There-fore, the belief that grace must destroy nature implies that God did not, in fact, create human nature; and *that* implies belief in a second, evil principle.

To commit the Pelagian heresy, on the other hand, is to lack a *"need of one single* Redeemer *[Bedürfniß eines einzelnen Erlösers]."*[12] Importantly, each component of this phrase ("need," "one single," and "Redeemer") identifies a distinct sense in which the heresy could be committed. And each involves some consideration of relations of dependence. Most obviously, if we are not in need of a Redeemer, we are not dependent on a Redeemer for our perfection. Our own persons are without lack with respect to the God-consciousness. But this is an extreme which for Schleiermacher is "no longer heretical, but anti-Christian."[13] One might, however, be committed, covertly, to the heresy proper by either denying a *need*, in a strict sense, for a Redeemer or else denying that that said Redeemer is one and one only.

To flatly deny a need for redemption would no longer be a merely implicit rejection of basic Christian beliefs, and so no longer be heresy. But Schlei-ermacher has a subtler charge in mind. The truly insidious problem comes when "the ability to receive redemption is assumed so absolutely" that "hindrance to the entry of the God-consciousness becomes so utterly infini-tesimal, that at each particular moment in each individual it can be satisfac-torily counterbalanced by an infinitesimal overweight."[14] That is, any given person might well be susceptible to "weak moments,"[15] but other individu-als, apart from Christ, might check this deficiency alone or together. The only alternative, according to Schleiermacher's elucidation of this heresy, is to affirm the absolute dependence of all on Christ for their salvation in exact parallel with our absolute dependence on God. But that is not all, for, as we have seen, Schleiermacher's notion of heresy grants that heretics are *ostensibly* good Christians. And so the real demand is not for the nominal affirmation of this dependence but for it to be borne out in content.

To affirm the absolute dependence of all on Christ in more than name only then requires that the redemption received (which we must, of course, be naturally *able* to receive) must have been received from Christ and Christ alone. In order to claim this with any necessity, Christians must also be committed to the claim that *all* humans, individually and collectively, *could not* receive redemption apart from Christ. The need is an impotence of a kind, yet one which cannot be an inability of human nature to *appropri-ate* redemption without once again becoming Manichean. Only if human nature includes a natural ability to receive redemption, but, at the same time, cannot activate or appropriate this power on its own, can we avoid both heresies at once. And so the Pelagian heresy leads us from the opposite direction to the necessity of explaining human nature's ability to appropri-ate redemption as a natural passive potency.

A natural passive potency allows for precisely the grounding of acts in natures that Schleiermacher accuses traditional accounts of Adam's fall of abandoning. Not only do our natures in this case explain our ability to do something – namely, to appropriate redemption – but they also explain our *inability* to do something: to redeem ourselves. And, in the more sophisti-cated formula of a natural *passive* potency, our natures specifically explain our ability to *become able* to do something.[16] Natural passive potencies are developmental powers. Thus, Schleiermacher implies a general evolutionary-developmental account of redemption, in which the starting point is not a *fall* but an *original* passive potency to appropriate redemption. And because of how Schleiermacher has delimited the Manichean and Pelagian heresies, this specific kind of developmental account is, he thinks, *necessarily* implied should Christians wish to avoid implicitly denying their most basic commitments.

Good cannot corrupt good

Having seen how Schleiermacher delimits any approach to sin and its ori-gins, we now begin to examine his own proposal for thinking about the origins of sin. In keeping with his criticism in previous chapters, Schleier-macher rejects the traditional doctrine that the first sin caused a change in human nature. He explains:

> Therefore, it is not *necessary* to hold that a change in human nature brought about by the first sin of the first humans belongs among the propositions which rank as utterances of our Christian consciousness. The less we found cause at a previous stage to ascribe a high degree of pious morality [*frommer Sittlichkeit*] and pious enlightenment [*from-mer Erleuchtung*] to the first pair before their first sin, and the less we are able to explain the first sin as proceeding from a perfectly sinless condition, the more decisively does every reason disappear for admit-ting that a change in human nature was then produced.[17]

There was, according to Schleiermacher, no change in human nature as a result of sin. Yet, alone, the lack of such a doctrine as an immediate deliv-erance of the God-consciousness is indecisive. The relevant role the God-consciousness might play – but doesn't – is to generate the notion of the fall as a necessary but inferential belief. As we saw in regard to the fall of the Devil, the main work the God-consciousness does as an authority is to require fewer beliefs by minimizing our explanatory obligations. In combination with the reasons proffered against a fall in the previous chapters, the effect is to rob every reason for being from such a doctrine. Because we needn't admit such a change, Schleiermacher thinks, we shouldn't.

Indeed, the conceptual basis of any version of a fall faces difficulties – especially in combination with Schleiermacher's tacit subscription to the principle of sufficient reason that we explored in the previous chapter. The principle underwriting any fall account, " 'The person corrupts the nature [*das Einzelwesen verdirbt die Natur*],' " Schleiermacher claims,

> clearly brings out the fact that, in this act [*Act*], if the nature corrupted in consequence of it was good, the person cannot have been good, for good cannot corrupt good [*weil Gutes nicht kann Gutes verderben*]; but if the nature was already bad, its corruption was not brought about by the action of the person.[18]

With this strong premise – "good cannot corrupt good" – we begin to see the introduction of Schleiermacher's own axiological commitments, commitments which, as we saw in the previous chapter, are *shared by Augustine*.

But we also see in this premise the work the principle of sufficient reason does. For Schleiermacher implies in his use of this principle to generate the conclusion that no change for the worse could have been brought about by the action of a good person that there must be some *reason* a good nature went bad. The good cannot simply degrade. In contrast to his pre-modern forebears, Schleiermacher's account of moral corruption parallels the physics of natural *conservation* of motion (or force). In just the same way that an object in motion stays in motion unless acted upon by another force, so too with the goodness of a thing. If it is to deteriorate or deform, it must be *made* to do so. Since good cannot corrupt good, no good person could be corrupted, except by something or someone that was already bad. And any appeal to such a preexistent bad begins an infinite regress.

Schleiermacher's arguments are intended to show that when Augustine's cutting question about how a good nature could go bad is combined with true principles (i.e., the principle of sufficient reason), no such cause can be found. And yet, Schleiermacher does not thereby avoid Augustine's question. On the contrary, as we will see, his account is specifically meant to offer a satisfactory reply to this deeply Augustinian concern about the sheer possibility of the good going bad. Schleiermacher's alternative account of the origins of sin is thus not meant to finish off the Augustinian tradition, but to rescue it.[19]

Evolutionary origins and absolute beginnings

Aiming to avoid the Manichaean and Pelagian heresies, and proceeding from the principle that good cannot corrupt good, Schleiermacher gives an *organic developmental account of a teleologically ordered world.*[20] That is, the development of the world as a whole is end-ordered, and the world, nature itself, is not only a necessary but also a sufficient condition for the attainment of this end. The world as a whole, like a life, intrinsically contains within itself the reason why its effects come to be. But unlike an ordinary life, the world is unique in kind; and so, unlike an ordinary animal, the world is the *sole* reason for what happens in it, unfolding in a unity of purpose and necessity. Its development is an *entailment* of its nature alone. And its development is *to*, not *from*, the good for which it was made.

Within this evolutionary-developmental account of the world (i.e., the nature system), there are nested, compatible, developmental processes. Within the overall development of the world, stars are formed, animals evolve, and particular animals grow from infant to adult. As I have shown, there were powerful theories and discoveries in the natural sciences of Schleiermacher's day that were (and remain) compelling reasons to see the world this way in principle.[21] And I have argued that Schleiermacher did, for these reasons (among others), conceive of the world in just this way.[22] Because he did, there is reason to think that human beings were not an exception to this rule; that humans, too, evolved from earlier lifeforms, and that this development, too, was teleologically ordered, and so justifiably described as a development from lower to higher lifeforms.[23] The *continuity* between humans and our prehuman ancestors, continuity upon which all developmental accounts depend, is a crucial plank in Schleiermacher's account of the origins of sin.

Perhaps perplexingly then, Schleiermacher declines to offer a contentful account of human origins. Indeed, he refuses to give *details* about human origins in principle. This might be taken to count against my interpretation as a whole by disrupting the developmental continuity on which it depends – *if* (but only if) Schleiermacher's refusal to give such an account follows from certain reasons, and not others: namely, if he denies that descriptions of humans' prehuman ancestors are pertinent because sufficient continuity does not obtain. Importantly, Schleiermacher does not refuse for this, or any related, reason; and the reasons Schleiermacher *does* give for declining a detailed account actually give his account greater utility in making sense of the difficulties pressed upon Christian accounts of the origins of sin by the natural sciences today. In order to understand Schleiermacher's account, and to derive as much from it as possible, it is important to understand the reasons behind the limits Schleiermacher imposes on himself.

Schleiermacher explains in §61 that, although the Christian religious consciousness develops in each individual "in virtue of this original perfection of human nature," an account of "history lacks an account of how, on the same presuppositions, the first humans have themselves developed, and the hints [*Andeutungen*] we have on that subject cannot form a religious doctrine in our sense of the word."[24] Such an account cannot be a Christian doctrine because it is not implied in the distinctively Christian religious consciousness. "[M]atters of fact in human development," Schleiermacher says, "are never questions of faith but rather of history."[25] The inclusion of such facts under Christian doctrine is a category error that risks reducing the content of faith to the merely historical.[26]

Schleiermacher's position, however, does not end with this warning. In fact, he admits a possible exception: "There could only be specific doctrines of faith concerning the first humans in so far as their unique manner of coming into being and of temporal existence might modify the application of our concept to them."[27] And even then, the bearing of such a doctrine would be specific and limited.[28] That is, *if* the first humans – for instance, Adam and Eve – came into being in a special way and enjoyed a distinct sort of existence, their origins would bear on Christian doctrine. However, the plausibility and relevance of this special origination are dismissed over the following sections.[29] What becomes clear then is that it is traditional accounts of Adam and Eve that are the real target of Schleiermacher's trepidation in making claims of human origins Christian doctrine. Any account of human origins that the God-consciousness might demand reduces to Schleiermacher's doctrine of the original perfection of the world and of human being (see ahead) – a doctrine, which as we will see, provides further evidence that Schleiermacher sees human beings in continuity with our evolutionary ancestors.[30]

The risk of demanding that a tenuous historical claim be made into Christian doctrine is, however, not Schleiermacher's only concern with details about the origins of the first humans. He also has another objection, related to the God-consciousness, but not limited to it. As he explains,

> [A]ll attempts to form a historical picture of the first beginnings of human existence must necessarily fail, because, as no absolute beginning [*absoluter Anfang*] is given to us, we lack any analogy [*Analogie*] by which we could make the absolute beginning of rational consciousness [*vernünftigen Bewußtseins*] intelligible. We do not even have a clear understanding of the consciousness of the child in the first period of life.[31]

Schleiermacher's protest in this case is, as the child development example makes clear, a principled protest, not limited to the origins of the human species, or limited to questions of what might specifically be described within the limits of Christian doctrine. Because it is principled, his objection is to *any and all* absolute beginnings. Because we can never point to *any* such *absolute* beginning, we can never explain the absolute beginning of human beings by comparison.

Denial of the intelligibility of absolute beginnings has important and far-ranging implications. First, the claim that we never experience absolute beginnings also bears on important issues we examined in previous chapters, in particular the issue of the beginnings of sin and the causal completeness thesis – namely, Schleiermacher's use of the principle of sufficient reason. Denial of the former, an absolute beginning of sin, is synonymous with the latter: on the supposition of the principle of sufficient reason there must be some reason why things begin to be or act as they do. When that state or act is sin, there is some reason for sin that precedes sin, out of which sin arises. The denial of absolute beginnings *is* simply the principle of sufficient reason put in other words. It is not a matter of mutually supporting commitments, or even mutually implied ones. Rather, commitment to the principle of sufficient reason and the denial of absolute beginnings are two ways to say the same thing.

Second, in respect of the question of human origins, Schleiermacher's denial of absolute beginnings is further evidence that he conceives of human beings in developmental continuity with our prehuman ancestors. Indeed, this principle necessarily implies it: the alternative to an absolute beginning is a relative one; and a relative beginning is, by definition, in continuity with what preceded it. And it is the synthesis of novelty and continuity that is the essence of a developmental account.[32] This also amplifies why Schleiermacher would be so concerned to exclude human origins from doctrine: *if* human origins mean the origins of the *absolutely first* humans, such an account, whether religious or otherwise, can never be made *intelligible*, because *no absolute beginning can ever be made intelligible*. Accordingly, Schleiermacher settles on a narrow formula, one that begins whenever humans begin – a point left intentionally vague:

> [T]he first humans themselves, when their influence on a second generation began, stood at some point in the line of development (even if we cannot determine it), and consequently they were in a position to influence the development of the God-consciousness in the next generation; that is to say, self-communicating piety is as old as the self-propagating human species.[33]

In short, far from undermining the evolutionary adequacy of his account, Schleiermacher's denial of absolute beginnings affirms total continuity of humans with prehuman species, and so of human sin with the history of the cosmos. And though this might, for the moment, look like an additional burden, it becomes crucial ahead when Schleiermacher considers the original perfection of the world. Before we can turn to that question, however, we need to see in detail how Schleiermacher thinks of the origins and development of sin, especially as it regards the priority of the good.

The origins of the incapacity for the good

Sin, according to Schleiermacher, is an arresting of the God-consciousness.[34] We explore what that means in much more detail in the following chapter. Yet why and how does it *come about* that the God-consciousness is *arrested?* This is the question we take up in this section, where we turn to Schleiermacher's own account of the *origins* of sin.

Having set multiple parameters within which any satisfactory account must hold, Schleiermacher's options are limited. He cannot propose that humans are in any way self-saving or naturally unredeemable without veering into either the Pelagian or Manichaean heresy. He cannot propose that human history in general or human sin in particular begins *de novo* without violating his strictures against absolute beginnings (and the principle of sufficient reason more generally). And he cannot propose that humans were born good but then corrupted themselves because *good cannot corrupt good*. Therefore, after dismissing all accounts of a fall, he dramatically concludes,

> If accordingly, no change in human nature took place as in the person of the first pair as a result of the first sin, and what is alleged to have developed from that sin must be assumed to have been in existence before it; and if this does not apply merely to the case of some first sin, but a like situation emerges (whatever the nature of that sin may have been) in the case of every individual; then the universal sinfulness that precedes every actual sin in the offspring is to be regarded not so much as derived from the first sin of the first humans, but rather *the same [dasselbige] as what in them likewise preceded the first sin*, so that in committing their first sin they were simply the first-born of sinfulness [*die Erstlinge der Sündigkeit sind*].[35]

There never was a change in human nature wrought by a disobedient will, or any other means. The first humans did not *become* sinners; *the first humans were themselves born sinners*; and the cause of sin in each new generation is *identical* with what made the first humans sinners too.

This is a stunning teaching – one with which thinkers of the last two centuries have become desensitized. Yet it is possible to interpret it in more than one way. Much of the remainder of this work will be occupied with establishing exactly what Schleiermacher meant by this teaching, correcting misinterpretations of it, and showing how at least one reading of his account of sin is plausible and defensible.

Indeed, in what follows I aim to show that Schleiermacher was deeply concerned to avoid misunderstandings of his teaching and held his own account of sin's origins as coextensive with the origins of humanity to a high standard of accountability to the tradition. It is because he recognizes the power and elegance of older accounts of sin, especially Augustine's, that he does so. We will see in what follows how, instead of divorcing his account of sin's origins as much as possible from Augustine, the truth is the reverse. Schleiermacher's account of sin is as Augustinian as possible *on the assumption that no account of a change in human nature is sustainable*. If so, every state or act is, in principle, explicable in terms of one or more determining causes grounded in a heritable nature – exactly what Schleiermacher explicitly claims earlier.

The quality of Augustinian insights explains why Schleiermacher is drawn to them, yet there are obvious differences; and what explains those differences is part of what makes Schleiermacher's account distinctive. One key feature of Schleiermacher's account is, as we saw, the minimalist role his gives to traditional authorities and how, when he does come into conflict with them, he navigates such conflict. We saw this clearly in Chapters 2 and 3 with respect to the fall of the Devil and the fall of Adam. In some instances, Schleiermacher argues that biblical texts or confessional documents are underdetermined. In other instances, he subordinates their authority. In few other instances is this clearer or more dramatic than in the case of the origins of sin, where Schleiermacher freely and simply admits that his account is, at least in some important respects, at odds with confessional authorities and at least some biblical passages.[36] Yet he is not dissuaded. And he is not over-occupied with explaining his account in such a way that disagreements with those authorities are minimized or explained away. Schleiermacher is, however, in contrast, very carefully attuned to *misunderstandings* his account might risk (as opposed to genuine disagreement), and deeply concerned to avoid those.

One of the most crucial points revolves around the *priority of the good* and the *naturalness* of sin. Schleiermacher, as we shall see shortly, thinks that natures are normative, and that sin is privative of that norm. Therefore, while he insists that there was never a change in human nature which caused humans to *become* sinners, he is nevertheless committed to explaining sin in such a way that the priority of the good is maintained, and that the naturalness of sin, in the normative sense, is denied, which is to say, he declines the principle of parallel priority (see Chapter 1).

Consider the following passage in which Schleiermacher specifies the relation of our inherited tendency to sin to the first act of sin:

> If then, on the one hand, we discard the idea that human nature changed, but, on the other hand, still maintain that an incapacity for the good [*eine Unfähigkeit zum Guten sei*] is the universal state of humans, it follows that this incapacity was present in human nature before the first sin, and that accordingly what is now inborn [*angebohrene*] sinfulness was something original also to the first pair. This we admit; yet it must be so determined as to be compatible with the likewise created original perfection, and in such a way that the state of the first human pair is understood to have been, through all time, like our own by analogy, as described above. In no sense, therefore, are we substituting for the idea of a longer or shorter state of perfectly vital piety, the idea that the first free act after the awakening of the God-consciousness was sin – a conception already eliminated by what has been said above. The truth is rather that the awakening of the God-consciousness implies also the

beginning of the good, which in turn could not remain without consequences that proved operative even after the first sin.[37]

Let us take this important and dense passage one claim at a time.

In the first place, notice how sin is described in terms of natures and powers, with sin specifically described as an "incapacity for the good." This
incapacity is "present" as a "state" from the first, "inborn" or "congenital"
in human being, and "original" to the first humans. It is an incapacity innate
in a nature *without being natural* – in the same way, apart from its origins,
that sin is innate to human beings for the Augustinian tradition post-fall.

In the second place, sin as native to human being is "compatible with,"
but not constitutive of, the original perfection of humanity. This crucial
point distinguishes Schleiermacher's account in important ways from some
of Schleiermacher's interpreters on sin and from other modern accounts of
sin's origins. Humanity, as we will see, will be *no less human* when sin
finally vanishes.

In the third place, notice that Schleiermacher explicitly denies that "the
first free act after the awakening of the God-consciousness was sin." On
the contrary, there could be no sin before there was a consciousness of
God – our highest good – and there could be no genuine consciousness of
God without genuine effects. Thus, though beset by this incapacity, the first
human beings were *limitedly* conscious of God and, therefore, were weakly
determined by that consciousness to act in accordance with the good in
some way before they sinned.

Of course, speculative natural history is not Schleiermacher's point here.
Rather, it is to begin to specify the different senses of the priority of the good
to which he subscribes as well as to qualify the ineluctability of sin. Humans
are at least sometimes not determined to act by their sin; and when we do
sin, the sin in question is dependent upon an already present perfection *to
be sin*.

One simply cannot sin if one is not conscious of God. "[Sin] can be present only simultaneously with and as related to the God-consciousness,"
Schleiermacher says.

> If our God-consciousness is not yet developed, there can be in us no
> resistance to it, but merely an independent activity of the flesh which,
> though in the future it will quite naturally come to act as a resistance to
> the spirit, according to the nature of the thing [*den Geist der Natur der
> Sache nach werden wird*], cannot at that stage be regarded as sin in the
> proper sense, but rather as the germ of sin.[38]

Even if the *germ* of sin is innate to human being, it cannot become sin apart
from the presence of the God-consciousness. The good must be prior to its
defect. And yet once the good is present, the resistance of the flesh to it is
unnatural.

However, Schleiermacher's correction might, in turn, mislead in the other direction. And so once more he offers precise qualification:

> Now if, on this view, the statement that man was created by God good, righteous, and holy means nothing more than that, in opposition to the Pelagian doctrine, the first actual state [*der erste wirkliche Zustand*] of humanity could not have been one of sin, we may unreservedly assent. For sin must have been preceded by knowledge and recognition of the divine will, and in that case it must have been preceded by free activity which was not sinful. But if what is meant is an actual power [*wirkliche Macht*] exercised by the higher faculties over the lower, then, the greater this power is taken to be (even if we do not conjoin with this the above Augustinian claim), it is from this point of view impossible to conceive of anything but a growing intensification of that power in the same regard.[39]

The mention of an "actual *power*" is key here. The idea is that, should the first state of humanity be one where the power of the God-consciousness is fully ascendant in its determining role, it could lead only to a positive feedback loop in attainment and exercise of that same power. And if that were the case, we would not stand in need of redemption, which contradicts the most fundamental deliverances of the God-consciousness and commits us to the Pelagian heresy.

Schleiermacher, instead, summarizes his own position as follows.

> If, accordingly, for the contrast between an original nature [*einer ursprünglichen Natur*] and a changed nature [*einer veränderten Natur*] we substitute the idea of a human nature, apart from redemption, everywhere and without exception unchanged; and if, for the contrast between an original righteousness that filled up a period of the first human lives and a sinfulness that emerged in time (an event along with which and in consequence of which that righteousness disappeared), we substitute a timelessly universal original sinfulness [*Ursündlichkeit*] adhering to human nature which exists along with the original perfection – though in such a way that from the concomitance and development of the two there could arise no active righteousness [*Thatgerechtigkeit*], but at best a vacillation between vitiated spiritual efforts and increasing and fully matured sin; if, finally, for the antithesis between an original guilt and a transmitted guilt we substitute the idea of an absolutely identical common guilt for all [*einer für Alle gleichen schlechthin gemeinsamen Schuld*]; then the confessional formulae in which this doctrine in its relation to the succeeding one is most succinctly expressed may be qualified and supplemented as follows.[40]

Schleiermacher's subsequent qualification and supplementation are not the headline. Rather, it is the dramatic summary he offers of his own account that should receive our attention. It consists of the following claims: (1) that sin "everywhere and without exception" adheres to human nature; (2) that, despite our original perfection, and because of sin, no *active righteousness* could be attained; and (3) that human beings' guilt for this state of affairs is not transmitted from a changed state, or from anyone else's guilt, but an "an absolutely identical common guilt." The rest of this chapter and the next will be devoted to explaining how Schleiermacher sustains these claims, and in what sense.

Schleiermacher's formula is a dramatic departure from the tradition in important respects – although it is not a total repudiation. The next section ahead, on the original perfection of the world and of humanity, emphasizes the continuity with tradition in Schleiermacher's account. But before we turn to the original perfection of the world and of humanity, which coexists with humanity's original sinfulness, another important discontinuity demands attention, a discontinuity between interpretations of Schleiermacher (and the broader Schleiermacherian tradition of thinking about sin) and Schleiermacher's own principles and specific claims.

There are two stories of what Schleiermacher thinks about sin that differ significantly enough from his claims and commitments that they could seriously mislead. The first is that sin is principally, or even solely, a *product* of social ill.[41] The second is that Schleiermacher conceived of human development as delivering human beings to an evolutionary and/or historical plateau where, at that point, our freedom *transcends* our natures, and so where our natures cease to explain our free acts, including those acts arising from sin.[42] Both stories are shown to be incorrect or incomplete by Schleiermacher's remarkable claims about the inherence of sin in human nature from the beginning, and how the sin that inheres in us strictly prevents righteousness proper.

Sin on Schleiermacher's account *is* linked to social ill, and Schleiermacher's doctrine on this point is important. However, sin is not, and cannot, according to Schleiermacher, be *grounded* in social ill or have *originated* from it. Societies explain the origins of our sinful natures only insofar as they explain the generation of human beings – namely, insofar as humans are birthed and raised in community. Natures, not contingent social arrangements or practices, explain sin.[43] Not only have we seen clear statements to this effect in this chapter, but also it follows from Schleiermacher's arguments in prior chapters against traditional accounts of sin.

One key example of this is Schleiermacher's dictum that acts cannot corrupt natures since every act proceeds *from*, and so is already *included in*, the nature of an agent. Social practices are acts or collections of acts. Therefore, social structures and practices cannot corrupt human nature (though, they can *amplify* sin – and more). If traditional explanations of Adam's fall can't succeed because we need something to explain *why* Adam willed what he willed, then accounts of the origins of sin that offer social ill as the basic explainer of sin can't succeed either *for the exact same reason*, for we must then ask why *whole societies* went wrong. And far from minimizing the difficulties posed by Adam's willing, social accounts exacerbate such fundamental problems in proportion to the number of sinners. Augustine only has to explain how two people willed what they willed. Socially grounded accounts of sin face Schleiermacher's same criticisms, only now multiplied by dozens, hundreds, or thousands of wills in sinful agreement. Thus, Schleiermacher's grounding objections applied to Adam's fall all the more rule out *grounding* sin in societies (of whatever scale).

Interpretations of Schleiermacher that read him as grounding sin in human freedom conceived in a particular way face similar problems. Again, there is the textual evidence to the contrary. Schleiermacher describes sin as an innate *incapacity* or *inability* – that is, an arrested power. Even if we think Schleiermacher subscribed to a view of freedom where our free acts are incompletely explained by our natures, circumstances, and motives – a view which this work in general, and the previous chapter in particular, has been concerned to argue against – such freedom would still not explain the origins of sin. For freedom, so conceived, is a power or ability. If we are free in this sense it is because we are *able* to be or do something. But sin is an inability: something which explains why we cannot exercise an ability. It is not clear how the possession and exercise of one ability explain another inability. It is even less obvious how freedom of this kind *grounds* an inability – that is, how it ends the explanatory regress and does so in such a way as to show why original sinfulness everywhere and always adheres to human nature, as Schleiermacher claims.

Further, if such freedom is not merely incompletely determined by our natures, and so forth, but actually, as John Hick argues, *unpredictable* in principle,[44] then not only does this go against everything Schleiermacher has said about the determining power of motives and more, but also it is not at all clear how, on this theory, the claim that sin is universal (apart from Christ) can be defended. It seems, rather, that the indeterminacy of freedom would make it not only possible but also nearly inevitable that at least *two* people (Christ plus someone, anyone, ever) would be without sin. And that not only contradicts Schleiermacher's stated commitment to the uniqueness of Christ but also obviates the need, in principle anyway, for "*one single Redeemer.*"[45]

It should be clear now: the risk of both alternative lines of interpretation is not only that they don't do sufficient explanatory work but also that at least some versions of those stories fall into the Pelagian heresy. Like all heresies, they do not intend but nevertheless amount to what Schleiermacher thinks are un-Christian claims. No, in order to avoid Pelagianism, Schleiermacher believes, with Augustine, that for the unredeemed it is not possible not to sin, and that what grounds this impossibility is an inability of humans to save themselves: not merely a coincidental inability but a necessary one, such that Christ *necessarily* is, by birth and by nature, he upon whom all depend absolutely for their salvation.

Original perfection

If Schleiermacher is going to err, he is going to err *against* Pelagianism.[46] But that means that he risks the Manichean heresy. And, indeed, I take it that, properly understood, Schleiermacher's account tilts, if anywhere, in that direction. Schleiermacher is, however, alert to the threat and determined to avoid the heresy.

His main resource for countering it is his doctrine of the original perfection of the world and of humanity (hereafter "original perfection of the world" for both, unless specified). With this doctrine, Schleiermacher aims to place the incapacity for the good within a teleologically ordered developmental scheme and to explain how that incapacity does *not* commit him, overtly or tacitly, to the idea that nature itself and human nature in particular are intrinsically beyond the possibility of salvation – that is, to Manichaeism as he understands it.

In so explaining the original perfection of the world, Schleiermacher will also specify in what sense sin is a privation – while continuing to deny the traditional claim that the origins of sin are causally incomplete. Privations are always dependent on goods of which they are privative; and so Schleiermacher will also begin to say more about the goods that are lacking. It is his account of sin as a privation apart from a fall that allows Schleiermacher to maintain the normativity of nature(s) and to explain how the original perfection of the world coheres with the fact of universal human sinfulness.

The doctrine of the original perfection of the world and humanity might easily mislead, however.[47] In the first place, it might be taken indeterminately as a claim that the world is perfect in every respect. It might also be taken as implying by the term *original* that there was a past in which the world was perfect, but now is no longer. Schleiermacher denies both senses.[48] The perfection in question is highly specific. "By the *perfection* of the world," Schleiermacher says,

> nothing is to be understood here except what we must name so in the interests of the religious self-consciousness, namely, that the totality of finite existence, as it influences us, and thus also all those human influences upon the rest of existence resulting from our place in the same, works together in such a way as to make the continuity of the religious self-consciousness possible.[49]

That is, the world is perfect insofar as it *facilitates* the God-consciousness. In combination with the original perfection of humanity (ahead), we will see how Schleiermacher adds to this idea the notion that human nature, as a product of the world, is likewise *sufficient* to develop the God-consciousness. In regard to both the world and human nature, the sense of *perfection* at hand is limited to the *natural ability to appropriate redemption*.

Schleiermacher also denies that by the *original* perfection he means to imply that there was a time when things were perfect (originally, in the past), but now are not. His explanation of this point is remarkable in its detail:

> It must be premised, however, that the term *original* does not refer to any definite state [*bestimmten Zustand*] of the world or of humanity nor of the God-consciousness in humans, all of which are a developed perfection admitting of more or less; the question is rather of self-identical perfection prior to all temporal development and grounded on the inner relations of the relevant finite existence.[50]

That is, Schleiermacher denies that the original perfection in question was a past Edenic state, because he denies that it refers to *any* particular time or place. What is noteworthy is, however, not merely that Schleiermacher is denying such a state – though this is certainly further evidence of Schleiermacher's denial of *any* corruption of a paradisiacal past, either by two people or by whole societies. No, what is most remarkable is his explanation of what was *original* about something that is normally thought of as past. For Schleiermacher, such a perfection is not only not *past* but also not even *temporal*. It is "prior to all temporal development [*aller zeitlichen Entwiklung vorangehenden*]"[51] for indeed it is grounded in the eternal omnipotence of God, whose relation to each moment of finite existence is undivided.[52] The world is *originally perfect*, therefore, because its suitability for facilitating redemption is its reason for being in the divine causality. It is, in order words, the eternal form of the world, its idea in the mind of God, as suitably ordered to this end, in which its *original* perfection lies.[53]

In what, then, does *perfection* itself consist? Schleiermacher explains his use in this context as follows:

> As to what in the sphere of experience we call perfection or imperfection, the former is only that which by means of the original perfection has already come to pass, the latter that which has not yet come to pass; both taken together, however, are the perfection which is coming to be. Hence we can say that for each given moment the original perfection is in that which underlies it as pure finite causality; but the definitive perfection is in the totality of all its resulting effects, its further development being thought of as included in the moment. But now what underlies each moment as finite causality is nothing but the totality of all persistent forms of being and all contrasted functions of the same; and consequently the original perfection is the unity of all these in virtue of which they are equal in compass to the divine causality, and because of the contrast evoke the consciousness of it.[54]

That is, the perfection and imperfection of our experience are greater or lesser approximations to the ideal related to the real perfection that has or has not *yet* eventuated, respectively. Only the totality of all that has happened and all that will ever happen approaches the ideal. The *original* perfection of the world is the source or ground of the perfection that is coming to pass. But that source or ground is just the ordered totality of existent things and what they do. Therefore, the original perfection of the world is the unity of all things in the way those things, as a totality in unity (i.e., a world), bring about the divinely ordained effects. *Perfection* is just the sufficiency of the nature system to its intended effects, its end or ends – specifically with respect to the God-consciousness. Thus, the original perfection of the world is fundamentally teleological.[55]

The original perfection of the world includes the original perfection of humanity. "It could of course be said that human being itself, with its constitution, is an integral part of the world," Schleiermacher says, "and that it is only in virtue of this constitution that it is precisely the part it is; and hence that the original perfection of humanity is already included in the original perfection of the world."[56] The original perfection of humanity is thus nested conceptually within the original perfection of the world in just the same way that it is nested causally.

The original perfection of the world and the original perfection of humanity are, however, distinguished not only as genus (world) to species (humanity) but also by their relative emphasis on (initial) action and passion. It is the power of the world to make possible and then *elicit* the consciousness of God that constitutes the original perfection of the world; and, conversely, it is the power of human nature to attain to the God-consciousness by its natural *receptivity* which partially constitutes the original perfection of humanity. The two, however, are not *really* different, only relatively distinct. The power of the world to develop the God-consciousness "by means of the human organism [*mittelst des menschlichen Organismus*]"[57] is included in the notion of the perfection of the world; and, likewise, the natural disposition to the God-consciousness attained by mutually perfecting aspects of consciousness can become actual only in connection with the consciousness of the world with which it ideally unites in every moment.[58]

Schleiermacher summarizes this relation in a grand unified vision:

> Passive states, however, can only arise through operative influences, and hence the original perfection of the world in relation to humanity consists principally in this, that in it is temporally grounded the excitation of passive states which are to pass into active states (these we name *incentives*), or, in other words, that they sufficiently determine the receptivity of humanity to the awakening and shaping of a person's self-activity. If now we take a person first of all purely on their inner side, as a self-active being in whom God-consciousness is possible, that is, as spirit; then, from this point of view that person's bodily [*leibliche*] side, which is not the person themselves, belongs originally to this material world into which the spirit enters, and only gradually does it [the body]

become the organ and means of presentation [*Organ und Darstellungs-mittel*] of the spirit, but prior and first of all it mediates the stimulating influences of the world upon the spirit. Thus the whole of this aspect of the original perfection of the world can be summarily expressed by saying that in it there is provided for the spirit such an organization [*Organisation*] such as the human is in living connection with all else which conducts the spirit into all the rest of being.[59]

That is, the world is originally perfect in that it contains all the necessary conditions for the union of not only human beings but also the world with the spirit of God: first as passive, then as active. The last point is critical, for Schleiermacher does not think of the eliciting of the God-consciousness as beginning and ending in passion, but as beginning with passion and ending in action, "[f]or," Schleiermacher says, "if all self-activity in humans were due to the effects of the world, it would be merely reaction, and every feeling of even partial freedom, would be illusion."[60] On Schleiermacher's account, humans must at least sometimes be the genuine proximate source of their own actions; and so, to the spirit, "the [human] organism is itself both the most immediate organ and the most immediate means of presentation."[61] As Schleiermacher further explains,

[I]t is only in connection with their organs that a human being realizes sovereignty over the world, of which they can only be conscious as something based upon the divine omnipotence; and it is only inasmuch as the simple activity of the spirit is presented through the medium of space and time that it awakens, as an image of the same, the consciousness of the divine causality.[62]

That is, although consciousness of the world and God can *begin* only with the organs of the human body (i.e., the senses, etc.[63]), it cannot but end in activity, activity which, in human beings, manifests as the consciousness of God and which, Schleiermacher hints, is at least part of what makes human beings in the divine image.[64]

Perfection is sufficiency. Thus, the original perfection of the world and humanity includes all the conditions, necessary and sufficient, for the development and sustenance of the God-consciousness in human beings, including also the *perfection* of the God-consciousness communicated through Christ.[65] And because this end is the sole end of concern to the Christian religious consciousness, when the world is found to be ordered to this end, its perfection, in the only relevant sense, is vindicated. The world is so ordered that it *shall* attain to this end. Because every actuality implies potentiality, the world, including human nature is, contra the Manichean heresy, naturally fit for this purpose at every level, both with respect to the cosmos in the widest sense and with respect to the human species; both with respect to the passive receptivity necessary to activate these states and with respect to the action that follows from them.

With the original perfection of the world guaranteeing that humanity not only *can* be perfected but also *shall* be, and that this potential is intrinsic to the world *and* human nature, Schleiermacher denies Manichaeism unambiguously. But it remains to be seen how, precisely, he explains the coherence of this natural perfectibility with the sinfulness endemic to all humans. Schleiermacher's explanation not only closes the loop on his account of the origins of sin but also returns us to an earlier theme in the chapter which both vexed and motivated Augustine's account: the priority of the good.

The priority of the good

Sin is privative of the good in two senses for Schleiermacher. It is privative of the complete ideal: the unbroken consciousness of God. It is also privative of the incomplete good already possessed by each person: an arresting of the God-consciousness that is already partially present in them. "Nevertheless," says Schleiermacher,

> we are not entitled to say that sin, on the view taken of it here, would conflict with the original perfection of humanity, and thus annul it. On the contrary, we must rather insist upon the fact that sin in general exists only insofar as there is a consciousness of it; and this again is always conditioned by a good [*durch gutes bedingt*] which must have preceded it and must have been a result of just that original perfection.[66]

Why sin exists only insofar as there is a consciousness of it is a topic we turn to in greater detail in the next chapter, but for now it is important to note the point, and how it coheres with the privative account of sin that Schleiermacher wants to maintain.

In an animal in which there is no consciousness of God whatsoever, there can be no sin, for sin is the incomplete development of the God-consciousness already present. To make for sin, the God-consciousness must be *present*, but *incomplete*. Moreover, in order for this consciousness of God to arise, it must have been conditioned by a prior good brought about by the likewise timelessly preexistent original perfection of the world. In other words, with some qualification, Schleiermacher can affirm a sense of the *temporal* priority of the good: there must be some consciousness of God at least weakly and intermittently present before its development can be accurately described as "arrested" as opposed to merely absent. And, without any qualification, Schleiermacher can affirm the logical and theological priority of the good: an absence depends on a presence, and the goodness of God grounds the development of the world and human beings in which sin is present as the incomplete development of the divinely ordained ideal, which is our highest good. "Thus," explains Schleiermacher,

> the state of sinfulness over its entire range actually presupposes the original perfection of humanity, and is itself conditioned by it; and

accordingly, just as the latter concept expresses the unity of our development, so sin in turn represents its intermittent and disjointed character, though without in any way abrogating the unity itself.[67]

The state of sinfulness presupposes the original perfection of humanity insofar as *any* privation depends on the good deprived.

Schleiermacher expresses this same doctrine psychologically in a discussion of *conscience* (not to be confused with consciousness). He explains:

> The "wicked conscience [*böses Gewissen*]" which we may have within
> us is there, for one thing, only because of our seeing the possibility of
> what is better, and this also by a different way, partly insofar as we have
> a conscience at all, i.e. the inward demand for harmony with the God-
> consciousness is implanted in us. Hence if in an individual, at a time of
> life when the God-consciousness could have been developed, or among
> a people still at an early age of development, the notion of that "better"
> has not been evolved in similar fashion, we regard their imperfection, and
> the violence of the flesh in them, not as sin, but as crudeness and igno-
> rance. *Sin, accordingly, manifests itself only in connection with and by
> means of what has already become good, and only inhibits future good.*[68]

We take up this topic in greater detail in the following chapter. But for now,
two important points from this rich passage require special attention. First,
for Schleiermacher, sin and the consciousness of sin are mutually entailing,
and the one cannot exist without the other. To find oneself a sinner *is* to be
conscious of the arresting of the God-consciousness, and vice versa. Second,
in every respect, sin stands dependent on goods, present and future. One
cannot sin if one is not at least limitedly conscious of God, and, as we shall
see in the following chapters, to be conscious of God is to share in God's
communicated blessedness, which is our highest good.

Nevertheless, in no way does Schleiermacher's account of privation depend
on the past *corruption* of goods already possessed. His distinct account of
privation coheres with his criticisms of traditional accounts of the fall of the
Devil and of Adam precisely because he agrees with Augustine that good
cannot corrupt good. But Schleiermacher's specific account gives him distinct advantages over Augustine's. Because Augustine was committed to the
idea that there was, in fact, a change in human nature, and yet, simultaneously to the dictum that good cannot corrupt good, he committed himself
to explaining the corruptibility of human beings in virtue of their deficient
wills and, ultimately, their creation from nothing.[69] While the being of the
finite creature does not corrupt, the admixture of nonbeing in every finite
thing does make corruption possible.[70] Thus, Augustine implied that there
is a fundamental susceptibility in creation, nonbeing, tending to the dissolution of created things, and actually occurring through the created possibility
of a deficient will. By this path Augustine came unintentionally to flirt with

the Manichaeism he rejected, despite using the basic concept of a change in human nature to explain the origins of sin. Because, for Schleiermacher, sin is not a dissolution or corruption of a temporally prior good nature, but an obstruction, arresting, or incapacity of a *present and future good*, he gains a double advantage over Augustine in this respect. In the first place, he has no need of any kind of fall or fall-like account to explain a change in human nature with which, in turn, to explain the origins of sin. And, in the second place, he has no need for a controversial account of the will or finitude-as-such that risks reintroducing cosmic dualism through the back door.

The final and most important sense in which sin is a privation of a good is its relation to the absolute perfection of Christ. On the one hand, acquaintance with Christ through his communicated God-consciousness provides privileged epistemic access. "[I]t is only from the complete sinlessness and the absolute spiritual power of the Redeemer," Schleiermacher says, "that we gain the full knowledge of sin."[71] And as consciousness of sin entails sin itself, it is only through our contrasting acquaintance with Christ's perfection that we are fully convicted. Most importantly, though, Christ's perfect God-consciousness is a perfection *of his humanity*. "[I]f we are to see everything that can develop out of such original perfection all together in a single human appearance," claims Schleiermacher, "it is not to be sought in Adam, in whom it must have been lost again, but in Christ, in whom it has brought gain to all."[72] Christ's perfection is human perfection. This perfection is not only ideal but also real, and in one and the same person. His humanity is as it should be. Christ is, indeed, the first true human.[73] And so it is his unbroken consciousness of God which is normative of all *human* nature. Thus, sin's privation (see earlier) is amplified: it falls further short of human nature; it is a privation of another already existent good – Christ himself; and it is an obstruction of a specific future good – Christ's communicated blessedness. The content of this good (i.e., the God-consciousness) is taken up in the following chapter.

The maintenance of the priority of the good is paramount. It shows that Schleiermacher is not, by rejecting a fall, committing himself to a disastrous account of nature and value. It also shows not only *that* but also *how* Schleiermacher aims to avoid Manichaeism. His tools for doing so are little other than what the tradition provided: that sin is a privation of an original good, a good possessed, and a good to come. Only, Schleiermacher is able to do so without appeal to either an independent will or the inevitable metaphysical tarnish of finitude. He is able to do so because he does not need to provide a story of the loss of these goods, only an account of their not yet having been gained. And last, the priority of the good brings Schleiermacher, albeit incompletely, back to the deficient cause tradition. For imperfect causes *are* deficient – only not in their origins. They are not ideal in themselves nor can they, by their own power, bring about their proper ends. They stand in need of perfection, of salvation. Yet they have sufficient reasons for being deficient, causes which are sufficient to determine them as they are, and yet also other causes which are sufficient to complete their creation and to bring about the ends for which they were made. In the end, Schleiermacher is confident his account avoids both natural heresies:

> [W]e may regard sin on the one hand as simply that which would not be unless redemption was to be and so any apparent necessity of approaching Manichaeism disappears; on the other, as that which, as it is to disappear, can disappear only through redemption, and so we can only wantonly fall into Pelagianism.[74]

Conclusion

Schleiermacher thinks there never was a paradise, that there never were humans without sin (apart from Christ), but that an account of the evolution of animals into human beings who could naturally, but not perfectly (by their own power), become conscious of God is sufficient to account for the origins of sin.

There are many potential objections to this account. It demotes biblical authority by substituting the Christian religious consciousness for the biblical text as the primary *explanandum* of Christian theology. It discards the story of the fall along with a certain sense of deficient causality. It could be taken to suggest that humans are delivered to a point where they could save themselves. It could be taken to imply that sin is natural to humanity, and so accompanies human nature even into heaven. It could be taken to suggest that God is a valueless omnipotence that stands in equal relation to the good as to the bad. Ultimately, it might lead the distrustful to assume that these commitments are *required* of an account of the origins of sin that places too much in the hands of external authorities like natural science.

As I have argued, however, only some of these possible objections have traction, and those objections that do are precisely the most difficult to maintain and explain for *traditional* accounts as well. Schleiermacher's account, therefore, does not accrue to it any *special* burdens in comparison to traditional accounts, yet does showcase unique strengths. Chief among those strengths is that, instead of taking a historical-degenerative form following Augustine (and the tradition more broadly), it takes a historical-developmental form. Because the development in question includes individual and specific development nested within the evolution of the cosmos, it is, in principle, compatible with not only an evolutionary account of human origins but also an evolutionary account of human wickedness – wickedness, which for Christians, is grounded in sin.

Finally, I have also shown that one reason traditional objections to Schleiermacher's account have little purchase is because Schleiermacher's account is generally *in agreement* with the Augustinian tradition. He agrees especially with basic traditional Christian claims about the priority of the good, logically, metaphysically, and even in some respects, temporally – insofar as the arresting of the God-consciousness depends on it being present, and insofar as Christ's temporal perfection is prior to our own. Along with his commitment to the priority of the good follows the normativity of natures, and an account of sin as a privation of the good. Sin is even a kind of deficiency in that what is sufficient to bring about our perfection is not (yet) within us.

The disagreements with traditional theological accounts that remain are specific, not general. And recognizing the specificity of what Schleiermacher maintains and what he discards allows us to see his project as surgical criticism, rather than wholesale destruction. At the same time, recognizing the specific differences in these accounts leads us to the most interesting and crucial decisions in Schleiermacher's theology. As we saw in the previous chapter, one of the most important differences is Schleiermacher's rejection of certain important senses of deficient causality as a corollary to a causal completeness thesis following from his affirmation of the principle of sufficient reason. This leads in two directions: first, to questions of freedom and culpability for states or actions issuing from states which were not, themselves, brought about by voluntary acts; and second, to serious and potentially all-important questions of divine justice as a consequence of God's connection to evil through sin. These two lines of inquiry respectively form the topics of the next two chapters.

Notes

1 *GL* §22.1; *The Christian Faith*, 97.
2 *GL* §22.2; *The Christian Faith*, 99, translation revised.
3 See Aquinas, *Summa Theologica*, II–II, Q. 11, a. 1, resp. On this point Schleiermacher is almost paraphrasing Aquinas. The difference is that Aquinas diagnoses the root of heresy as pride, and sees its fault as consisting in deviation from true doctrine, whereas Schleiermacher thinks of heresy as historically rooted (in syncretism, diversity of circumstances, misunderstanding, etc.) and sees its fault as consisting in incoherence with the essence of Christian piety (i.e., faith in the one Redeemer and absolute dependence on God). Among other important consequences, this suggests that heresy is best cured not by excommunication or extermination but by education and argumentation. See also Aquinas, *Summa Theologica*, II–II, Q. 11, a. 3, resp.
4 *GL* §22.2; *The Christian Faith*, 98, translation revised.
5 *GL* §22.2; *The Christian Faith*, 98, translation revised.
6 *GL* §22.2; *The Christian Faith*, 98, translation revised.
7 *GL* §22.2; *The Christian Faith*, 98–99, translation revised.
8 *GL* §22.2; *The Christian Faith*, 98, emphasis added.
9 See Aristotle, *Metaphysics*, IX.1, 5.
10 See Aquinas, *Summa Theologica*, Ia, Q. 1, a. 8, r. o. 2.
11 A thing cannot coherently be said to both be *incapable* of becoming something and, in fact, become that thing. Specifically applied to redemption, this means that if humans are, in fact, redeemed, they must be capable of being so; and if they are not capable of being redeemed, none can be. See Aristotle, *Metaphysics*, IX.3–4.
12 *GL* §22.2; *The Christian Faith*, 98, emphasis added.

13 *GL* §22.2; *The Christian Faith*, 99.
14 *GL* §22.2; *The Christian Faith*, 98.
15 *GL* §22.2; *The Christian Faith*, 98.
16 See Aristotle, *Metaphysics*, IX.1.
17 *GL* §72.3; *The Christian Faith*, 298, translation revised, emphasis added.
18 *GL* §72.3; *The Christian Faith*, 298, translation revised.
19 This in contrast to Hick's general interpretation. See Hick, *Evil and the God of Love*, 219–20, 225–26, 232, 236–40.
20 See Pedersen, *The Eternal Covenant*, 82–85.
21 See Pedersen, *The Eternal Covenant*, 19–35.
22 See Pedersen, *The Eternal Covenant*, 35–45.
23 This, as I have shown, was perfectly possible well before Charles Darwin's day. See Pedersen, *The Eternal Covenant*, 35–42.
24 *GL* §61; *The Christian Faith*, 247–48, translation revised.
25 *GL* §61.1; *The Christian Faith*, 248, translation revised.
26 *GL* §61.1; *The Christian Faith*, 248.
27 *GL* §61.1; *The Christian Faith*, 248–49, translation revised.
28 *GL* §61.2; *The Christian Faith*, 249.
29 *GL* §§61.2–4; *The Christian Faith*, 249–52.
30 *GL* §61.3; *The Christian Faith*, 250.
31 *GL* §61.3; *The Christian Faith*, 250–51, translation revised.
32 See Pedersen, *The Eternal Covenant*, 43–45.
33 *GL* §61.4; *The Christian Faith*, 252, translation revised.
34 *GL* §§66, 66.2; *The Christian Faith*, 271, 273.
35 *GL* §72.4; *The Christian Faith*, 299, emphasis added.
36 *GL* §72.4; *The Christian Faith*, 299–300.
37 *GL* §72.5; *The Christian Faith*, 301–2, translation revised.
38 *GL* §67.1; *The Christian Faith*, 273, translation revised.
39 *GL* §61.5; *The Christian Faith*, 255–56, translation revised.
40 *GL* §72.6; *The Christian Faith*, 303–4, translation revised.
41 For example, see McFarland, *In Adam's Fall*, 39–42; Wyman, "Sin and Redemption," 135–36.
42 For example, in the style developed from Schleiermacher's thought as found in Peterson, "Falling Up," 273–86; Hick, *Evil and the God of Love*, 276–80. See also Mariña, "Where Have All the Monads Gone?."
43 Evidence against this claim might include the following: "The sinfulness that is present in an individual prior to any action of his own, and has its ground outside his own being, is in every case a complete incapacity for good, which can be removed only by the influence of Redemption." It seems that Schleiermacher is saying sin is *not* grounded in our natures. But this is misleading. Instead, Schleiermacher is saying that an *individual*'s being does not ground *their own sin* because that sin is, as he puts it in the next sentence, "present from the first in every human being." *GL* §70, 70.1; *The Christian Faith*, 282.
44 Hick, *Evil and the God of Love*, 276.
45 *GL* §22.2; *The Christian Faith*, 98.
46 This in contrast to, among many, McFarland, *In Adam's Fall*, 42.
47 Unrelated to the present argument is the potential of the doctrine to mislead in a different way: by suggesting that *only* humans are perfect in this sense or even that humans are "the central point of all finite existence." Schleiermacher denies this. *GL* §58.2, postscript; *The Christian Faith*, 236–37.
48 *GL* §59, postscript; *The Christian Faith*, 241.
49 *GL* §57.1; *The Christian Faith*, 233, translation revised.
50 *GL* §57.1; *The Christian Faith*, 234, translation revised.

51 *GL* §57.1; *The Christian Faith*, 234.
52 *GL* §§52, 54; *The Christian Faith*, 203–6, 211–18.
53 See Aristotle, *Metaphysics*, IX.8.
54 I take it that by "its further development being thought of as included in the moment," what Schleiermacher means is that the perfection which is to come is already nascent in any given moment of a thing's development as the sufficient grounds for its perfection and that this generalizes to the world as a whole. *GL* §57.2; *The Christian Faith*, 235, translation revised.
55 Hence I disagree in part with Adams when he claims that "Even 'the original perfection of the world,' treated by Schleiermacher in connection with the doctrines of creation and preservation, is not presented, so far as I can see, as involving any teleology in the divine causality; it is simply a matter of the evaluation of the results of divine causality in relation to what is seen as the good for human life." Schleiermacher does present his account in causal terms, and certainly the good regarded is *our* good, but a cause ordered to some good is the essence of a teleological account, not a denial of one. See Adams, "Schleiermacher on Evil," 571.
56 *GL* §58.1; *The Christian Faith*, 236, translation revised.
57 *GL* §60; *The Christian Faith*, 244.
58 *GL* §60.1; *The Christian Faith*, 244–45.
59 *GL* §59.1; *The Christian Faith*, 238–39, translation revised.
60 *GL* §59.2; *The Christian Faith*, 239, translation revised.
61 *GL* §59.2; *The Christian Faith*, 240, translation revised.
62 *GL* §59.2; *The Christian Faith*, 240, translation revised.
63 See Aristotle, *De Anima*, III.8; Aquinas, *De Veritate*, Q. 2, a. 3, 19.
64 *GL* §59.2; *The Christian Faith*, 240, footnote 2.
65 *GL* §60.3; *The Christian Faith*, 247.
66 *GL* §68.2; *The Christian Faith*, 277, translation revised.
67 *GL* §68.2; *The Christian Faith*, 278.
68 *GL* §68.2; *The Christian Faith*, 277, translation revised, emphasis added.
69 See Wetzel, "Augustine on the Origin of Evil."
70 Augustine, *City of God*, XII.1, 6.
71 *GL* §68.3; *The Christian Faith*, 279, translation revised.
72 *GL* §61.5; *The Christian Faith*, 256, translation revised.
73 *GL* §89; *The Christian Faith*, 365–66.
74 *GL* §65.2; *The Christian Faith*, 270, translation revised.

References

Adams, Robert Merrihew. "Schleiermacher on Evil." *Faith and Philosophy* 13, no. 4 (1996): 563–83.
Aquinas, Thomas. *De Veritate*. Translated by James V. McGlynn. S. J. Chicago: Henry Regnery Company, 1953.
———. *Summa Theologica*. Translated by the Fathers of the English Dominican Province. New York: Benziger Bros., 1947.
Aristotle. *De Anima*. Vol. 1. Edited by Jonathan Barnes. Princeton: Princeton University Press, 1984.
———. *Metaphysics*. Vol. 2. Edited by Jonathan Barnes. Princeton: Princeton University Press, 1984.
Augustine of Hippo. *The City of God*. Part I, Vol. 7. Translated by William Babcock. New York: New City Press, 2013.
Hick, John. *Evil and the God of Love*. Third edition. London: Macmillan, 1977.

Mariña, Jacqueline. "Where Have All the Monads Gone? Substance and Transcendental Freedom in Schleiermacher." *The Journal of Religion* 95, no. 4 (2015): 477–505.

McFarland, Ian A. *In Adam's Fall: A Meditation on the Christian Doctrine of Original Sin*. Oxford: Wiley-Blackwell, 2010.

Pedersen, Daniel J. *The Eternal Covenant: Schleiermacher on God and Natural Science*. Berlin: De Gruyter, 2017.

Peterson, Gregory. "Falling Up: Evolution and Original Sin." In *Evolution and Ethics: Human Morality in Biological and Religious Perspective*, edited by Phillip Clayton and Jeffrey Schloss. Grand Rapids, MI: Eerdmans, 2004.

Schleiermacher, Friedrich D. E. *The Christian Faith*. Edited by H. R. Mackintosh and J.S. Stewart, translated by D. M. Baillie, et al. Berkeley: Apocryphile, [1928] 2011.

———. *Der christliche Glaube nach den Grundsätzen der evangelischen Kirche im Zusammenhange dargestellt*. Second edition (1830/31). Edited by Rolf Schäfer. Berlin: Walter de Gruyter, 2008.

Wetzel, James. "Augustine on the Origin of Evil: Myth and Metaphysics." In *Augustine's City of God: A Critical Guide*, edited by James Wetzel. Cambridge: Cambridge University Press, 2012.

Wyman Jr., Walter E. "Sin and Redemption." In *The Cambridge Companion to Friedrich Schleiermacher*, edited by Jacqueline Mariña. Cambridge: Cambridge University Press, 2005.

6   Schleiermacher on what sin is

> Then he who chooses thus would choose generation and destruction rather
> than that third sort of life, in which, as we were saying, was neither pleasure
> nor pain, but only the purest possible thought.
>
> – Plato, *Philebus*

In the previous chapter we saw how Schleiermacher gave an account of
sin as a privation of a good, while rejecting the idea of a fall into a state of
sin. In its stead Schleiermacher substitutes an evolutionary-developmental
account. In this chapter we examine more closely how Schleiermacher thinks
about the particulars of sin: the good(s) it regards, the way it misinforms
the operations of the mind, the way it yields particular acts, the propagation
and exacerbation of sin in community, and how sin is reckoned as guilt. As
in previous chapters, such exposition will serve not only to clarify Schleiermacher's thought but also as evidence of what I argue makes Schleiermacher's
account so controversial, and yet so distinctive and alluring.

Throughout we will see that, once again, Schleiermacher's account is not
made powerful, interesting, or scandalous by wholesale criticism of the
tradition, but by the way he denies *select* traditional claims and commitments while defending others. In this chapter, for example, we will see how
Schleiermacher thinks of sin as a privation of our highest good caused by a
state of *akrasia*, a lack or failure of self-control. That account bears a great
deal of resemblance to an account as traditional as, for instance, Thomas
Aquinas'.[1] In fact, on the whole, we will see once again how Schleiermacher's account is substantially *closer* to the tradition in many respects than is
sometimes thought.

And yet, at the same time, the theme of Schleiermacher's denial of states
or acts without sufficient causes will become even more apparent as the
state of sin, its yielding specific thoughts and volitions, and its spread by
and through societies are all explained by what is, in principle, a causally
complete structure. His denial of deficient causes is not a loose generaliza-
tion, or a thesis asserted only with respect to sin's origins. Instead, he denies
deficient causes in detail by offering a causally complete account each step

of the way. Causal completeness, as a corollary of the principle of sufficient reason, links sin to some prior sufficient cause at every level, from the will to the individual, to social forces, and ultimately to nature as a whole. Controversially, this links faults of the will to faults of nature,[2] and fully commits Schleiermacher to claiming that God is the author of sin.

The structure of this chapter is as follows. First, we will examine what, exactly, Schleiermacher thinks sin *is*, particularly as it relates to the God-consciousness. Second, we will see how Schleiermacher explains the moral psychology of sin, in particular the relation of the arresting of the God-consciousness to the intellect and will, and to thought and action. In the third section, this and the prior chapter will be integrated into a holistic picture linking Schleiermacher's larger notion of nature with his account of particular sinners and their acts by examining Schleiermacher's account of the relation of original to actual sin, and its mediation through social groups and practices.

The arresting of the God-consciousness

Sin, Schleiermacher tells us, is a "state of alienation [*Zuständen Abwendung*] from God."[3] And we count "everything as sin that has arrested the free development of the God-consciousness."[4] In contrast to sin, Schleiermacher says, "that absolute facility [i.e., ease – *Leichtigkeit*] of the development of the God-consciousness from any given stimulus and in every given situation, which is set as the goal, is constant communion with God."[5] Sin is an arresting of that facility, and is, therefore, a hindrance to that communion, a hindrance which, in and of itself, alienates us from God. In this section we see in what sense sin is an arresting of the God-consciousness, how it comes about that the God-consciousness is arrested, and we begin to see what Schleiermacher takes this to imply for our ultimate well-being and our guilt.

As an *arresting*, sin is a lack or hindrance of another thing: the God-consciousness. In order to understand sin, we must first examine the God-consciousness and see how exactly, in the nested developmental account Schleiermacher wants to give, alienation takes form, and what it consists in. In particular, parallels will be drawn to traditional accounts of sin, for, once again, the novel appearance of Schleiermacher's account of sin belies its traditional content.

Sin is a matter of consciousness. Because sin is an arresting or hindrance of a state of consciousness, "sin in general exists only in so far as there is a consciousness of it."[6] One must, in other words, not only be *capable* of being conscious of God but also actually be so – only incompletely – in order to find oneself in a state of sin.[7] And "[w]e have the consciousness of sin," Schleiermacher says, "whenever the God-consciousness which forms part of an inner state, or is in some way added to it, determines our self-consciousness as pain."[8] Conscious alienation from God is misery.[9]

But what gives rise to such a condition? Such a state occurs when the God-consciousness "has formed part of our self-consciousness, but this God-consciousness has not been able to permeate the other active elements therein, so as to determine the moment."[10] Despite any sensuous pleasure that may attend such a state, due to the "impotence [*Unkräftigkeit*] of the God-consciousness" in forming the moment, such a state is also accompanied by a simultaneous and compatible pain [*Unlust*] of the higher consciousness.[11] The God-consciousness is present, but powerless; and this powerlessness, and consciousness of powerlessness, is what generates the aforementioned pain.

The impotence of the God-consciousness in question regards the *power* of the God-consciousness to *determine* (or *inform*) a given moment – a moment itself specified by the sensuous self-consciousness under particular circumstances.[12] This impotence *is* the arresting Schleiermacher speaks of: "sin [is] a hindering of the determinative power of the spirit caused by the independence of the sensuous functions."[13] That is, sin *consists in* a lack of power on the part of the God-consciousness to determine the moment, to make the moment one thing and not another, a moment consisting of both thought and action, due to the inhibiting, because competitive, determining power of the sensuous self-consciousness. In short, Schleiermacher explains, sin is "a positive antagonism of the flesh against the spirit."[14] We look much more at the details of the moral psychology Schleiermacher deploys to explain this understanding of sin in the following section. For now, what is most important to note is that the God-consciousness is *actively hindered*, or arrested, by another determining cause.

The arresting of the determinative power of the God-consciousness stands in contrast to the ideal state, where the consciousness of God and the sensuous self-consciousness are rightly ordered.

> If we conceive now a state in which the flesh, i.e. the totality of the so-called lower powers of the soul, were susceptible only to impulses proceeding from the quarter of the God-consciousness and were never an independently motive principle [*ein selbständig bewegendes Princip*], a conflict between the two would not be possible, but we should again have conceived a sinless state. In every possible moment in this self-consciousness the two powers would be perfectly at one [*vollkommen eins*], every moment beginning in the spirit and ending in the spirit and the flesh serving only as a living intermediary, a healthy organ, and never exhibiting anything not initiated and directed by the spirit, whether as an act of its own or as an intrusive extraneous element in an act proceeding from the spirit.[15]

In this ideal state, the higher self-consciousness and lower self-consciousness, as powers of the soul, are arranged properly. The God-consciousness and the sensuous self-consciousness never conflict because they are nested hierarchically, and within that hierarchy they are rightly ordered: the God-consciousness informs, and so determines, the sensuous self-consciousness – but not the other way around. There is no *conflict* because the flesh has taken its rightful place as instrument of the spirit; and because there is no conflict created by the flesh as "independently motive principle,"[16] there is no *arresting* or *hindering* of the determining power of the God-consciousness.

This ideal state is, however, found only in Christ.[17] In contrast, for all others,

> [a]s long, however, as spirit and flesh have not in this sense become one, they co-exist as two agents [*Agentien*] opposed to each other, and in so far as the spirit presses towards the perfect unity indicated, this state can only be characterized as an incapacity of the spirit.[18]

To be sure,

> [r]esistance, as an activity by which an opposed activity is to be neutralized, has naturally its degrees of more and less, and is thus an intensive phenomenon conditioned by time, and when present in a living thing advances by repetition in time to proficiency.[19]

Thus, the determining power of the God-consciousness can be ranked two-fold: on the one hand, as ideal and anything less than ideal; and on the other hand, as a greater or lesser degree of impotence, such that while all but Christ are sinners, not all are sinners to the same extent or degree. That is, not all sinners stand in the same relation to the *initial appropriation* of redemption, even while they all remain alike as sinners in need of redemption.[20]

Notice what Schleiermacher's description of the God-consciousness and the sensuous self-consciousness implies. First, and very importantly, there is no in-principle incompatibility between the sensuous self-consciousness and the God-consciousness. Their conflict arises not from their coexistence but from their disordered ranking. Schleiermacher is clear: the flesh's proper place is as an *instrument* of the God-consciousness, subordinate to the God-consciousness. Indeed, the sensuous self-consciousness plays an essential *mediating* role in determining the moment in which the God-consciousness finds expression in the sensible universe as "a living intermediary, a healthy organ" to communicate the spirit to the world.[21] It is, therefore, not only good but also indispensable. Yet it becomes a source of sin when it assumes pride of place, when it sets its own motive principle in competition with the God-consciousness as the principle determining thought and action. As the human organism is ordered to mediate not only the spirit to itself but also to the world, the internal disorder of the flesh and the spirit amounts to a description of the soul at war with itself, and of creation in rebellion against God.

The basis of this disordered power of the flesh is, however, not utterly unreasonable. The sensual self-consciousness issues in "the antithesis of the pleasant and the unpleasant, or of pleasure [*Lust*] and pain [*Unlust*],"[22] and it does so "according to *whether life is furthered or hindered* by [feelings of relative freedom or dependence]."[23] That is, the sensual self-consciousness is a good-tracking power. Insofar as it generates awareness of a furtherance of life under particular circumstances, it issues in pleasure; and conversely, from a hindrance of life, it issues in pain. In itself, it is a superior state of consciousness over what Schleiermacher calls the "animal confusion" of lower states of consciousness.[24] Indeed, it is the first state of *consciousness*, properly speaking – all other antecedent states being dim or confused approximations of it. The sensual self-consciousness is thus a genuine perfection, both intrinsically and instrumentally. Yet the goods it tracks are merely terrestrial goods, the perfection it amounts to is a strictly terrestrial perfection – albeit a perfection which is a necessary developmental condition of the higher consciousness, and which persists alongside it.

In contrast, once attained the God-consciousness is not indexed to, or dependent upon, individual fortunes. "Its effect," says Schleiermacher, "is simply an unchanging identity of life [*unveränderliche Gleichheit des Lebens*], which excludes any such antithesis [of pleasure and pain]."[25] Its good is supreme: "This state we speak of under the name of the blessedness of the finite *as the highest summit of its perfection*."[26] And indeed, humanity's highest good is supernatural, "since union with the Supreme Being is absolute satisfaction."[27] The sensual self-consciousness is necessary to mediate the God-consciousness, and "all activities of the flesh are good when subservient to the spirit,"[28] but "to the person who once recognizes what piety is, and appropriates it as a requirement of their being, every moment of a *merely* sensual self-consciousness is a defective and imperfect state."[29] Thus the disorder involved in the antagonism of the flesh against the spirit is a disordered ranking of *genuine goods*. Though in itself good, and though necessary to mediate the God-consciousness, the sensual self-consciousness becomes an ill when, and only when, it is exchanged for our true supreme good: the consciousness of God, which is blessedness itself. Thus sin regards a *specific* disordered ranking of the sensual self-consciousness in service to "what Christian piety regards as alone good in the strictest sense": communion with God.[30]

Both the sensual self-consciousness and the God-consciousness *determine* thought and action.[31] They thus *inform* both (i.e., they determine both with respect to their objects); but both sorts of consciousness provide the intellect and the will with something more than content alone.[32] The interpretation I wish to advance (on the basis of its explanatory power) is that the God-consciousness and the sensible self-consciousness deliver *principles* of thought and action. In the following section I explain how this works in more detail. But, for now, notice that on this hypothesis, when the sensual self-consciousness resists the determining power of the God-consciousness, it *misinforms* human being with respect to its proper objects (of knowledge, or action, or both). Our consciousness of God is confused with the consciousness of sensible things, and thus we find ourselves in a greater or lesser idolatry.[33] Likewise, the goods we pursue in action are improper. We exchange actions informed by our highest good for the desire for lesser goods, for actions informed by the consciousness of mere sensible things.

Only when the mediating sensual self-consciousness assumes its proper role as providing mere *mediating* principles, subordinate to the *first* principles of thought and action provided by the God-consciousness, do our thoughts and actions conduce to their proper ends – our natural good in service to our highest good. When they do, there is no conflict. The determining power of the sensual self-consciousness is compatible with the determining power of the God-consciousness because it is included within it: when an animal life is informed by the consciousness of God, it does not cease to be an animal life with natural needs and vulnerabilities. So long as the principles provided by the sensual self-consciousness fall *under* those principles provided by the God-consciousness, there is no contradiction. The ranking of principles then reflects the ranking of goods: natural goods, such as the seeking of pleasure and the avoidance of pain, are subordinate to our highest, supernatural end.

Accordingly, sin, as a hindrance of our highest good, is a privation of both the right ordering of goods and the further good that right ordering brings about – namely, the assumption of all activity within the determining power of the God-consciousness. The source of this privation is behind and before us, inherited and exacerbated by the whole human race, but the state is ours, and the sinful acts which follow from it are likewise ours, and so the guilt attending it is ours. "[W]hatever alienation from God there is in the phases of our experience," Schleiermacher says, "we are conscious of it as our original act, which we call sin."[34] Indeed, it is an important contention of Schleiermacher's that, whatever the *ultimate* source of this disordered ranking of goods, the state of sin belongs to us, and the sins that issue from such a state are actions attributable to us as issuing voluntarily from such a state; and so our sinful acts are both determined and free, acts for which we can be blamed by others and punished by God – albeit not, in the case of the latter, in an altogether traditional sense.

In the following section, we look to the moral psychology of sin to see exactly how Schleiermacher explains that the arresting of the determining power of the God-consciousness issues in thought and act.

The moral psychology of sin

Sin, for Schleiermacher, is a state and function of mind. Yet his account of consciousness is distinctive. Schleiermacher, therefore, explains how sin functions within a unique moral-psychological framework where the classic faculties of intellect and will account for how sin arises under particular circumstances in their relation to the God-consciousness as a third term. The conceptual overlap with traditional moral psychologies offers important insight into Schleiermacher's notion of sin and its relation to his rejection of aspects of the deficient cause tradition. In particular, we see that although Schleiermacher's moral psychology is strictly anti-voluntarist, it is not reducible to the determination of the intellect, for reasons we will see ahead. In this way, his account of the specifics of the moral psychology of sin coheres neatly with his general account of sin as a sufficiently caused deficiency.

We begin piecing together Schleiermacher's complex moral psychology with the simple elements of intellect and will. Sin, Schleiermacher says, is "a result of the unequal development of insight [*Einsicht*] and willpower [*Willenskraft*]."[35] However, Schleiermacher warns against the mistaken *reduction* of his account to "intellect and will" [*Verstand und Willen*][36] in parallel with his resistance of the reduction of piety to either knowledge alone or action alone.[37] Instead, the immediate self-consciousness is the *tertium quid* in this relation, and is the measure of the discrepancy of the intellect and will.[38] Whereas the right ordering of the God-consciousness to the sensuous self-consciousness is a nested hierarchy, it is the role of the immediate self-consciousness in action to not only inform but also coordinate and modulate the intellect and will.

This mediating role of the immediate self-consciousness is key. The immediate self-consciousness forms the "conscious beginning [. . .] which is represented in every intellectual determination of the will."[39] This conscious beginning, this "taking command of oneself,"[40] Schleiermacher describes as "simply the understanding [*Einsicht*] of the *exclusive excellence* of those states which unite with the God-consciousness without hindering it."[41] That is, what the understanding grasps is the *unique value* of states compatible with the consciousness of God. However, "That understanding [*Einsicht*] cannot emerge without the individual appropriating it," Schleiermacher says, "which only happens through an act of self-consciousness, in which, under the form of approval and recognition, this insight now becomes a command."[42] *That* the immediate self-consciousness does a great deal of work is plain, even if the specifics are unclear. Let us, then, unpack this dense account in its entirety in detail, one step at a time.

First, sin is a result of *unequal development* of insight (or understanding) and willpower. That is, there is an improper discrepancy between insight and willpower, a discrepancy that is explained by their developmental irregularity. In this case, what Schleiermacher has in mind is the development of these powers within an individual's life from birth to adulthood, although this kind of developmental account also fits within expanding concentric evolutionary considerations from a single person's life to the emergence of humans in the universe. It is, after all, only when an animal is capable of self-consciousness that it achieves the clarity of consciousness necessary to generate self-control – the "taking command of oneself" [*Sich selbst gebieten*] that Schleiermacher describes earlier.[43] Moreover, it is only with this middle stage of consciousness reached that an animal can attain the next stage, the consciousness of God;[44] and it is only with these developmental prerequisites satisfied that an animal can find its consciousness of God arrested. Therefore, disordered principles in competition generate simultaneous and nested dilemmas at every step. Sin, resulting in an unequal development of insight and willpower, reflects this broader developmental pattern within an individual life.

Second, and crucially (as mentioned earlier), sin does not merely regard the unequal development of intellect and will, but their unequal development *in relation to the immediate self-consciousness*. The immediate self-consciousness is the principle that informs, and so finds expression in, the intellectual determination of the will.[45] But the immediate self-consciousness itself includes both the sensuous self-consciousness and the God-consciousness.[46] Ideally, they are hierarchically ordered, and so noncompetitive: the sensuous self-consciousness is subordinate to the determination of the God-consciousness. But, in a state of sin, the sensuous self-consciousness competes with, and so hinders, the God-consciousness as the *first* principle informing intellect and will. It is the competition from the sensuous self-consciousness – the "violence of the flesh" [*Gewalt des Fleisches*][47] – that results in a case where "the act does not correspond to that [intellectual] determination."[48] We return to this last sentence ahead, but before we do, let us reexamine the third and final step more closely: *how* the immediate self-consciousness informs the intellect and will.

Third, as Schleiermacher explained earlier, "understanding [*Einsicht*] cannot emerge without the individual appropriating it," and this "only happens through an act [*Act*] of self-consciousness in which, under the form of approval and recognition, this insight now becomes a command."[49] That is, the individual must first attain those states of understanding of "exclusive excellence"[50] which do not conflict with the God-consciousness. But that understanding has to be appropriated to become a person's own. It is not simply given.[51] Such an understanding is so appropriated when the self-consciousness *acts* to approve and recognize it. It is the immediate self-consciousness that determines the understanding by doing that work of approval and recognition – that is, by assigning identity and approbation under the relevant principle, either the sensuous self-consciousness or the God-consciousness. At the same time, the appropriation of this understanding under the relevant principle *makes it* a command. This "commanding recognition" [*gebietende Anerkennung*] then becomes an "impulse" [*Stoß*] given to the will.[52] A state of sin occurs whenever this complex series of relations is interrupted.

The sheer number of moving parts here might, however, mislead, for Schleiermacher discards a greatly complexifying possibility: namely, "a lagging of the understanding behind the will [*ein Zurückbleiben des Verstandes hinter dem Willen*]."[53] Any supposed instance of this "would only *seem* to be the case [*dies nur scheinbar wäre*]."[54] In fact, according to Schleiermacher, the will never does outrun the intellect. And this coheres perfectly with what one would expect from what we saw in previous chapters of

Schleiermacher's account of reasons determining action. Yet something nevertheless goes wrong in the case of sin. And given the elimination of a will willing contrary to, or beyond, the intellect's judgments, that leaves only two possibilities: first, misinformed understanding, or second, a will which somehow lags behind the intellect in intensity.

Although Schleiermacher does think one especially pernicious effect of sin is intellectual distortion,[55] sin is principally an *intensive* discrepancy between the determinations of the intellect and the will. "Now the fact that this excitation of the self-consciousness follows on the understanding [*Einsicht*] more rapidly than it is able to determine the excitations of the will," Schleiermacher says, "*is* just that inequality along with which sin and the consciousness of sin are given."[56] That is, as earlier, the self-consciousness, through an act of approval and recognition, both (1) appropriates an understanding and (2) becomes a command *through* that recognition. When (1) occurs more readily than (2), we have the *only* sort of discrepancy between the intellect and the will that *can* occur once it is conceded (as Schleiermacher claimed earlier) that there are no genuine cases of the intellect lagging behind the will. What Schleiermacher describes is, then, an account of *akrasia*, a weak will, in terms unique to his own moral-psychological framework.[57] We *know* what we should do, but we do not *will* (and so act) to do it.

Schleiermacher provides two counterexamples of how this state of sin might *not* arise that help to clarify how he thinks sin in general and *akrasia* in particular work. The first, a Christological allusion, is most illuminating for present purposes. As Schleiermacher explains,

> Thus if one were gradually to reach an understanding of the relationship of their various states to the God-consciousness, but only as well as their recognition can set the will in motion, then for that person no consciousness of sin could arise, as indeed they could never imagine a more divine life than that which they actually exhibit at every moment.[58]

What makes this life divine and what, at the same time, makes it free from sin is that there is perfect fluency between the recognition reached and the will exercised, no discrepancy between the recognition commanding and the will commanded. No human life but Christ's reaches this perfection in this life. "[E]ven in a state of grace, when the knowledge of the sinfulness of one's usual states is perfected," Schleiermacher says, "still, the power of the will lags behind the understanding [*noch immer ein Zurückbleiben der Willenskraft gegen die Einsicht entsteht*]."[59] Even the will of sanctified sinners remains intermittently weak in this way.

But how does this account of the weak will lagging behind the intellect comport with Schleiermacher's earlier description of sin as an arresting of the God-consciousness? Specifically, how does the independence of the sensuous self-consciousness contribute, thus resulting in a conflict between flesh and spirit? While the general outlines are clear enough, to see how the specifics work in detail, we have to connect the dots that Schleiermacher laid down ourselves.

In order to see how Schleiermacher's account works on the whole, we will work backwards from the resultant weakness of will to the conflict of flesh and spirit as motive principles. To do this I will assume that Schleiermacher's description of a weak will follows traditional conceptions in its general outline. The justification for this latter hypothesis is, once again, its explanatory power. If Schleiermacher's description is treated as a roughly typical description of *akrasia* (as everything seems to indicate), modified by the terms of his own moral psychology, the result will be a robust connection between the conflict of flesh and spirit and the *state* of sin (which *is* that fundamental conflict) on the one hand, and that state's issuing in sinful *acts* on the other, which, because those acts "owe [their] occurrence solely to voluntary action,"[60] are deeds for which we are liable to blame.

Sinful acts happen when we act against our better judgment – when, as Schleiermacher puts it, "the act does not correspond to that [intellectual] determination."[61] We know this because Schleiermacher restricts candidates for sin to those who possess a God-consciousness. Without such a consciousness, we cannot sin. Indeed, it is a central feature of Schleiermacher's doctrine of conscience that "the 'bad conscience' which we may have within us is there, for one thing, only because of our seeing the possibility of what is better."[62] We also know this because acts of sin occur when determinations of the self-consciousness excite the intellect easier than they excite the will. We thus *know* what we should do more readily than we are stirred to do it. As we saw earlier, the reverse situation does not occur: the will never outruns the intellect. And if there is an equality between the insight and willpower because *both* are weak, such a condition is not sin either. That latter condition is, according to Schleiermacher, simply a blameless state of incomplete development, such as children enjoy.[63] Therefore, sinful acts only ever occur when our judgment is determined by our self-consciousness with greater facility than our will brings that determination into effect in an act. And that is a condition of *akrasia*.

However, if it is true that sin consists in acting against our better judgment, and yet it is also true that the will never outruns the intellect, Schleiermacher has to have some way of explaining how this discrepancy comes about without recourse to an independent will – for an independent will *might* outrun the intellect, and Schleiermacher has denied this possibility. Aristotle's solution to this puzzle was to argue that *akrasia* occurs when two principles compete to be the major premise in a practical syllogism.[64] For example, if I hold that it is good to pursue the pleasurable, and good to pursue the healthy, then I may find myself an akratic should I act to pursue some delicious but unhealthy chocolate cake (following one principle of action, delivered by my appetite) at the expense of my health (contradicting another principle of action, delivered by my better judgment).[65] I can be said to have acted against what I *know* not because I acted against everything I know (e.g., I *know* that cake is delicious and that this *is* cake) but because I acted against at least one recognized principle of action. And yet it cannot therefore be said that I acted entirely apart from or against what I know (and so involuntarily or nonvoluntarily) because I still acted on the basis of another *known* principle of action: that it is good to pursue the pleasurable. Schleiermacher's account of the will lagging behind the intellect makes best sense if we suppose that he has an account like this in mind. If so, the sensuous self-consciousness and the God-consciousness are the relevant competing principles.

Moreover, there is good reason, besides its explanatory power (see ahead), to think Schleiermacher believes the sensuous self-consciousness and the God-consciousness function as competing *principles*. The best evidence is his foregoing description of the "flesh" as an "independently motive principle" [*ein selbständig bewegendes Princip*],[66] which, by implication, stands in conflict with the God-consciousness as another *motive principle*. The problem with the "flesh" in this case is its independence. If it were properly subordinate to the God-consciousness, "both powers would be perfectly at one [*Beide Potenzen würden . . . vollkommen eins*]."[67] The conflict between the flesh and the spirit, which is to say between the sensuous self-consciousness and the God-consciousness, is thus a conflict between competing motive principles. Because both are competing *motive* principles, they are almost certainly best understood, in this case, as competing first principles of action. And that is, again, precisely what gives rise to *akrasia*.

The explanatory power of this reading adds further to its persuasiveness. Sinful acts come about because of a discrepancy between insight and willpower. That discrepancy, on this reading, consists in the will lagging behind the intellect. The will so lags because, since it is akratic, it and the intellect are simultaneously informed by two competing principles. The intellect is excited by the proper principle (the God-consciousness) more readily than the will is. The will, instead, acts according to the other principle at hand: the sensuous self-consciousness. Because Schleiermacher thinks of these powers as developing unevenly in all humans but Christ, "here the flesh has habit on its side as the real law in its members"[68] and so the will more readily follows the flesh than the spirit, despite the intellect's recognition of the proper place of the God-consciousness. It is the fact that the flesh is developmentally prior to the spirit, and is further nurtured by habit, that makes the will more receptive to the impulses of the flesh than to the spirit.

The sensuous self-consciousness is a candidate for akratic conflict in the first place because, as a good-tracking power (see earlier), it is a genuine perfection for it to guide human action – only not as an *independent* principle. The disordered independence of the sensuous self-conscious comes about for a variety of reasons – erratic individual development, social influence, and more – but, once independent, it *arrests* the *determining power* of the God-consciousness by competing with it *as a principle with its own determining power*, and so *misinforms* human action with respect to its true good. Nevertheless, the sinner is neither compelled nor ignorant. They act for reasons, though they know better, because both the God-consciousness and the sensuous self-consciousness are present. Accordingly, sinners are, for Schleiermacher, blameworthy for their sin since, "The actuality of everyone's sin has its ground in the same way in themselves."[69] Thus, reading Schleiermacher's teaching as a species of *akrasia*, the whole moral-psychological chain from the arresting of the God-consciousness to the issuing of this state in blameworthy acts is explicable.

Nevertheless, it might be objected that this picture risks misconstruing Schleiermacher's account of *sin* as either a matter of false belief or bad action as opposed to the arresting of a third thing, the God-consciousness. If so, this contradicts Schleiermacher's clear statement that piety is neither a knowing nor a doing. But not only is this an objection that can be satisfied, but also it is actually another aspect of Schleiermacher's thought that can be explained *better* on my interpretation. Recall that Schleiermacher claims that the functions of the immediate self-consciousness, whether the God-consciousness *or* the sensuous self-consciousness, somehow come to simultaneously determine and also mediate between the intellect and the will; and also recall that Schleiermacher insists on this third element, the immediate self-consciousness (including both the God- and self consciousnesses), in his moral psychology. The akratic reading I propose depends on taking Schleiermacher's description of the sensuous self-consciousness and the God-consciousness as "motive principles" straightforwardly and seriously. And so the immediate self-consciousness, which in itself is neither a knowing nor a doing, has everything to do with action and thought because, as a principle, it *informs* them both.

But what if Schleiermacher described the God- and sensuous self-consciousnesses as *motive* principles only because he happened to be speaking specifically about the will? In other words, what if the reading I advance makes too much of this one phrase? This is where the akratic reading fits into a larger picture. As I have argued elsewhere, the sensuous self-consciousness and the God-consciousness deliver principles.[70] As principles, they are neither thought nor action but the major premises of both. When cast under the aspect of goods to be pursued, the God-consciousness and the sensuous self-consciousness become principles of action, or "motive principles," generating definite actions under particular circumstances. When cast under the aspect of knowledge, the respective consciousnesses become principles of thought, yielding definite conclusions through particular inferences. I have argued at length that the God-consciousness and the sensuous self-consciousness deliver principles which, in the strict sense, *inform* thought about God and the world.[71] If I am right, Schleiermacher is making a parallel claim about how the God-consciousness and the sensuous self-consciousness *inform* action that would place his account squarely in the Scholastic *synderesis* tradition.[72] Not only does this parallelism result in mutually supporting interpretations of the way the God-consciousness and sensuous self-consciousness function in relation to thought and action, but also it completes Schleiermacher's specific account of sin by offering an explanation for how the two species of consciousness can ultimately coincide in a sinful act which *involves* a discrepancy between the intellect and will related through the immediate self-consciousness generally. In short, the very basis of the discrepancy between intellect and will results from two principles vying to determine both thought and action at once.

If Schleiermacher's account of sin generally follows the *akrasia* tradition, then his account can be elucidated further still. According to Aristotle, the principle of an action is the final cause of that action.[73] And final causes are goods to be pursued.[74] That means that the principle of an action, which is some good, is an *object* of action. Principles, then, are specified *by their objects*. But as we have seen, for Schleiermacher, the God-consciousness and the sensuous self-consciousness are competing principles of action. If Schleiermacher's account is read in this largely classical light, these two species of immediate self-consciousness are likewise to be distinguished by their *objects*, which is to say, *by the goods they regard*.

If the God- and sensuous self-consciousness are so distinguished by the goods they regard, the competition between the God-consciousness and the sensuous self-consciousness can be specified as competition between goods. But Schleiermacher is clear that the sensuous self-consciousness is a good-tracking power.[75] Moreover, in one without sin, the power of the flesh is not *absent* but *subordinate* to the spirit. The conflict between flesh and spirit cannot, therefore, come about from a complete incompatibility between goods, only incompatibility in a certain respect. The problem, as earlier, must be a matter of disordered ranking of genuine goods. But the God-consciousness is our greatest good, "the highest summit of a person's perfection."[76] Therefore, it is that good to which all other goods *should* be subordinate. Because sin is a conflict of principles in themselves *good*, only one of which is rightly accounted *highest*, the conflict between the sensuous self-consciousness and the God-consciousness arises only when two principles *both* claim to be the *first* principles of action – that is, when we pursue both the spirit and the flesh as our *highest good*. The stronger the claim of the sensuous self-consciousness, the lesser the claim of the God-consciousness – and so the arresting of the latter. A state of sin occurs when God and the things of this world, including our merely natural well-being, are alike ranked highest – though with greater or lesser degrees of confusion – and *only in that case* can they compete in the relevant way.

Schleiermacher's evolutionary-developmental account explains how this akratic state comes about. Within evolutionary history, animals very early develop a sense of pleasure and pain, respectively indexed to genuine goods to be pursued and ills to be avoided: things like food, sex, health, and sociality on the one hand, and hunger, disease, injury, and loneliness on the other.[77] Though theirs is a state of "animal confusion," creatures pursue the goods of pleasure and avoid the ills of pain unconsciously.[78] Very young humans share this state of consciousness.[79] By (at least) one point in evolutionary history, animal confusion gives rise to clarity in self-conscious pursuit of pleasures and avoidance of pains.[80] At the same time, the God-consciousness arises as its corollary.[81] But because in the history of life, animals have deeply evolved to follow pleasure and avoid pain, and because in an individual's life a person is born doing the same (and further determined to do so by personal habit and social formation), the pursuit of pleasure comes first and easiest, with that facility which first nature confers and second nature strengthens. And so the flesh is primed to compete with the spirit.

Yet, at the same time, all of this is for the animal's good. Animals pursue pleasures and avoid pains because those pleasure and pains are indexed to the goods and ills to which they pertain. The same is true with children. Animals, including humans, *require* such appetitive powers in order to stay alive, to grow, to reproduce, and eventually, in the case of humans, to become the sorts of things that *can* apprehend a higher good. In short, Schleiermacher's evolutionary/developmental account explains the power, urgency, and even providential necessity of the sensuous self-consciousness, which in turn explains its competition with the God-consciousness when the God-consciousness finally arises.

Because Schleiermacher can give a complete account of how this competition comes about, he can explain how a deficiency can arise through sufficient causes. Because, at one developmental stage, the sensuous self-consciousness in a state of "animal confusion" *does* rightly pertain to an animal's highest good (i.e., the preservation and propagation of the individual and species), the sensuous self-consciousness has a power to inform appropriate to its station and to the creature. This motivating power simply retains its efficacy even when its object is demoted in rank when another, better, object is offered in its place. And so, as a human being awakens to consciousness of God, the *power* of the sensuous self-consciousness is undiminished. It is only its suitability to the final end of the human animal which has changed – because a higher end has been superadded.

Original sin and actual sin

According to tradition, humans are blameworthy for their voluntary sin despite being born in a state of sin because, on accounts like Augustine's, inherited sin is a perversion of nature, distinct from human nature as created by God.[82] Because humans distorted what God had made, they, but not God, can be blamed for their state and the acts that follow from it. When Schleiermacher denies a story of the fall, he is also required to explain how a state of sin, which is, in one sense, natural,[83] can also yield the sorts of acts for which *we* can be held responsible. In the previous section we saw how the *state* of sin, the arresting of the God-consciousness, issues in specific acts and thoughts. In this section we bring the theme of the origins of sin from the previous chapter together with Schleiermacher's account of what sin consists in from this chapter to connect *original* and *actual* sin, for, as Schleiermacher says, "In all humans original sin is always issuing in actual sin."[84]

The aims of this section are threefold: first, to add the final link in explaining how the *origins* of sin yield a *state* of sin which issues in *actual* sins; second, to explain how, given our determined sinfulness, we can be *guilty* for our sinful acts; and third, to explain how the connection between original and actual sin secures our corporate guilt for sin. As we will see, these connections are fully illuminated only given Schleiermacher's account of the moral psychology of sin which secures our agency, and so our culpability, even for those acts which we are by nature determined to do.

As we saw in the previous chapter, Schleiermacher has an evolutionary-developmental account of the origins of sin. In that account sin is a privation not of a past state but of the ideal for which the world was made and to which it is providentially ordered. And, as we saw in the foregoing sections, that privation *consists in* an incapacity of the determining power of the proper first principle of thought and action. The result is that our thoughts and deeds are, in this state of impotence, ill-*informed*. What is still missing, however, is an explicit link between our incomplete development and the inevitability of our sinfulness. Schleiermacher clarifies this connection with a very strong, very distinctive doctrine of original sin's connection to actual sin – a doctrine elaborated in causal terms, indeed, in terms of necessity. This doctrine follows from another application of the principle of sufficient reason, a use of that principle which renders the causal story complete from beginning to end – that is, from the origins of sin to the issuance of a state of sin in particular acts.

Schleiermacher's account of the relation of original and actual sin becomes clear when we see where the distinction between the two lies. "Thus," Schleiermacher explains,

> under the one head [original sin] the state is considered as something received and brought with us before all action, yet at the same time something in which our guilt is latent; under the other [actual sin] it is set forth as becoming apparent in the sinful acts which are grounded in the individual himself, but in that which is received and brought with us is revealed.[85]

While a superficially standard description, Schleiermacher's account is extraordinary, for, as we discover, he means to make the connection between original and actual sin very close indeed, so that original sin is *revealed* in actual sin in the sense that actual sins *merely* make patent what was latent in us as original sin. Indeed, Schleiermacher claims, "Any explanation of actual sin, whether more or less general, will be right only in so far as it teaches that actual sin is grounded in an underlying sinfulness."[86] That is,

Schleiermacher thinks that every actual sin *arises from*, in the sense of find-ing its source in, an underlying sinfulness: original sin.

But how close does Schleiermacher understand this connection to be? Consider this extended passage:

> For the disposition [*Richtung*] to sin, which we apprehend as purely inward and timeless, would not be actual at all unless it were also, at the same time ever manifesting; and conversely, that which does mani-fest itself would merely be something adhering to us from without, and therefore no sin, unless it was part of the manifestation and temporal process of original sin. And just as all that is manifest in original sin must manifest itself somewhere in the measure in which it is distributed among people, so it necessarily has a part in every motion [*Bewegung*] of every person in whom it is present and makes some element thereof to manifest sin.[87]

It is not merely that the potential, in a general or vague sense, must be the condition of sin's manifestation if and when it does manifest but rather that where there is such a disposition to sin, it is *always* manifesting itself such that there is no act of a sinner that is not in some sense mixed with sin as its underlying disposition. "Thus," Schleiermacher concludes,

> throughout the entire range of sinful humanity there is not a single per-fectly good action, i.e. one that purely expresses the power of the God-consciousness; nor is there one perfectly pure moment, i.e. one that does not exist in secret antagonism to the God-consciousness.[88]

Original sin is thus constantly informing states and acts in which it becomes actual sin to a greater or lesser extent. It is a possibility that is always actual-ized, and an actuality which is always comprehended by its ground – that is, by original sin. And thus, Schleiermacher is clear to avoid what he calls the "repellent and offensive" teaching that original sin can be considered apart from actual sin.[89]

Yet, at the same time, Schleiermacher is careful to avoid the opposite mis-understanding: "that original sin is not guilt until it breaks forth in actual sins, for," Schleiermacher claims instructively,

> the mere circumstance that there has been no opportunity for and no outward incentive to sin cannot increase the spiritual worth of a person; but, rather, original sin is the sufficient ground [*hinreichende Grund*] of all actual sins in the individual, so that only something else outside of them, and not anything new within them, needs to be added for the generation of actual sins.[90]

It is original sin as the *sufficient ground* of actual sins for which we are guilty. And yet, since a sufficient ground necessarily comes to expression under ripe circumstances, the connection between original sin and actual sin is something that *shall* manifest so long as it *can*. Remarkably, yet in perfect accord with the principle of sufficient reason, Schleiermacher's account of original sin follows the same principle of plenitude that his account of creation follows.[91] All that can happen will happen. And it is the powers and dispositions of things, together with their circumstances, which explain why they do what they do with such sufficiency so as to *complete* the explanation. Nothing more is needed.

Yet this might suggest that sinners are mere patients in respect to their sinful acts, victims either of their created natures or of their circumstances. However, Schleiermacher does not secure causal completeness at the *expense* of agency, but rather *through* it. Recall that in order for original sin to become actual all that is necessary to bring it about is a change in the person's circumstances, not the person. That means that the basic explanatory work lies on the part of the agent themselves. And so, Schleiermacher claims, accordingly, that "Original sin is purely a thing received [*ein rein empfangenes*] only in the degree in which the individual is not yet spontaneously active, and it ceases to be such in the degree in which that activity is developed."[92] As soon as the person in whom original sin resides is spontaneously active – that is, as soon as the person in question begins to be the genuine proximate cause of their own effects – their original sin ceases to be merely *originated* and instead becomes *originating original sin* "since it brings forth and increases sin in oneself and others."[93] What "has its cause outside the individual [*ihre Ursache außer ihm selbst hat*],"[94] and so is originated, becomes originating as soon as it itself becomes a cause, and so produces sin as its effect, within the individual.

What is most striking about this account is not the way it reckons guilt – itself an important point to which we will return ahead – but rather the way in which the agency of a sinner acting in, because of, and *from* a sinful nature coheres with both Schleiermacher's accounting for agency on a spectrum from mere spontaneity to self-conscious activity and his warning not to count natural necessity against freedom.[95] Neither the principle of alternate possibilities or a theory of incomplete efficient causes is required to secure the agency required for us to become the agents of our own sin – even sin which is ultimately of natural, not solely voluntary, origins.

Schleiermacher has more still to say about how the agency of a sinner connects to their guilt which further illuminates his account of the relation of original sin to actual sin. As he explains,

Since, then, this later sinfulness which has issued from the individual's spontaneous activity is one and the same with that which was congenital in origin, it follows that, just as the supervening sinfulness has arisen within them from free acts based upon the original sinfulness, so the latter, which in fact falls more and more into the background in comparison with the former, and which always forms his starting-point, does not continue in them, and therefore would not have arisen in him, apart from their will [*Willen*]. So it is with justification called the guilt of each person.[96]

Let us examine this very important passage point by point.

First, originating original sin arising from the sinner as agent is "one and the same [*eine und dieselbe*]" as originated original sin – the sin which is inherited. Clearly, however, these two species of original sin can't be the *same* in the sense that they both arise in the same way. That would annul the distinction. Therefore, they have to be one and the same in some other, non-trivial, sense. Given Schleiermacher's foregoing descriptions of original sin as the *sufficient ground* of actual sin, it is most likely that he means the same sufficiency to hold between originated and originating original sin – that is, between sin in us as patients and sin in us as agents. If so, Schleiermacher is claiming that whatever we take up as sinful agents was already implicit in human nature – either in us or in our communities. The difference between the two is then not in content but simply that sin becomes *originating* when it begins to inform our actions.

Second, Schleiermacher implies once more in this passage that what makes us agents in the relevant sense is that our acts be *voluntary* – that is, that the agent acts by the agent's *will*. But notice that Schleiermacher can't mean acting by the will in a sense which runs counter to what he has said earlier about the necessity by which original sin *shall* become actual sin, or about how originated and originating original sin are "one and the same." Indeed, it appears that Schleiermacher thinks we *necessarily will* our sinful acts. Minimally, what he says implies that to will in the relevant sense need not mean that this will was insufficiently determined by the sinful nature of the agent. That is, even if sinful act *S* is a matter of choice, Schleiermacher seems to think that we are determined to choose *S* by our own natures as sinful agents. And because he is clear that we need only act *from* our natures to be free, he seems to think our voluntary sin is determined by our being created as agents who, by our own misinformed wills, cannot not sin.

Further evidence for this interpretation comes from the handful of sentences which follow the foregoing passage, where Schleiermacher entertains the idea of sin in the immature ("children and the unborn").[97] While Schleiermacher grants that they are not guilty in *exactly* the same sense as mature actors (see ahead), he does claim that they can nevertheless be considered latently guilty because "actual sin proceeds unfailingly from original sin" and, therefore, "that of them [children and the unborn] it may be said that they *will* be sinners because of what is already within them."[98] What is most important about this pair of claims for our purposes is: (1) how it eliminates any possibility of the immature willing anything other than sinful acts; and (2) that Schleiermacher claims this necessity because of "what is already within them [*was jetzt schon in ihnen ist*]." This not only is further evidence for my interpretation of Schleiermacher's account of our *necessarily willing* to sin but also will bear further on how we understand Schleiermacher's account of the propagation of sin in community ahead.

No matter how we interpret Schleiermacher's connection of the voluntariness of our sinful acts to the details of the will as a faculty, he is clear that it is the voluntariness of our acts that makes us guilty because the original sin that is within us passively is made active with our will: "So it is with justification called the guilt of each person."[99] And yet, as earlier, this does not distance original sin from actual sin, but, in fact, brings the two closer together. For if original sin is the sufficient ground for all actual sins, then sinful acts are simply the latent content of our original sin, appropriated through the will, and revealed in acts. Because of the plenitudinal relation of original to actual sin, there is, in the end, no meaningful difference in *content* between what is in us as disposition, what we will and so appropriate, and what we do. Because what we *are* as sinners is the sufficient ground for what we *do*, even children are not exempt from a certain sort of anticipatory guilt, according to Schleiermacher, since they are rightly counted guilty for what they will (eventually) do on account of their original sin – an inference which is warranted only if original sin generates actual sin with necessity.[100]

This justification for the guilt of children can, of course, apply *only* to those children who live long enough to commit actual sins. As for those children who die before they commit actual sins, Schleiermacher must articulate their original sinfulness differently. Interestingly, however, he cannot articulate their guilt in terms of hypothetical counterfactuals – that they can be reckoned guilty because of what they *would have done had they lived long enough to do so* – because Schleiermacher has committed himself to the strong metaphysical claim that the possible does not extend beyond the actual. On the other hand, Schleiermacher is still free to articulate this guilt in terms of original sinfulness as the sufficient ground of actual sins, as we will see he does shortly. But in that case his reasoning is somewhat odd, for then the original claim that children are reckoned sinners because of what they (eventually) will do is unnecessary. Schleiermacher could simply have said they are guilty for their sinfulness, and this sinfulness, *should it give rise to actual sin*, is always the sufficient ground of actual sin.

This last point returns us once again to the passage cited earlier where Schleiermacher denies that anything new on the part of the sinner is needed to bring forth sinful acts. The passage deserves quoting again at length:

> Yet this is not to be understood in the sense that original sin is not guilt until it breaks forth into actual sins, for the mere circumstance that there has been no opportunity for and no outward incentive to sin cannot increase the spiritual worth of a person; but, rather, original sin is the sufficient ground [*hinreichende Grund*] of all actual sins in the individual, so that only something else outside of them, and not anything new within them, needs to be added for the generation of actual sins.[101]

In its larger context, this passage is the best evidence for this reading of the necessity and completeness of the explanatory power of original sin in bringing forth actual sins. By denying that original sin *becomes* guilt only in sinful acts, Schleiermacher eliminates a possible close cousin of the view he apparently wants to advance: that we are guilty solely for acts, not for our natural dispositions.[102] Instead, Schleiermacher affirms the complete equivalence between the two: an act is simply what a disposition yields under given circumstances.[103] And because nothing more is, or need be, contributed *on the part of the agent* for a disposition to become an act – because it is the *sufficient ground* of an act – there is "not anything new within them." Therefore, because all the requisites for the act on the part of the agent are included in original sin, nothing about the actuality of the act *adds* to their guilt. What was latent simply becomes patent.

Original sin and social sin

According to Schleiermacher, our own voluntary sins perpetuate and exacerbate sin in ourselves and others. What is *originating* in us as cause (once appropriated voluntarily) becomes *originated* in others as effect. And in all by exercise and habit, "there is growth in congenital sinfulness."[104] It is this power of voluntary sin to engender and encourage further sin that is the ultimate basis of Schleiermacher's famous social doctrine of sin. Yet this well-known teaching, too, might lead to misunderstandings. On the one hand, Schleiermacher's account might be taken to be something like what some Reformed theologians taught as a *federal* account of sin: that sin is *imputed* to us representatively.[105] On the other hand, it might be taken in the vein of more recent social accounts of sin where social sin is the basic *explanans*. However, Schleiermacher's teaching subtly but crucially runs against both more traditional and more recent accounts of corporate sin.

Famously, Schleiermacher describes sin as "each the work of all, and all the work of each" and that "only in its corporate character can it be properly and fully understood."[106] And, importantly, this is because sin is not something that "pertains severally to each individual and exists in relation to them by themselves."[107] Indeed, Schleiermacher claims that

> [T]he total power of the flesh in its conflict with the spirit (it being the ground of everything in human action [*menschlichen Handlungen*] which is incompatible with the God-consciousness) can be understood only by the totality of all those sharing a common life, and never completely in any one part; and whatever appears in an individual, whether a personal or a composite one, is not to be attributed to, or explained by, them alone.[108]

That is, no one person will be the complete explanation for their own sin. This is true whether we consider the whole of humanity across either space or across time.[109]

Where this statement might mislead, however, is if the denial of any one individual sufficiently explaining their own sin is taken further as the denial that there is not an explanatory basis for all sin in the aggregate of individuals and that, instead, corporate sin – conceived either as federal representation or social practices that are not grounded in individuals' innate sinfulness – is a real thing or power above and beyond that aggregate. But this is not Schleiermacher's claim. Instead, Schleiermacher's account of the universal character of sin is of mutually informing individual causes. The totality of individuals (including their attributes and characteristics) itself explains their collective character. It is an account of universal sin that parallels Aristotle's doctrine of concrete universals, the precise account of natural kinds we saw Schleiermacher refer to in the context of the fall of Adam.

There are several further pieces of evidence which support this reading, and which count against what I have claimed are misunderstandings. The first, against federal accounts of sin, is that Schleiermacher thinks that, despite the fact that no one person ever completely explains their own sin, it is always the person's *own* sin that generates *that person's* guilt. The second reason, which counts against both abstract and imputed corporate accounts of sin, is Schleiermacher's consistent order of explanation (i.e., what explains what), and its parallel in his chronological ordering of sin's engendering and imputation. These factors all go hand in hand for Schleiermacher. We look at each in more detail ahead.

Consider, first, the passage that immediately precedes Schleiermacher's famous statement on the corporate character of sin earlier:

> Now, on the one hand, the sinfulness which is prior to all action works in every individual through the sin and sinfulness of others; but, at the same time, it is implanted and fixed in others through the free actions [*freien Handlungen*] of every individual: so it is something absolutely common to all.[110]

Notice the details of the premises that lead to the conclusion, "so it [sinfulness] is something absolutely common to all." Every sinful action is (logically) preceded, and sufficiently explained by, a sinful ground in the sinner (as we saw earlier). This sinfulness operates through the sin and sinfulness of others. It does so by – and this is key – being transmitted through the voluntary acts of others, and so is implanted. This, it appears, is intended as adequate reason to subscribe to the conclusion that sin is common to all.

This is significant because what Schleiermacher describes is a *concrete* account of the transmission of sin. While by no means a merely mechanical account, it includes a specific mechanism for the transmission of sin sufficient to make sinfulness genuinely common to all: namely, sinful acts. Nothing but agents, their dispositions, and their acts is referenced in describing how sin can be "genuinely common to all," which is to say, no abstract corporate sin exists apart from or beyond these concrete particulars. And it is, once again, these dispositions, voluntarily appropriated, which are sufficient to render us guilty, because they are the sufficient ground on the part of the sinner of all sinful acts. Every step of Schleiermacher's account is susceptible to explanation through sufficient concrete causes – including agents' motives, judgments, dispositions, and acts.

The concrete causal structure of Schleiermacher's account is especially clear in the passages where Schleiermacher details the operation and transmission of social sin chronologically. For example, in the earlier cited passage, sinfulness is *prior to all action* [of an individual].[111] More importantly still, when Schleiermacher explains the intelligibility of sin with reference to the whole causal network of sin, he claims that "The same is also true of time. What appears as the congenital sinfulness of one generation is conditioned by the sinfulness of the *previous [früheren]* one, and itself conditions the *later [späteren]*."[112] That is, earlier generations' sin explains later generations' sin, but not the other way around. The transmission of sin, and so also the imputation of guilt, goes only one way.

Finally, Schleiermacher claims that

> It is precisely in virtue of this connection, in fact, that the individual is the representative of the whole species [*ganzen Geschlechts*] in this regard, for the sinfulness of each points back to the sinfulness of all, both in space and time, and also goes to condition all both *beside* [*neben*] them and *after* [*nach*] them.[113]

Once again, the power of sin behaves like any other efficient cause: it affects things around it and after it, but not before it. And so when Schleiermacher says that the individual is the "representative" of the whole species, he cannot mean it in a federal or abstractly collective sense because of the way he ties the imputation of sin to a causal account of its propagation in time and space like other causes. Instead, an individual is representative *only insofar as they are causally implicated.*

The point of pressing this detail is twofold. First, it distinguishes Schleiermacher's account in subtle but important ways both from at least some of the tradition that came before him as well as some of the tradition which has taken inspiration from him. It is important to recognize that Schleiermacher is advancing a very particular account of corporate sin, its transmission, its causal structure, and the ways it generates, and, by implication, does not generate, guilt.[114] Second, and just as crucially, this concrete account of sin working across space and time as other causes coheres with the same premises Schleiermacher summons in criticism of traditional accounts of sin's origins. There are always causes sufficient to explain a given state or act, and these causes are *prior* to the things they explain. Since, just as at every other step in the consideration of the origins of sin to particular sinful acts, corporate sin is causally complete, it is no exception to sin's natural origins.

Conclusion

This concrete causal account of sin and its transmission integrates Schleiermacher's moral psychology with his broader developmental framework using the exact same premises. Natures logically precede acts in the order of explanation, but do not differ from them in content. Acts *depend on* the nature of the agent for their intelligibility. No animal can do more than is included in the notion of the species, and no agent could be tempted to voluntarily sin were they not already susceptible.

Instead, animals evolve who become ordered to two competitive, ostensibly ultimate ends. The determining power of their true end is inhibited by a natural, necessary, genuinely good, but disordered, power. In thought and action, this power functions as a principle. In a given circumstance, this disorder causes actual sins as their sufficient ground. We are left akratic: unable to judge and act well according to our true end because, although we know better in a sense, our appetites render us impotent to act on what we know as readily as we know it.

The cause of the disordered ranking of our highest good is prior to ourselves, but becomes ours as the will approves, and is aggravated in ourselves and others through action hardened into habit. Though we inherit our sin, we are guilty through our own wills, as we ourselves sin and form new sinners. Like children learning to talk, we are all born disposed and *able to become able* to exercise our natural powers, but we nevertheless fail to develop our natural potencies with grave consequences for ourselves and for others. And it is this vast natural network of mutually informing agents and actions, of which we are all part, which perpetuates the guilt, corruption, and disease of human nature.[115]

There is therefore, in principle, for Schleiermacher, an explanation for (1) the origin, (2) the expression, and (3) the transmission of sin. In part, it is simple generation. Children are rightly, according to him, counted sinners because of what they *shall* do by virtue of their innate sinfulness, by the way they were born (indeed, even *prior to their birth*). In part, this is because of the inescapably mixed and reflexive influence of culture and biology on one another. Yet biology and sociality are alike *natural* in the sense that both are included in the notion of a human being. Humans across time and space form and inform one another with consequences for our character, our actions, our deepest loves, and our highest good. Schleiermacher describes how this works both in the history of the cosmos and in the soul, mediated through social relations by action, speech, habit, and circumstance – and, at bottom, by the generation of new individuals who are born unable not to sin.

And yet, something more important and more controversial lingers over his account: it is *causally complete*. That is, as Schleiermacher turns from his criticism of the tradition to his own account, he *adopts* many traditional notions that might be superficially incompatible with his earlier criticism. It is clear by now, for example, that his is a broadly Augustinian account in many key respects: natures norm, the good is prior, and good cannot corrupt good. Yet the all-important Augustinian deficient cause is not to be found. There is no moment of mystery, no rift of insanity, no inexplicable swerve of the will. In its place Schleiermacher not only maintains the principle of sufficient reason but also emphasizes it doubly when it comes to social and psychological causes. There is no step in his account – whether cosmic, evolutionary, social, or individual – where a sufficient reason for our sinful states and acts cannot be assigned in principle. Sin is deficient with respect to human's proper ends but is causally complete with respect to its origins.

Accordingly, there is no disjuncture between nature as created by God, and humans as agents disposed to sin. Instead, every act is grounded in a preexistent potency, and every specific natural potency is nested within the natural order. Sin, in all its inevitability, is something created. It is not merely foreseen and permitted but foreordained and caused. God is, Schleiermacher claims, the author of sin.[116] In the following chapter we will take up that claim and explore in detail his treatment of sin and evil. For now, however, it must be reemphasized that Schleiermacher makes very clear that sin is a sufficiently caused *lack*. Though not a corruption of a historical past, it is a privation. Indeed, it is a privation of our highest good, an impediment to that blessedness for which we were by nature made, but which by nature we cannot attain.

Notes

1 Aquinas, *Summa Theologica*, II–II, Q. 156, a. 1, resp.
2 See Aquinas, *Summa Theologica*, Ia, Q. 49, a. 1, resp.
3 *GL* §63; *The Christian Faith*, 262.
4 *GL* §66.1; *The Christian Faith*, 271.
5 *GL* §62.2; *The Christian Faith*, 261, translation revised.
6 *GL* §68.2; *The Christian Faith*, 277.
7 *GL* §68.2; *The Christian Faith*, 277.
8 *GL* §66; *The Christian Faith*, 271.
9 Compare, for instance, to Aquinas, *Summa Theologica*, Ia, Q. 98, a. 7, resp.
10 *GL* §66.1; *The Christian Faith*, 271, translation revised.
11 *GL* §66.1; *The Christian Faith*, 271.
12 *GL* §§5.3–5; *The Christian Faith*, 22–25.
13 *GL* §66.2; *The Christian Faith*, 273, translation revised.
14 *GL* §66; *The Christian Faith*, 271.
15 *GL* §66.2; *The Christian Faith*, 272.
16 *GL* §66.2; *The Christian Faith*, 272.
17 *GL* §89.2; *The Christian Faith*, 367.
18 *GL* §66.2; *The Christian Faith*, 272, translation revised.
19 *GL* §67.2; *The Christian Faith*, 274, translation revised.
20 *GL* §68.3; *The Christian Faith*, 278–79.
21 *GL* §66.2; *The Christian Faith*, 272.
22 *GL* §5.4; *The Christian Faith*, 23.
23 *GL* §5.4; *The Christian Faith*, 23, emphasis added. See Aristotle, *Nicomachean Ethics*, II.3.
24 *GL* §5.3; *The Christian Faith*, 20–22.
25 *GL* §5.4; *The Christian Faith*, 23.
26 *GL* §5.4; *The Christian Faith*, 23, translation revised, emphasis added.
27 *GL* §110.3; *The Christian Faith*, 510.
28 *GL* §74.1; *The Christian Faith*, 307.
29 *GL* §5.3; *The Christian Faith*, 21, translation revised.

30 GL §70.3; *The Christian Faith*, 284.
31 GL §68.1; *The Christian Faith*, 275–77.
32 GL §68.1; *The Christian Faith*, 275.
33 GL §68.1; *The Christian Faith*, 277.
34 GL §63; *The Christian Faith*, 262, translation revised.
35 GL §68; *The Christian Faith*, 275.
36 GL §68.1; *The Christian Faith*, 275.
37 GL §3; *The Christian Faith*, 5–12.
38 GL §68.1; *The Christian Faith*, 275.
39 GL §68.1; *The Christian Faith*, 275, translation revised.
40 GL §67.2; *The Christian Faith*, 275.
41 GL §68.1; *The Christian Faith*, 275, translation revised, emphasis added.
42 GL §68.1; *The Christian Faith*, 275, translation revised.
43 GL §67.2; *The Christian Faith*, 275.
44 GL §5.3; *The Christian Faith*, 20–21.
45 GL §66.2; *The Christian Faith*, 272.
46 GL §5.1; *The Christian Faith*, 18–19.
47 GL §67.2; *The Christian Faith*, 275, translation revised.
48 GL §67.2; *The Christian Faith*, 275, translation revised.
49 GL §68.1; *The Christian Faith*, 275, translation revised.
50 GL §68.1; *The Christian Faith*, 275, translation revised.
51 See West, "Schleiermacher's Hermeneutics and the Myth of the Given."
52 GL §68.1; *The Christian Faith*, 276.
53 GL §68.1; *The Christian Faith*, 276, translation revised.
54 GL §68.1; *The Christian Faith*, 276, translation revised, emphasis added.
55 GL §68.1; *The Christian Faith*, 277.
56 GL §68.1; *The Christian Faith*, 275–76, translation revised, emphasis added.
57 See Aristotle, *Nicomachean Ethics*, VII.1; Davidson, "How Is Weakness of the Will Possible?"; and for a selection of recent work on *akrasia* see Stroud and Tappolet, *Weakness of Will and Practical Irrationality*.
58 GL §68.1; *The Christian Faith*, 276, translation revised.
59 GL §74.2; *The Christian Faith*, 310, translation revised.
60 GL §68.2; *The Christian Faith*, 280.
61 GL §67.2; *The Christian Faith*, 275, translation revised.
62 GL §68.2; *The Christian Faith*, 277.
63 GL §68.2; *The Christian Faith*, 277. Which is to say, those in such a condition are what Aristotle would call "brutes." See Aristotle, *Nicomachean Ethics*, VII.1.
64 See Aristotle, *Nicomachean Ethics*, VII.3.
65 For more examples, see Aquinas, *De Malo*, Q. 3, a. 9, r. o. 7.
66 GL §66.2; *The Christian Faith*, 272.
67 GL §66.2; *The Christian Faith*, 272, translation revised.
68 GL §68.1; *The Christian Faith*, 276.
69 GL §69.2; *The Christian Faith*, 280, translation revised.
70 See Pedersen, *The Eternal Covenant*, 70–87.
71 See Pedersen, *The Eternal Covenant*, 156–62.
72 See Aquinas, *Summa Theologica*, Ia, Q. 79, a. 12.
73 Aristotle, *Metaphysics*, V.2; Aristotle, *Nicomachean Ethics*, I.1, III.3.
74 Aristotle, *Nicomachean Ethics*, I.1, 7.
75 GL §5.4; *The Christian Faith*, 23.
76 GL §5.4; *The Christian Faith*, 23, translation revised.
77 See Aristotle, *Nicomachean Ethics*, II.3.
78 GL §§5, 5.1, 5.4; *The Christian Faith*, 18–19, 22–24.
79 GL §5.1; *The Christian Faith*, 19.

80 *GL* §5.3; *The Christian Faith*, 20–21.
81 *GL* §5.3; *The Christian Faith*, 21.
82 Augustine, *City of God*, XI.17; XII.3.
83 This one sense is, of course, *only* in respect to its origins, and does not refer to normal human nature, of which it is a privation.
84 *GL* §73; *The Christian Faith*, 304, translation revised.
85 *GL* §69, postscript; *The Christian Faith*, 281, translation revised.
86 *GL* §73.2; *The Christian Faith*, 306, translation revised.
87 *GL* §73.1; *The Christian Faith*, 305, translation revised.
88 *GL* §73.1; *The Christian Faith*, 305.
89 *GL* §71.1; *The Christian Faith*, 286.
90 *GL* §71.1; *The Christian Faith*, 286, translation revised.
91 See *GL* §54; *The Christian Faith*, 211–18; see also Pedersen, *The Eternal Covenant*, 98–126.
92 *GL* §71.1; *The Christian Faith*, 286.
93 *GL* §71.1; *The Christian Faith*, 287.
94 *GL* §71.1; *The Christian Faith*, 286.
95 *GL* §49.1; *The Christian Faith*, 191–92.
96 *GL* §71.1; *The Christian Faith*, 287, translation revised.
97 *GL* §71.1; *The Christian Faith*, 287.
98 *GL* §71.1; *The Christian Faith*, 287, emphasis added.
99 *GL* §71.1; *The Christian Faith*, 287, translation revised.
100 See *GL* §54.2; *The Christian Faith*, 213–15.
101 *GL* §71.1; *The Christian Faith*, 286, translation revised.
102 See Zwingli, "On Original Sin," 4–5.
103 See Aristotle, *Metaphysics*, V.12, 19; Zwingli, "On Original Sin," 9–10.
104 *GL* §71.1; *The Christian Faith*, 287, translation revised.
105 For the origin and development of federal theology, and sin in particular, see Weir, *The Origins of the Federal Theology in 16th Century Reformation Thought*.
106 *GL* §71.2; *The Christian Faith*, 288.
107 *GL* §71.2; *The Christian Faith*, 288, translation revised.
108 *GL* §71.2; *The Christian Faith*, 288, translation revised.
109 *GL* §71.2; *The Christian Faith*, 288.
110 *GL* §71.2; *The Christian Faith*, 287–88, translation revised.
111 *GL* §71.2; *The Christian Faith*, 287.
112 *GL* §71.2; *The Christian Faith*, 288, translation revised.
113 *GL* §71.2; *The Christian Faith*, 288, translation revised.
114 *GL* §71.2; *The Christian Faith*, 289.
115 *GL* §71.2; *The Christian Faith*, 289.
116 *GL* §79; *The Christian Faith*, 325.

References

Aquinas, Thomas. *On Evil*. Translated by Richard Regan, edited by Brian Davies. New York: Oxford University Press, 2003.
———. *Summa Theologica*. Translated by the Fathers of the English Dominican Province. New York: Benziger Bros., 1947.
Aristotle. *Metaphysics*. Vol. 2. Edited by Jonathan Barnes. Princeton: Princeton University Press, 1984.
———. *Nicomachean Ethics*. Vol. 2. Edited by Jonathan Barnes. Princeton: Princeton University Press, 1984.

Augustine of Hippo, *The City of God*. The Works of Saint Augustine, Part I, Vol. 7, Translated by William Babcock. New City Press, New York, 2013.

Davidson, Donald. "How Is Weakness of the Will Possible?" In *The Essential Davidson*. Oxford: Oxford University Press, 2006.

Pedersen, Daniel J. *The Eternal Covenant: Schleiermacher on God and Natural Science*. Berlin: De Gruyter, 2017.

Schleiermacher, Friedrich D. E. *The Christian Faith*. Edited by H. R. Mackintosh and J. S. Stewart, translated by D. M. Baillie, et al. Berkeley: Apocryphile, [1928] 2011.

———. *Der christliche Glaube nach den Grundsätzen der evangelischen Kirche im Zusammenhange dargestellt*. Second edition. Edited by Rolf Schäfer. Berlin: Walter de Gruyter, [1830/31] 2008.

Stroud, Sarah, and Christine Tappolet, eds. *Weakness of Will and Practical Irrationality*. New York: Oxford University Press, 2003.

Weir, David A. *The Origins of the Federal Theology in 16th Century Reformation Thought*. New York: Oxford University Press, 1990.

West, Cornel. "Schleiermacher's Hermeneutics and the Myth of the Given." *Union Seminary Quarterly Review* 34, no. 2 (1979): 71–84.

Zwingli, Ulrich. "On Original Sin." In *On Providence and Other Essays*, edited by William John Hinke. Durham, NC: The Labyrinth Press, [1922] 1983.

7 Schleiermacher on sin and evil

O my beautiful Philebus, the goddess, methinks, seeing the universal wantonness and wickedness of all things, and that there was in them no limit to pleasures and self-indulgence, devised the limit of law and order, whereby, as you say, Philebus, she torments, or as I maintain, delivers the soul.

– Plato, *Philebus*

Schleiermacher has secured an account of sin linking individual and social development to the evolutionary history of life. Explained using a detailed moral psychology, his account shows not only how but also why our natural and supernatural ends inevitably compete to determine our thoughts and deeds. This is an achievement. It preserves the best insights of the Augustinian tradition while recasting the basic account of sin's origins in a causally complete account coherent in principle with the history and science of human origins. But it does so at the expense of a theory of deficient causes. The most important consequence of the rejection of deficient causes is that it makes God the author of sin and the cause of evil. Indeed, Schleiermacher does not merely imply this, but explicitly claims it as a consequence of his account. If so, Schleiermacher's doctrine of sin and nature faces a series of daunting objections.

Throughout the history of theology, the accusation that "God is the author of sin" has been hurled in many debates from all sides of the theological spectrum. Schleiermacher's explicit adoption of what is usually an opponent's worst accusation demands our attention. The aim of this chapter is, therefore, to clarify *what exactly* Schleiermacher means by this idiom and how he shoulders its explicit avowal. As we shall see, Schleiermacher's account not only *agrees* with many features of traditional accounts but also does so with fewer added burdens and fewer moving parts. In fact, I argue that Schleiermacher's account comes with no greater burdens on the whole than related traditional claims about evil, divine causality, and divine intention, while it comes with its own advantages: namely, an account linking evolution to redemption which is, in principle, causally complete.

I also return to questions of human determination and argue that God as the author of evil offers yet another reason to think that Schleiermacher does not intend to secure an account of freedom which exempts human beings' states or acts from the determined natural order. The single greatest theological incentive to secure such freedom would be to guard God against responsibility for sin and evil. But Schleiermacher claims that God is the cause not only of evil but specifically of *moral, or social, evil* (see ahead) and the author of sin. Therefore, he has declined a major motivating reason for theologians to secure indeterminate freedom.

Schleiermacher thinks that evil – all evil – depends, like all things, on God, which is to say that Schleiermacher believes that God is the *sufficient cause* of evil. This is a remarkable claim. It will require explanation of what Schleiermacher means and why he thinks this is the case. It will also require an explanation of how this claim coheres with the goodness and justice of God. Finally, it will require explanation of whether, and if so how, the dependence of evil on God coheres with the claims I have made about Schleiermacher's subscription to the normativity of natures and the priority of the good. Whatever advantage Schleiermacher's account possesses in its power to situate sin in evolutionary history and human development depends on its ability to reply to these important matters.

The structure of this chapter is as follows. First, we will not only see *that* God is the cause of sin and evil but also examine *how* God is so in some detail. Second, we will explore whether, or in what sense, God *intends* sin and evil. Next, we will look at Schleiermacher's account of how God's justice relates to evil. And finally, we will see what Schleiermacher's accounts of God's holiness and our power of conscience imply for questions of value in Schleiermacher's overall account.

Evil, sin, and God's causality

Evil has a specific meaning for Schleiermacher. He defines it as "conditions which lead to a persistent and regularly renewed consciousness of hindrances to life."[1] Because moral evil and social evil, like natural evil, are such conditions, they are also included, in the same way, under the genus "evil."[2] Indeed, Schleiermacher thinks, from the standpoint of evil's dependence on God, there is no difference between the two.[3] They are only to be relatively distinguished.[4] Therefore, when Schleiermacher claims that "evil" should be "placed in absolute dependence on God"[5] he means *all* evil, without exception, including moral evil.[6]

Neither should a difference be drawn, Schleiermacher thinks, in the *way* good and evil alike depend on God. Rather, evil should be considered "just as much universally dependent on God as that which is opposed to it, namely, the good."[7] This point is more controversial. It risks implying that evil as such can be an object of divine action, which contradicts the metaphysical priority of the good: if evil is an object, it *is* a *thing*, not merely a privation. Unless Schleiermacher can explain this equality of dependence in such a way that he is not committed to evil's real subsistence, he cannot have recourse both to the priority of the good and to the notion that not only are good and evil dependent on God but also they are *equally* so.

Schleiermacher offers such an explanation – or, more specifically, two mutually supporting explanations. The first of these is a description of the general conditions of finite life and its interrelatedness. The second is an elaboration on the metaphysical conditions of evil in an effort to clarify in what sense (as opposed to the *way* – the manner or degree) evil is dependent on God. Both together serve not only to defend but also to specify Schleiermacher's account of evil and God's causality.

The first explanation of the remarkable claim that evil is *equally* an object of divine preservation is an account of finite life as such. Such life is "fluctuating and transitory [*wechselnden und vergänglichen*]."[8] It develops and degrades, comes nearer to a perfection of life sometimes, nearer to the loss of life at others.[9] It is a basic condition of human life to experience the source of both life-furthering and death-furthering causes in one and the same natural world and society.[10] "And thus," Schleiermacher explains, "both modes of life [*Lebensformen*], furtherance and hindrance [*Förderung und Hemmung*] of life, are each conditioned by the other."[11] This seems to settle the point for Schleiermacher. Presumably he thinks "are each conditioned by the other" is a suitable place to end the argument because his audience would be unlikely to contest the claim. I also suspect, however, that he has further assumed the very strong metaphysical claims he advances elsewhere in *The Christian Faith* – namely, that the world could be no other way in whole or in part by absolute necessity and that there are no other possible worlds.[12] With that premise, his argument becomes more convincing because it doesn't rely on us weighing the relative good or ill that attends parts of the world *in relation to possible alternatives* – for there are no other genuine possibilities. On the supposition of the absolute necessity of all things, such a task is utterly fruitless.

Neither does Schleiermacher think it is possible to think of a finite life free from the bad in the world, but benefiting from the good. Here he appeals not so much to the absolute necessity of the world but to the idea that there is a *world*. The world, or nature system, is the mutually conditioned whole of all finite being. There is only one world (which is to say, creation is a *universe* in the strict sense), and all created things are, *by definition*, members of it.[13] We delude ourselves, according to Schleiermacher, either when we think that we are exempted from the "mutual limitations of the finite"[14] or when we think we can abstract the sources of life's repressions (i.e., evil) away from the conditions of its progress.

The former delusion, that we could isolate ourselves from part or all of the world, is impossible on the description of the world that Schleiermacher is committed to. We are "only relatively self-existent."[15] He explains, therefore,

> [T]here is no absolute isolation [*schlechthinige Vereinzelung*] in the finite: each is only self-existent in so far as it conditions another, and is in turn only conditioned in so far as it is self-existent. But another thing is only conditioned by me if it can be promoted [*gefördert werden*]

through me; but then this equality implies that I can be a hindrance. The whole relation can be presented to consciousness in so far as both terms (in both forms, that of self-existence and that of conditioned-ness) are presented; therefore, hindrances are just as ordained by God as furtherances.[16]

That is, finite life is relatively self-existent. But it can be this only if it can act. If it can act, it can affect other things. The best finite life can act in such a way that it betters other things. But this power to act also implies the power to hinder. And so the world cannot be free from the evils of life without being deprived of its perfections since all finite things depend on this exhaustive network of action and passion to *be* and to be as they are.

The mention of the conditions of life's progress and regress leads to the latter delusion: that the hindrances to life "could be isolated and eliminated – in short, that the world could exist apart from evil."[17] Schleiermacher denies this possibility because "if one wanted to remove the sources of hindrances to life, the sources by which furtherances to life are conditioned would also be missing."[18] With this claim, Schleiermacher seems to skirt very close to the doctrine that evil as such contributes to progress. But that is neither what he says nor what he means. No, evil is not necessarily required in order to further good. Rather, *the conditions* of evil are required because they are the same *conditions* that are needed to further good. Evil, in itself, is a hindrance to life and nothing else – this much Schleiermacher makes very clear. But those things which are necessary as the cause of our good are also sometimes, under some circumstances, the cause of ills. Consider, for instance, the case of sunlight. Without sunlight, there would be little life on earth (geothermal-based life being an exception). But if there is sunlight, there are also the attendant ills of sunlight: heat exhaustion, sunburn, and dehydration. In order to have a planet without *any* sunburns, the sun must be darkened or extinguished. The same kind of *indirect* necessity applies to *all* evil, Schleiermacher thinks, with varying degrees of proximity to the good it also implies. Perhaps sometimes they follow so closely that, as per the Stoics (and Augustine), evil can sometimes even bring about a good, but the standard case Schleiermacher has in mind is a remote, indirect, tragic necessity.

Importantly, this applies not only to natural evil but also to moral evil. "[A]nd this is not only by chance because sin produces charitable works sometimes in individuals and sometimes as a great historical lever," says Schleiermacher, "but in general; for sin only comes to be done by virtue of that capacity of humans to express their inner being, which is the cause of all good."[19] The subsuming of moral evil into this scheme brings Schleiermacher closer to the view that even moral evil *brings about* good. In particular, the idea that this connection is not merely accidental risks implying that evil yields good essentially. That is, Schleiermacher might be taken as claiming that good follows upon ill with such necessity that evil is *required* to bring about good. But despite closing the distance with that view, Schleiermacher does *not* commit himself to the idea that evil brings about, or causes, good; or even that evil follows from good essentially. No, despite superficial appearances, Schleiermacher's claim here regards only the necessary conditions of moral evil. Humans' capacity to express our inward life outwardly is our capacity for properly human action. In order to have moral evil, we must have moral agents. To "remove the sources of hindrances to life" in the case of moral evil would require the elimination of agency altogether – the ability of anything *to be done voluntarily*. And to draw that inference does not commit Schleiermacher to the idea that *all* agency *essentially* yields sin, or that such sin necessarily contributes to the good, or that moral evil is required as means to the good as end. Even if committed to a controversial view of moral evil, Schleiermacher is not committed to a straightforwardly Stoic view, but a mixed view akin to Augustine's in this respect. More, however, will be said about evil vis-à-vis God's intentional action ahead.

The foregoing series of claims is, collectively, Schleiermacher's first explanation of how his view of God as the cause of evil coheres with the priority of the good. His second explanation directly connects to the first, but emphasizes the metaphysical conditions of finite evil.

Schleiermacher begins by refusing to distinguish between God's merely *material* cooperation with evil versus God's *formal* cooperation with everything else. His reason for doing so is that merely material cooperation is not cooperation at all but *bare* preservation – which he does not admit, and thinks no Christian should admit, since it divides the being of things from their activity.[20] Further, Schleiermacher argues that "there is no activity [*Thätigkeit*] without form [*Form*], so that there can be no cooperation [*Mitwirkung*] with an activity which is not also cooperation with its form."[21] And since Schleiermacher thinks that *being* and *activity* imply one another,[22] that means that *being*, *activity*, and *form* are all mutually implicative. If so, this has very interesting consequences, for where there is merely material preservation, and not also formal cooperation, there is not only no *activity* with which God cooperates (or *could* cooperate) but also no *thing* which God could preserve. Therefore, Schleiermacher recommends the abandonment of this and related distinctions.[23]

Schleiermacher instead proposes that we claim that

> everything actual [*wirkliche*] without exception is the result of divine cooperation, and this can suffer no diminution; but all evil, including the bad as such, has its ground in mere defect [*bloßen Mangel*]; and divine cooperation cannot be directed at such a partial nonbeing [*partielles Nichtsein*].[24]

Evil is a matter of defect. Defect is not a *thing* at all.[25] Because it isn't a thing, it cannot be an object of divine cooperation – either formally or materially.

This explanation is more than merely superficially traditional, but is a definite effort, on Schleiermacher's part, to join his view with accounts like Augustine's.

Yet, as we discover, Schleiermacher's view is still not *entirely* traditional either, for Schleiermacher cautions elsewhere that if we take the nonbeing of defect to imply that such defect is not itself ordained by God, then we face a problem with finite things in general, and hence with creation as such. His reasoning is that "every finite nature is a combination [*Ineinander*] of being and nonbeing."[26] And although "nonbeing can likewise not be the divine purpose,"[27] there is, nevertheless, "in regard to every finite nature a creative divine will."[28] And so, if we disclaim any kind of involvement of God with nonbeing in general, we must also deny that things which necessarily involve nonbeing – that is, creatures – can be the object of the divine will. Plainly this is unacceptable; and, so, Schleiermacher recommends that we instead think of the divine will as creating things *with definite limitations* – that is, as creating finite natures wherein defect and natural limitation imply one another. That means that God causes evil, Schleiermacher thinks, in *formally* the same way as God causes any creature to exist: not by causing the creature to fail, or with defect as such an object of the divine will, but by willing to create a finite nature as a member of the world.

Evil is not intrinsic to a particular finite nature, or finitude considered in itself, but arises only once a finite thing finds itself in the world of mutually determining finite causes. For while Schleiermacher thinks that evil is, in itself, mere defect, he consistently maintains that its causes are not merely deficient. Rather, the natures of finite things are the limits of those things' powers. Finite things sometimes bear upon one another in such a way that one is "attacked in a way which exceeds its resistance."[29] The partial nonbeing of created things is implied by their finitude. That finitude is limitation. Limitation makes a thing *vulnerable* to harmful external influence because finitude implies a limitation of power. But it is some *other* power or thing which actively causes the evil in question. And as the *being* (and power and activity) of that other thing *is* an object of divine cooperation, God brings about evil, a deficiency, through an efficient, not a deficient, cause.[30]

As a concrete case, consider a person's violent encounter with a bear. Say this person is innocently enjoying the woods. A bear is also present without fault and without particular defect, except perhaps that it is hungry. The bear attacks the person. The person is maimed or eaten, suffering a significant and persistent hindrance to life – that is, the person suffers what could be considered an evil (see ahead for qualification). The bear causes it, though not by a *fault* of being a bear, but rather through a perfection of its kind. The evil was brought about solely through the *power* of the bear relative to the *power* of the person to resist – that is, through the confrontation of two particular animals, two determinate powers, both of whose forms and activities are the objects of not only divine preservation *but also cooperation*. When a person with natural limitations is placed in the mutually determining nexus of finite causes that is the world, such evil *shall* occur, not because evil as such is a matter of divine intent, let alone *this* or *that* evil, but because *bears* are, with all having bears in the world entails.

Moral evil and God's causality

All evil, Schleiermacher thinks, works like this; and the description of not only natural evil in these terms but also moral evil in the same terms is where he parts ways with Augustine.[31] Schleiermacher's strategy for explaining our hypothetical bear encounter is relatively uncontroversial. Instances like this are exactly what Augustine has in mind with his aesthetic account of natural evil. Such evils are bad only relative to specific ends and are only a double effect of other worthwhile goods that are good not only intrinsically but also for how they inform the world as a whole.[32] Schleiermacher's account differs in that he applies this same general explanation to natural *and* moral evil, and so to sin itself.

Schleiermacher can apply claims about natural evil to moral evil with ease because, he claims, natural and moral evil are only relatively distinct. "The difference," Schleiermacher explains, "consists principally in this, that the one is much more caused by the entirety of the forces of nature, and the other by the general conditions of human activity."[33] It is not that there is no difference, but the difference is a matter of emphasis and the

> two kinds of evil not only give rise to each other [. . .], but they also overlap in concept [*Begriff*], for the being of a person consists only in the totality of their activity [*Gesamtheit seiner Thätigkeit*] and *vice versa*.[34]

This is a remarkable claim worth examining more closely. It is not altogether unusual to think that moral and natural evils give rise to one another. Starvation brought about by drought or plague may prompt murder for scant resources. Or, conversely, greed might spur the exploitation of natural resources which, in turn, causes drought and disease. Both kinds of cases are well known and often lead directly into the other. But Schleiermacher's claim that the two not only give rise to one another but also *overlap in concept* is much more unusual. And his justification for this claim is as informative as the claim itself.

The two kinds of evil are not *really* different for Schleiermacher but only relatively distinguishable, because the being (or nature) of a thing of a kind (like a human person) is not different in content from the totality of that thing's activities. While we might consider a thing according to its being or nature – what it is – or according to its powers and activities – what it does – we are still considering only one and the same thing whose being and activities are, at bottom, identical. There isn't a *real* difference between being and activity, only a conceptual distinction. The distinction between natural evil and moral evil is, in turn, a distinction between the total forces of nature on the one hand and human activity on the other. But human activity *is* human being made manifest. And human being is a natural occurrence, which is to say, *part of* the total forces of nature. Therefore, a distinction between the forces of nature and human activity is only a matter of emphasis. Instead, the one always implies the other: human activity *is* a force of nature. And since the distinction between natural evil and moral evil depends on this merely relative distinction between nature and action, natural and moral *evil* are, themselves, only relatively distinct.

If so, then moral evil, as we saw in previous chapters, has causes sufficient to determine it as it is. And if so, the causes sufficient to determine humans to sin are real, not privative, just as the powers of the bear are not privative, though they sometimes bring about a privation in human life. But what powers could Schleiermacher have in mind?

Here is where his account of the meaning and origins of sin from the previous two chapters becomes crucial, for there we saw that the reason why the sensuous self-consciousness was able to arrest the determining power of the God-consciousness was that it had its own *determining power*. And, moreover, the reason the sensuous self-consciousness was so able to determine was because it tracked genuine, even indispensable, goods, though it ranked them improperly. Last, the reason for this improper ranking in the first place was developmental: both evolutionarily and in an individual human life, the well-being of animals' bodies is a necessary condition of them developing the power of spirit – that is, the consciousness of God. And it was this early development and practice which led to the *facility* of the flesh, and thus to its over-ease in determining thought and action. But notice: every step in this process is explained by pointing to some good or advantage at a particular point which later becomes an ill in light of a more distant end. It is *good* that the sensuous self-consciousness develops early and well. It is *good* that it tracks genuine, if penultimate, goods. It is *good* that it determines thought and action. Because both the sensuous self-consciousness and its objects are truly good, there are real, non-privative causes to this story at every turn in just the same sense as natural evil because all these causes – both the agent themselves and also their objects as proximate final causes – are, like bears, *finite forms*. Like any natural evil they have a *power*, a power which is a good, which gives rise to privation only when, like natural evils, they *overpower* to the loss of some other good.

The connection between sin and evil

All evil, Schleiermacher claims, is an effect of sin, which is to say that, without sin, there would be no evil of any kind. This is a remarkable claim – and *prima facie* dubious. Traditional accounts of the origins of sin were able to make claims like this plausible by explaining that the origins of sin in the first humans had altered human nature *and* the cosmos insofar as it bore on or related to human nature. But Schleiermacher has rejected all accounts that depend on a fall, let alone a change in human nature or the world. That leaves Schleiermacher with the difficult task of explaining how all evil nevertheless depends on human sin without appeal to traditional resources.

Schleiermacher's explanation depends heavily on his account of sin that we examined in prior chapters. Sin is an arresting of the determining power of the God-consciousness, which, recall, means an inability to rank our ends properly and think and act by them in their proper order. Communion with God through consciousness is our supreme good. Yet sin inverts the hierarchy of flesh and spirit such that we are determined to think and act by our sensuous self-consciousness *as our highest good*. When this occurs – and only when this occurs – evil results. Schleiermacher's account at this point depends on several moving parts: his definition of evil; his account of evil and the good; and his account of human perfection relative to our distinct ends. We look at each now in turn.

Evil consists of *all* "persistent causes of hindrance to a person's life."[35] This includes not only wrongdoing[36] but also those features of created existence which are "a hindrance of our bodily and temporal existence,"[37] things like "disease and debility [*Krankheit und Schwäche*]," and "natural death [*natürlicher Tod*]."[38] These examples of natural ills are, however, contained in the original perfection of the world. The suffering of them shall never cease in this life because they are included in the necessity of the world. Our regarding them *as evils*, however, depends solely on sin.[39]

Evil arises when, and only when, our temporal good is improperly ranked as our highest good – that is, when what "prevails is not the God-consciousness, but the flesh."[40] In this case, the well-being of the flesh, our "bodily and temporal existence,"[41] is exchanged with the consciousness of God as our highest good. What we come to regard as our *life* follows our ranking of those goods. And, once so ranked, we (falsely) *identify* that life which ills obstruct – our "bodily and temporal existence," the life of the flesh – with our highest end. And that means that things like disease, debility, and death all come to persistently hinder the attainment of what is our (improperly ranked) highest good – what has become our *life* in the relevant sense. Therefore, on the supposition that our natural and supernatural ends are disordered, natural ills *become* evil.[42]

This disordering of ends that causes the merely bad to become *evil* is exactly what Schleiermacher thinks sin *is*. When the determining power of the God-consciousness is arrested by the sensuous self-consciousness, the flesh prevails. Because natural and supernatural ends can be ranked only two ways (one above the other), the state of sin Schleiermacher has described is the only condition that *could* amount to this disorder and so the only state in which evil *could* arise. If evil regards the persistent hindrance to our highest good – to our life considered as "spiritual life"[43] – then all evil necessarily depends on sin because it depends on our misranking of the flesh and the spirit in order for mere obstructions to our temporal life to *become* hindrances to our highest good.[44]

But why should evil regard hindrances to only our *highest* good in the first place? Aren't all genuine goods – of which the temporal life of humans surely is one – susceptible to the kind of hindrance that would amount not merely to loss but to *evil*, no matter how conscious of God we were? What, in short, are Schleiermacher's reasons for thinking some things we reckon evil would cease to be so if it were not for sin? His reasoning, it turns out, revolves fundamentally around the relation between humans' distinctive ends and the necessary conditions of created life, conditions which are also necessary to bring about our ultimate ends. In other words, the issue is the relation between nature and grace.

Schleiermacher has good reason to think that *any* created life will determine and be determined by other created things. We will necessarily, he thinks, live finite lives characterized by growth and gain, loss and decay. Creatures will necessarily die. Humans will necessarily err to our detriment. His views about human life follow what we might take to be facts about the natural world: that all other animals live like this, and limitations of all sorts are inbuilt to the "life of sense [*sinnliches Leben*]."[45]

Life is not only like this but also *supposed* to be like this. Not only has Schleiermacher already denied what theologians would traditionally appeal to in such cases – that the conditions of human life differ from what they were in paradise – but also he has denied all possible grounds for *any* such transformation in principle (see Chapters 2, 3, and 4). Schleiermacher's view that error, debility, disease, and death are features of the natural world follows necessarily when theories – *all* theories, not only Augustine's in particular – of the corruption of human nature in the fall are denied. And, as we have seen, Schleiermacher denies these at length.

Supposing Schleiermacher's denial that the world or human nature were or even could have been transformed for the worst, consider what choices remain. On the one hand is the theory Schleiermacher advances: that at least some clear cases of loss and sorrow are not intrinsically *evil* but only evil on the condition of sin, because they are unavoidable features of a teleologically perfect creation and so do not prevent the attainment of humans' highest ends (on the condition that our ends are rightly ordered). On the other hand is the contrary theory: that features of the world *as created* not only cause grievous loss, depriving us of all sorts of natural goods and thwarting our natural ends, but also threaten to prevent the attainment of the highest ends for which we were made by the very same created conditions. In other words, on the assumption that the voluntary act of the first human beings did *not* bring about a change in human nature or the world as a whole, we face a choice between the conditions of creation *as God made it* sometimes preventing the attainment of some natural human ends alone, and those same conditions potentially hindering not only humans' natural ends *but humans' highest ends also*.

Contrary to the second option, God, Schleiermacher thinks, created the world (minimally) for the attainment of humans' highest ends: our blessedness in communion with God. If at least some features of the natural world are not merely bad but intrinsically *evil*, the world that God made *for* our redemption might *prevent* our redemption. Because Schleiermacher is committed to the notion that the divine end for creation is *one and one only*, and that end is redemption, the latter option implies that the world that God made, as God made it, is insufficient to bring about the ends for which it was made. Therefore, it must be rejected.[46] The only alternative is the admission – at least as burdensome as the hints of Stoicism in Schleiermacher's account – that the grief and loss that at least some of us will encounter in this life will crush us body *and soul* and could be sufficient to permanently thwart the attainment of our highest ends and to forever deprive us of blessedness.[47]

That then leaves the former option: that, apart from sin, the bad does not prevent the attainment of our beatitude. And if the ends of human life which the world sometimes prevents us from attaining are to be distinguished non-arbitrarily from those which it does not, they must be so distinguished *in kind*, according to whether the world *can* and *does* sometimes prevent their attainment. But, according to Schleiermacher's account, the divine wisdom assures the attainment of any divinely appointed end.[48] Indeed, the actual achieving of divine ends is the very reason for the world in the first place. So there must be at least one end *for which* the world is made and, therefore, which no feature of the world can ultimately hinder. But plainly our natural ends are not of this kind. They are manifestly obstructed, and routinely so. Therefore, *if* the world was made for an end or ends that the world as created cannot obstruct (without contradiction), such an end or ends must be what the tradition calls "supernatural" and what Schleiermacher calls "spiritual."[49]

Finally, we come full circle, for if there are some goods, the loss of which obstructs our attainment of natural ends, but the loss of which does *not*, at the same time, obstruct our spiritual ends, then we have the grounds for distinguishing between categories of evils according to whether they are of this kind or not. If they are of this kind, Schleiermacher calls them hindrances to the life of sense. If they are not of this kind, then they *always* (minimally) involve the obstruction of our highest, spiritual ends, and Schleiermacher calls them hindrances to the life of spirit. In both cases, however, for a thing to be *evil* (and not merely an ill) *depends on* its obstruction of our *de facto* highest good. And for the ills of the life of sense to be reckoned as such can occur only by the disordered ranking of the God-consciousness and the sensuous self-consciousness as our highest ends – that is, *by sin*, in which our natural ends are improperly ranked as our highest ends. Therefore, all evil depends on sin; and any loss, however genuine, which is not a hindrance to our highest end is not ultimately evil to the rightly ordered soul.

While surely not the final word on the matter, this explanation reveals that Schleiermacher's superficially implausible claim that all evil depends on sin, with its attendant distinction between evil and the merely bad, is actually a natural conclusion from his premises: (1) that the world is perfectly ordered by God to bring about its ends; (2) that the world, including human nature, was not fundamentally altered by sin in a fall or fall-like event; and (3) that we do, in fact, sometimes suffer losses and hindrances to our natural and spiritual lives. Indeed, the options for explaining the coherence of these claims are surprisingly limited. And those paths Schleiermacher does not take – such as suggesting that terrestrial misfortune might prevent the attainment of our supernatural ends, or even that God ordained *through* such misfortune to bring about our spiritual misery – are far less palatable than the course he pursues. And since Schleiermacher provides powerful arguments for his premises, his conclusion that all evil depends on sin is much more plausible than is typically credited, and is arguably superior.

Schleiermacher's position, in sum, is this. That all evil depends on sin, and that

> without sin there would be nothing in the world that could be rightly considered an evil, but that whatever is directly bound up with the transitoriness of a human life would be apprehended as at most an unavoidable imperfection [*unvermeidliche Unvollkommenheit*].[50]

Sin equally (though indirectly) includes both moral/social evil *and* natural evil because not only are the two only relatively distinct[51] but also natural and social evils bear upon and reinforce one another.[52] God, Schleiermacher claims, is the author of sin.[53] But all evil depends on sin. Therefore, evil, like sin, wholly depends on God[54] – though neither sin nor evil is an object of divine intent.

Evil and intentional divine action

Even if Schleiermacher's account of the dependence of sin on God is coherent, it might also be thought perverse. God, it might appear on this account, uses – or perhaps, abuses – humans (and more) for the divine ends through their subjection to grievous loss and terrible wickedness. Is such a description of God *recognizably good*? If not initially so, how might Schleiermacher explain the worthiness of not only awe before the power of God but also reverence before the divine goodness in light of such an account of evil? This section will analyze sin and evil within a holistic description of divine action in an effort to make Schleiermacher's view as plausible as possible – especially for those who share his Augustinian commitments and sensibilities, including, but not limited to, Augustine himself, Thomas Aquinas, and Schleiermacher's own Reformed tradition.

The mention of tradition is important in this connection because objections to Schleiermacher's account of sin as dependent on God might take the closely related form of objections to its novelty. That is, it might be a bad idea – full stop; or it might be a plausible, but proscribed, explanation of sin in relation to God's causality *given the stipulations of tradition.* These two charges dovetail. Plainly, Schleiermacher's account is not straightforwardly traditional (in the broad sense), and the greater theological tradition of thinking about sin was developed, in part, to explain the relation of sin to God that, above all, preserved the divine goodness. The novelty and possible perversity of Schleiermacher's account go together. But there is also another sense in which they go together, for any attempt to answer the objection on the grounds of perversity is likely to succeed only on the condition of novelty – of being at least somewhat *un*traditional – otherwise the tradition will be convicted of the same perversity charged. Therefore, both accusations must be addressed together and at once.

Schleiermacher's overall strategy is to give a double-effect account of sin: an account where sin is foreseen and caused, but where it is not, in itself, an object of divine intent. Insofar as he does, his account is, once again, traditional. This is exactly the general strategy employed by thinkers like Augustine and Aquinas.[55] If Schleiermacher can sustain this strategy, he has a strong claim to have defeated the charge of perversity. And yet, as we have seen, he thinks that sin (and with it evil) depends on God, that God is even the *author* of sin – a term which, if anything, seems to imply intent. Thus, if Schleiermacher means to give an account where sin is a double effect of the divine intent, he will face special burdens that the deficient cause account of sin does not. In particular, Schleiermacher will be obliged to explain how his account does not devolve into a consequentialist account given his claims about sin as a possible object of the divine will – that is, given that his account makes it seem like God both *uses* sin *and intends to use it* for some greater gain.

An important first step is to reiterate a point made earlier: that *in itself* sin is mere nonbeing. And while the nonbeing of sin might seem to disqualify sin from the divine willing, "the same might be said of every finite nature,"[56] and finite beings *are* objects of the divine will. Therefore, Schleiermacher's claim depends on a distinction. The nonbeing of sin, like the nonbeing of finitude, is never in itself intentionally willed by God because nonbeing is never an object of divine intent generally.[57] But *both* cases of nonbeing are willed insofar as they are conceptual entailments of creation ordered to its true purpose, redemption. As Schleiermacher explains,

> The sinful nature is a combination of the being and the nonbeing of the God-consciousness, but in the same way every finite nature is a combination of being and nonbeing; and nonbeing can, no more than sin, be the divine purpose. Yet in regard to every finite nature there is a creative divine will – not however as something existing in and for itself, but as contained in the divine will producing the entirety of differentiated being. In the same way, the divine will can be thought of producing the sinful nature as contained in the production of the entirety of the finite God-consciousness, which also contains redemption in its conclusion.[58]

As before, part of Schleiermacher's argument here is to emphasize that there is no *special* burden to explaining how God can be the cause of sin, because the nonbeing of sin is to the God-consciousness what nonbeing in general is to any finite nature. In order to deny that God is the cause of sin, we would be forced to deny that God is the cause of finite things, which implies the Manichean heresy.[59]

However, Schleiermacher makes another very interesting claim in relation to the divine intent. And that is not only that "in regard to every finite nature there is a creative divine will" but also that *this will*, the will to create any finite thing, is "contained in the production of the entirety of the finite God-consciousness."[60] What is remarkable here is the subtlety of Schleiermacher's explanation. He could have couched the divine will to create the God-consciousness as simply falling under the divine will to create anything *ad extra*. But instead, the divine will to create "every finite nature" is *contained in* the divine will to create the finite God-consciousness "which also contains redemption."[61] In other words, the order of divine intent is strictly supralapsarian: God properly intends the ultimate end of redemption, and then wills creation as means to that end as its necessary and, in Schleiermacher's view, sufficient condition. It is not only that, supposing God wills to create something finite, then God must create a thing which is a mix of being and nonbeing. No, Schleiermacher's view is that, supposing God wills to share the unclouded blessedness of unbroken communion with God, then God must make *certain sorts* of creatures, which in turn implies making creatures in general, which *only then* implies making finite things combining being and nonbeing. Therefore, sin is, on Schleiermacher's supralapsarian account, *more distant* from the object of divine intent than in accounts in which creation, not redemption, is first in the order of decrees.

Such an account, however, does not yet exonerate Schleiermacher from charges of consequentialism: that God uses sin for the divine ends and such use of sin as means is justified solely insofar as it brings about sufficiently desirable ends, outweighing the harm caused in good wrought. For even if sin is more distant to the true object of divine intent than would at first appear, it might still be the case that God makes use of it *and intends it for its use*. Remarkably, Schleiermacher addresses this charge explicitly and his denial could not be stronger or more revealing:

> It is even more confusing, however, to accept, instead of mere approval, that God indeed ordained sin, but only as an unavoidable means to otherwise important ends, making the evils consequent upon sin a source of greater gain, and, through Christ, completely repaying the damage of sin itself. But quite apart from the fact that the contrast of means and end cannot exist for a pure and all-creating will, we could not well imagine a more erroneous presentation of Christian thought than to say that Christ came only to make good the damage incurred from sin, while God, considering the manifold gains to come thereby, could

not do without sin itself. As against this, our own presentation is that
sin is ordained only with a will to redemption, and that, accordingly,
redemption shows forth as the gain connected with sin, in comparison
with which there can be no question whatever of damage due to sin,
for the merely gradual and imperfect development of the power of the
God-consciousness belongs to the conditions of the stage of existence at
which human kind stands.[62]

Several points in this important passage require exploration in detail. Schleiermacher's first and most obvious objection to this line of reasoning is that:
(1) consequentialist accounts of sin necessarily assume an *antithesis* between
means and ends. As I have discussed elsewhere, this is not a blanket disa-
vowal of explanations in terms of divine practical reasoning, but of the
idea that, for God, means and ends are (or could be) *opposed*.[63] God does
not create already existing things within already existing circumstances, but
creates the very things and their circumstances themselves. Insofar as this
kind of consequentialist reasoning implies the competition of means against
ends (i.e., that ends would have to *counterbalance* means), and vice versa, it
cannot be applied to God. Schleiermacher's second and third objections are
tightly connected to his first. The view to which he is opposed claims that:
(2) Christ came *ex post facto* to make good on the damage done by sin; and
(3) though God brings good out of this, God cannot *eliminate* sin itself, only
compensate for it. Schleiermacher denies all three ideas.

The specific contrast with his own theory is revealing. Schleiermacher's
theory does not involve denying that redemption is worthwhile, that the
end is *worth* the means. Nor does it involve disconnecting sin from redemption such that redemption could have been attained without sin as a consequence. As I have argued previously, the denial of these related claims
would safeguard God against the accusation of consequentialism only at the
expense of an account of God as a practical reasoner.[64] And, indeed, what
Schleiermacher objects to in the contrast between ends and means in divine
action is not the fitting use of means to bring about divine ends but the idea
that the means might *not* bring about the divine ends, or at least might not
do so *well*. In other words, this problem of *contrast* between God's ends and
means arises only when God is described as an *imperfect* practical reasoner
and *that*, according to Schleiermacher, is what consequentialist justifications
for evil applied to God suggest.

Instead, on Schleiermacher's view the incomplete development of the
God-consciousness is a necessary condition. But like all developmental conditions, the consequences attending its imperfection – in the case of sin,
evil – are generally not means to the perfection of a thing, and are so only
insofar as they incentivize perfection through the recognition of imperfection as ills. And that means that sin and evil are developmentally necessary
only in the sense that the weakness of a sapling is accidentally necessary
for it to become an oak. Its weakness is certainly *consequent* upon the

incompleteness of its development, but the attainment of its perfection depends on what it *is* or *has*, not what it *lacks*. And so the straightforward divine *use* of sin as such to bring about some good is not at all what Schleiermacher has in mind, despite the fact that God is its cause, even its author.[65]

This further explains why Schleiermacher anticipates the consequentialist criticism that might be leveled at him, for, taken together, claims (2) and (3) imply a certain view about the balance of goods and harms such that an unrecoverable loss is outweighed by a greater gain. The result of such a story of loss and gain is, then, to imply claim (1): the view that the divine means and ends are opposed. Schleiermacher does not deny that redemption is gain – indeed, he ardently affirms it. But he does deny that sin and redemption are incommensurate, such that the loss incurred by sin is different in kind from the gain won by redemption. Rather, Schleiermacher's view is that the ill of sin is precisely that imperfection which redemption makes whole; and therefore, that the process of redemption is neither making up for sin nor using sin to acquire an unrelated, though superior, good, but the *disappearance* of sin and evil altogether as perfected human nature comes to attain its divinely appointed end of communion with God.

God is the author of evil

There are many potential objections to Schleiermacher's account of the dependence of sin and evil on God. We have seen a number of them entertained earlier. Yet there is a further objection which is not so important for Schleiermacher himself, but for readers wishing to evaluate his view: that whatever the merits of his position, it is so untraditional that it is not a possible option, or at least not a licit one. In this section we compare one account given by John Calvin to Schleiermacher's with an eye to evaluating how different the two accounts really are.[66] The aim, however, is not exhaustive but illustrative. I do not argue that this comparison settles the matter, but only that it unsettles it, such that it should give adherents to traditional accounts, especially in the Reformed tradition (though also Augustinian accounts more broadly), pause before rejecting Schleiermacher's account merely on the basis of its supposed divergent innovation.

Calvin, in contrast with Schleiermacher, denies that God is the author of evil.[67] That might seem to be the end of the comparison. But Calvin also makes a number of claims that raise questions about whether he is truly entitled to this conclusion, for, while arguing that God is not the author of evil, he claims that: (1) the will of God is the cause of all things;[68] (2) no created causes, including free agents, fall outside of the divine will;[69] (3) no appeal to mere permission is possible;[70] and, therefore, (4) "the will of God is the chief and principal cause of all things."[71] Given claims 1–4, it is not at all clear that Calvin can sustain his denial, or at least it is not obvious in what sense he can. In what follows we look at these claims in more detail.

"First," Calvin says, "it must be observed that the will of God is the cause of all things that happen in the world; and yet God is not the author of evil."[72] This claim requires explaining and Calvin has two possible strategies for doing so, one of which he mentions but declines to pursue. That first strategy is to put the Augustinian deficient cause tradition to use: to emphasize that God is the cause of all *things* in contrast to the nothingness of evil, which is not a thing. In this sense, God could be the exhaustive cause of all *things* that happen, while in no way being the cause of evil. Although Calvin accepts this explanation, he pursues it no further and makes no use of it, "for this subtlety does not satisfy many."[73]

In its place, he offers his own theory: "Whatever things are done wrongly and unjustly by man, these very things are the right and just works of God."[74] Calvin offers many brief samples of what he might mean by this, mainly in the form of created causes unintentionally (from the point of view of the evildoer) bringing about divine ends. That might show that God *permits* evil; and it might show that God might make subsequent *use* of sin, but it does not yet show that, or how, God is not the cause or author of sin and evil. What is more, Calvin explicitly denies that "evils come to be not by [God's] will, but merely by His permission," because "Scripture shows Him not only willing but *the author* of them."[75] In this breathtaking reversal, Calvin seems to explicitly deny his own initial claim. God is, he says here, the author of evil. But, on the assumption that Calvin is not flatly contradicting himself, this passage at least eliminates the possibility of explaining the will of God as merely permissive and also qualifies the sense in which God makes use of sin: for God cannot merely make use of sin in the very same sense in which God does not merely permit it. Instead, God must be the cause, *in some sense*, of that of which God makes use.

Calvin recognizes the difficulty he is in. "But the objection is not resolved," he admits, "that if all things are done by the will of God, and men contrive nothing except by His will and ordination, then God is the author of all evils."[76] In hopeful reply he offers his best example:

> To come to a closer analogy: the prince is praised who repels rapine and pillage from his borders in a just and legitimate war. For this purpose he will arm many soldiers whose lust to shed blood, to plunder the goods of the poor and for every kind of violent lawlessness are certainly not praiseworthy. Suppose that two armies engage in battle; suppose you discern in the general, under whose auspices and by whose command the battle is joined, an upright disposition though he be only a mortal man; do you not absolve him, while condemning the soldiers who set their hands to murder for shameful reward? And do you defraud God of the glory of His justice because He works by means of Satan?[77]

The analogy is limited. It is not at all obvious that one would, in fact, absolve a prince or general under whose command troops committed such atrocities.[78] Importantly, we are told nothing of the general's efforts to restrain or mitigate the evils of his own army – whether any such efforts were made, whether they were successful, and if not, why. And so it is not clear that, having used such an army in such a way, we *could* discern "an upright disposition" in such a leader. Last, and most importantly, the analogy with God breaks down in that it addresses only the just *employment* of already existing soldiers under already existing circumstances. But God, uniquely, *creates* all things and all circumstances.

Nevertheless, let us suppose that, given the opportunity, Calvin could improve the analogy, or at least that he means for it to work in only very limited respects. After all, Calvin's main aim is to show that the *active* (not merely permissive) use of evil for divine ends does not imply the transitivity of blame, such that to make use of evil makes one evil.[79] Calvin's main argument for this is to distinguish between the *intent* of the general and the *intent* of the soldiers.[80] Suppose, for instance, that the general faced a dire invasion threatening the wholesale destruction of life and the political community. Suppose also that the soldiers at hand were the only ones available. Suppose, finally, that the general takes all reasonable measures to restrain and mitigate his own soldiers' wrongdoing. Under circumstances of overwhelming obligation and strict constraint, do the sins of the soldiers redound to the general? Calvin thinks we should answer in the negative, and the distinction in blame he thinks we should make is key to understanding his case.

The importance for Calvin's case is this: that the difference between our condemnation of the soldiers who committed wrongs and our (assumed) praise for the general who used such soldiers' wrongdoing to further the common good implies a distinction in their acts, even though all were engaged in one common cause under one common command bringing about one common effect. Because, on the surface, what the soldiers did and what the general did *through* the soldiers was not different (to draw the analogy to God closer), the distinction between the praiseworthy and the blameworthy must lie elsewhere. And that leaves the main distinguishing work to the *intent* of each party: the good general *intended* good, the wicked soldiers *intended* evil. All-importantly on this account, therefore, *the authorship of sin is a matter of intent.* Supposing we can distinguish between what look like the very same actions, including any evil involved, *according to intent*, we can distinguish between one agent who is *not the author* of said evil, despite causing it and making use of it, and other agents who are both agents *and authors* of evil. On a view like this, Calvin's distinction might be defensible; and if his distinction is defensible, then his claim that God is not the author of evil might be too.

If so, Calvin *claims* something markedly different than Schleiermacher. But is the difference in their accounts borne out in content? Recall that Calvin, like Schleiermacher, claims that God is the *cause* of sin and evil and, indeed, that God *wills* sin and evil. Recall also that Calvin, like Schleiermacher, denies that God merely permits sin and evil. Recall that both Calvin (in this work) and Schleiermacher decline to make use of Augustine's deficient causal explanation of the *origins* of evil while both affirm that evil is, in itself, a deficiency or nothingness. Recall, finally, that both Calvin and Schleiermacher affirm that God can make good use of sin and evil (though not necessarily that sin and evil are *for* said use), and that this can be true of the very same sin and evil which God both wills and causes. If so, then the sole difference between Calvin's account and Schleiermacher's is the matter of divine authorship of sin *in the sense of divine intent*.

Here too, however, the contrast fades – but from the other direction, for Schleiermacher offers a nearly identical qualification of divine intent in his distinction between God's *commanding* and *efficient* will.[81] "Now it must of course be added," he says, "that the will of God which commands [*gebietende*] others, though we call it will, and the efficient will [*hervorbringende Wille*] of God are not identical [*nicht identisch*]."[82] Indeed, Schleiermacher's account of sin *depends* on just this distinction because "sin is committed only where there exists a commanding divine will to which some expression of life [*Lebensäußerung*] conflicts."[83] That is, we can sin only given the presence, but impotence, of the God-consciousness, the proper rule of which is God's commanding will, but which is not efficient in the sinner. The commanding will regards divine intent as the difference between command and effect implies. Therefore, Schleiermacher is committed, like Calvin, to denying that God is the author of evil *if by "authorship" we mean only this very narrow notion of intent* – that is, if intent is understood solely as the term of an act apart from its means and conditions.

More specifically, what Schleiermacher and Calvin both ultimately deny is that sin and evil could be God's *antecedent* will – God's naked intent apart from other conditioning intentions. But they both affirm that sin and evil are God's *consequent* will – the concrete effects brought about by the sum of divine intentions and their mutual limitations and requisites. This not only brings Calvin and Schleiermacher yet closer on the matter but also explains both of their positions best, for both want to claim that sin and evil are not proper objects of divine intent while maintaining that God actively wills and causes sin and evil. But the same hypothetical objection will arise in both cases: that "though the commanding will and the efficient will are not the same, still the latter cannot be opposed to the former; for there could be no truth in the prohibition if God brought the transgression to pass."[84] That is, God's consequent will can *qualify* God's antecedent will, but it cannot contradict it. The two wills must cohere. And the conditions of attaining God's ends cannot ultimately prevent their attainment or else God cannot be described as a competent practical reasoner. In reply to this objection, Schleiermacher offers a line that could have come straight from Calvin's quill:

> We must say that the restriction is to be understood only in the sense that an inadequacy [*Unangemessenheit*] to the commanding will of God

can nonetheless be brought about by God's efficient will, thus in this respect sin is grounded in the divine causality.[85]

This is to say that sin *both* is a deficiency *and* has causes sufficient to bring it about.

Although many points of disagreement remain between Calvin and Schleiermacher, especially Schleiermacher's account of authority, the foregoing discussion raises doubts about whether their respective accounts of sin and evil rank among them. And even if they did, it is not obvious that Schleiermacher would be the worse for it as, unlike Calvin, he emphasizes the tragic necessity of sin over God's employment of it (see earlier). Again, however, this does not so much conclude the discussion as reopen it. It requires criticisms launched from the position of tradition, especially Schleiermacher's own Reformed tradition, to be very careful that they do not condemn themselves when they condemn him and to not merely note nominal differences but make sure that any apparent contrasts are born out in content. In doing so, champions of that tradition (and others) will have to explain not only what complex and occasional writers like Calvin mean but also why they are entitled to their conclusions and whether, given their conceptual entitlements, their position does not amount to Schleiermacher's all the same. Until this is done adequately, the objection that Schleiermacher's account is perversely untraditional should be met with skepticism.

Drawing Schleiermacher closer to Calvin might, however, raise other objections, for Calvin's view is famously an account partly intended to explain the justice of the punishment inflicted by God: both the this-worldly punishment for sins and, especially, everlasting damnation. If Schleiermacher's account works like Calvin's, it raises grave concerns about the divine justice. Since *justice* is a notion whose moral species is included in the word (it is always good to be just and always bad to be unjust),[86] the discussion of justice once again returns us to explicit questions of *value*. In order to sustain his description of God as more than bare power, Schleiermacher will have to explain how, despite being the cause of sin and evil, God is just.

Evil and the justice of God

Among Calvin's many motivations is the desire to answer the question, in his words, "How then is God to be exempted from the blame to which Satan with his instruments is liable?"[87] Supposing Calvin's account, where everything happens by the will of God, in which God is the cause of evil, it is a serious matter to answer what he calls "the greatest ambiguity; namely, how God may be free of guilt in doing the very thing that he condemns in Satan and the reprobate and which is condemned by men."[88] What Calvin articulates here is an important feature of traditional theological accounts of divine justice, especially in respect to divine *punishment*. Traditionally, divine justice is maintained by securing *asymmetrical fault*: that we are blameworthy (and so possible candidates for punishment), but God is not blameworthy.

On any account where God is the cause of evil, however, this simple solution is hard to sustain. Calvin is deftly attuned to the difficulty facing accounts like his: if we are blameworthy (and also liable to punishment) and God is *also* at fault (because God is *also* the cause of the fault in question), then God is *also* liable to the same blame. If we are liable to *condemnation* because of God's *will* and *causality*, then, it seems, God is liable to *self-condemnation*, which contradicts the divine goodness and justice. The problem is only made worse with traditional assumptions about hell and its conditions. For, according to the majority tradition, at least some people are handed over to extraordinary and everlasting torment for those states or acts which are perverse and unnatural, for which they are to blame but God is not. If God *wills* and *causes* those states *and their punishment*, it seems God is as perverse as they. Calvin's distinction of divine causality from divine authorship (understood as narrow intentionality) is his primary tool for replying to this puzzle.

Augustine, too, recognized the need to generate asymmetrical fault. His account, however, aims to do this slightly differently than Calvin's: by combining the aphorism that "no one is punished for faults of nature but only for faults of will"[89] with his theory of deficient causes, thus denying that God is, in any sense, the cause of evil. If Calvin's solution does not appeal, Augustine's might. Augustine's rule is elegant and consistent. It in no way hints of the *ad hoc* and the arbitrary. What applies to human justice likewise applies to divine justice: we cannot be blamed for how we were made, but only for what we are or do voluntarily, by our wills. Since God is the creator of our natures, the rule applies to God with a unique strictness. Because God follows this rule, God can be described as *just* in a recognizable sense. But for Augustine, faults of the will are different. Faults of the will are unnatural and their causes are merely deficient. Therefore, God is in no way implicated in such faults, even remotely or unintentionally; and it is perfectly just, according to Augustine, for God not only to blame but also to damn for vices of the will.

When Schleiermacher replaces Augustine's theory of deficient causes with his own causal completeness thesis, he denies the premise that is crucial to the justice of Augustine's account. Faults of the will are not, according to Schleiermacher, uncaused or of unnatural origin. Instead, a complete causal line can be traced from voluntary acts to the arrested God-consciousness, from the arrested God-consciousness to conditions of individual and evolutionary development, and from the cosmic history of this development to God. Likewise, when Schleiermacher refuses Calvin's tenuous distinction between God as willing and causing, *but not authoring*, evil, he denies the premise that is crucial to the justice of Calvin's account. God is, rather, the cause of sin and the author of evil and, if condemning, must be self-condemning. How then does Schleiermacher explain God's justice in light of his account of sin and evil?

Schleiermacher first gives an account of divine justice in general. Broadly, Schleiermacher explains, "The justice of God is that divine causality in virtue of which in the state of universal sinfulness there is ordained a connection between evil and actual sin."[90] That is, God's justice ordains that "all sin is reflected in evil, and that all evil is explained by sin."[91] What Schleiermacher has in mind here by "connection" [*Zusammenhang*] is a *causal* connection. Sin is cause, evil effect. And God's justice consists in guaranteeing (1) that there *is* such a connection; and (2) that it is universal and exceptionless such that there is no sin which is not attended by evil and no evil which is not explained by sin. Perhaps surprisingly, that means that Schleiermacher thinks God's justice "can only be retributive [*vergeltende*]."[92] Moreover, even as retributive (as opposed to distributive), God's justice cannot regard *reward*, which is always unmerited and is due to divine grace alone,[93] but solely regards retributive *punishment* [*Strafe*].[94] Indeed, divine punishment *is* that fundamental causal necessity by which sin *yields* evil; and, therefore, all evil is divinely ordained punishment for sin.

Both the sin in question and the evil inflicted are *social* in nature.[95] Indeed, although all evil is punishment for sin, "only social evil is directly so, and natural evil only indirectly."[96] But the infliction of social evil on groups of people for sin is rarely, if ever, directed to the exact source of the sin. And, as a rule, "on no account must the evil affecting the individual be referred to that individual's sin as its cause."[97] Rather, "If sin as a whole system can be rightly understood only as the collective action of the human race," Schleiermacher says, "its causality in relation to evil can only be understood in the same way."[98] This causal action is complex. It involves nested and overlapping groups, from the nation to social groups within nations.[99] The way the justice of God ordains that evil follow from sin is, correspondingly, not straightforward. In no way is the suffering of individuals, for instance, rightly "meted out to each individual in proportion to their share in the collective fault,"[100] for not only does this run against Christ's teaching on the matter,[101] but also it contradicts the key Christian idea

> that within a common sphere of sin it is possible for one to suffer for others, so that all evil justly due to the sin of many often falls upon one [*oft über Einem zusammenschlägt*] who is himself most free from the common guilt and who most firmly opposes sin.[102]

Therefore, it is only on the whole that evil follows from sin, yet in every case sin is its cause, and punishment – in this case, of whole societies – its purpose. Because *all* sin is, directly or indirectly, reflected in the evil suffered by groups of people as a whole, all guilt is perfectly met by punishment due; and thus the justice of God is complete *in this world*, even if not in the life of each sinner themselves.[103]

But how is God's punishment just if God is the cause of both punishment and the sin? For it seems that if Schleiermacher thinks of the divine justice exclusively as *punishment* for sin, then he faces the problem of securing punitive divine justice without the traditional notion of asymmetrical fault. Schleiermacher's answer lies in the ultimate ends of divine justice. He entertains three candidate ends of divine punishment for sin and settles on the third.

The first possible, but unsatisfactory, candidate end is that punishment for sin is "ordained by God as reformative [*Besserungsmittel*]";[104] that is, that the suffering of the penalty would serve in itself to secure the obedience of the flesh to the God-consciousness. But Schleiermacher denies this option on two grounds: one, that pitting fear against pleasure does nothing to liberate the God-consciousness from the determining power of the flesh, but only continues the state of sensuous domination in the form of sensuous fear; and two, that if the sufferings of punishment could elicit the power of the God-consciousness, then, in lieu of redemption, God would need to construct "a system [*System*] of divine penalties as perfect as possible,"[105] which is to say, that if suffering could provide sufficient *positive* incentive, then, in order to redeem us, God should place us all in hell. Hence, describing the aim of divine justice as reformative (in this sense) will not do.

Similarly, Schleiermacher entertains, but rejects, the idea that divine justice is "merely vengeful or retaliatory [*bloß rächende oder wiedervergeltende*]."[106] This species of vengeance or retaliation is distinguished from the retributive punishment Schleiermacher endorses by the pleasure on the part of the wronged party it is supposed to bring about; that is, "only insofar as the offended person regards their pleasure [*Lust*] in the woe [*Wehe*] of the offender as an annulment or assuaging [*Aufhebung oder Versüßung*] of their own woe [*Wehe*]."[107] Schleiermacher considers this view especially untenable when applied to God. It is a "very undeveloped [*sehr untergeordneten*]" idea which assumes that God is "still irritable and not above the feeling of offense and above having other passive states."[108] That is, Schleiermacher's principal objection to the *theological* application of vengeance as the aim of justice is the passivity (and hence dependence) that vengeance, bringing about real pleasure, relief, or other satisfaction on the part of God, implies. God's well-being is, on the view Schleiermacher opposes, quite literally made dependent on *our* unhappiness; and it is this relation of dependence, as much as any moral questions about the notion of God who would find the suffering of creatures pleasurable, to which Schleiermacher objects.

The final possible aim of divine justice, and that to which Schleiermacher subscribes, is punishment ordered to protection or deterrence [*abwehrenden oder einschrekkenden*].[109] "Punishment is, in fact, that which must of necessity be interposed wherever and insofar as the power of the God-consciousness does not yet show itself alive in the sinner," Schleiermacher explains, "in order to stop their prevailing sensuous tendencies from growing to dominate through unchecked habit."[110] That is, God's justice takes the form of retributive punishment *in order to* militate against the domination of the flesh. Unlike reformative punishment, it does not attempt to *strengthen* the

God-consciousness through incentives or disincentives but, rather, attempts to *weaken* the determining power of the sensuous self-consciousness through the necessary association of the misranking of the flesh and the spirit with the suffering of evil.

Notice what this means. Evil follows sin of necessity. This entailment is an effect of divine justice. This evil is punishment for sin. But the *aim* of this punishment is to check the disordered determining power of the sensuous self-consciousness, the power of the flesh which arrests our consciousness of God. Thus, God ordains the connection between sin and evil *for the sake of* guarding the God-consciousness from complete domination by the arresting power of the flesh, which is to say that God ordains evil, as the punishment for sin, for our good. Because evil is ordered to punishment, and punishment to deterrence, God's punishment is ordered to the ultimate aim of the disappearance of sin through the contestation of its dominance, and hence to the eventual complete cessation of divine punishment.

Schleiermacher stresses the point that the *connection* between sin and evil holds whether sin grows or diminishes, and so the same divine justice is also the basis of divine forgiveness. That is, because sin and evil are *exactly proportionate*, when sin grows, evil increases. But, by the same token, when sin diminishes, evil, too, abates. And so, "this abrogation, i.e. the forgiveness of sin, falls under the very same divine causality," Schleiermacher says, "for it is in this that the recompense [*Belohnung*] of Christ lies."[111] As the divine justice ordains that evil should be found in proportion to the presence of sin, so too does the justice of God ordain the disappearance of evil in exact proportion to the disappearance of sin; and so the redeeming power of Christ, his power to save all from sin, is also his power to deliver us from evil by one and the same justice of God. Because the *justice* of God is already punishment for sin ordered to the cessation of sin, *mercy* is not a distinct attribute of God but, according to Schleiermacher, "[W]e cannot allow mercy to rank as a distinct attribute," he says, "since we have already included that [remission of punishment] at the same time as the enactment of the penalty in the divine justice."[112]

Accordingly, Schleiermacher's reply regarding the justice of divine punishment for sin, in light of his declining to maintain asymmetrical fault, is that: (1) because evil is always exactly proportionate to sin, all divine punishment is complete in this life, and thus all divine punishment is restricted to this life; (2) divine punishment has the specific aim of *deterrence*, not the vengeful enjoyment of suffering on the part of God – or the enjoyment of just suffering on the part of the blessed, as in an account like Aquinas's;[113] and (3) the same ordinance of divine justice that causes evil to necessarily follow upon sin as a natural consequence also causes it to cease by the same correlated necessity: therefore, our punishment is ordered to *nothing but our good*.

Notice how his reconfigured account gives Schleiermacher very different explanatory obligations than Augustine and Calvin. Because he has not only accounted for the punishing justice of God without recourse to hell and damnation but also, in fact, explained the justice of God in a way such as to make it *incompatible*, in principle, with eternal punishment, Schleiermacher simply does not need to justify extreme forms of divine punishment. Because, for Schleiermacher, the *sole* use of divine punishment is deterrence, he need not be able to show, for instance, that the punishment suffered is sufficient to satisfy all loss, or to meet other possible criteria of just punishment. Finally, because deterrence is itself ordered to *the creature's* good – as opposed to, for example, the cosmic order, the divine justice in the abstract, or the good of the community considered over and apart from the sinner – there is no absurdity generated by God's co-operating with sin and evil as tragic concomitants of redemption. Schleiermacher has, in other words, taken a very different approach to securing the divine justice than the tradition: rather than deny a premise of the dilemma, or rather than attempt to defend the justice of damnation with hairline distinctions, he has insisted on God as the author of sin and evil, but declined to defend damnation at all. In reply to Calvin's question, "How then is God to be exempted from the blame to which Satan with his instruments is liable?,"[114] Schleiermacher can answer quite simply that the ordination of God which inflicts evil in proportion to sin applies no less to God, Christ, and the blessed in heaven than to sinners: it is that very justice of God which, by ordaining that evil and sin should be necessarily conjoined, also ordains that their sinlessness should be utterly free from evil.

Sin and evil, conscience, and the holiness of God

Schleiermacher gives an account of *conscience* (not to be confused with consciousness) which explains our *sense* of sin, or how our state of arrested God-consciousness comes to be apprehended as sin by us. Instructively, Schleiermacher includes his account of conscience under the divine attribute of *holiness*. It is the holiness of God that ordains the necessity with which this sense of sin accompanies our genuine need for redemption. But how does conscience and the holiness of God bear on questions of sin and evil? Most basically, conscience matters because sin explains evil, and conscience in part explains sin. Without conscience, therefore, there would, in an important sense, be no evil – a point that harkens back to Schleiermacher's distinction between evil and the bad. But, moreover, in his doctrine of conscience and holiness Schleiermacher makes his most explicit claims about *value*. And any discussion of evil will have to address what, if any, notions of value are at work. Schleiermacher's doctrine of conscience and the correlated divine attribute of holiness are some of the best evidence of the role of value in his account of sin and evil.

Spelling out the place of value in Schleiermacher's account wards off potentially severe misunderstandings. Schleiermacher's distinction between evil and the bad, his account of the divine causality in relation to sin and evil, and his account of the divine justice ordaining evil in (indirect) service of the divine ends might all lend the impression that Schleiermacher thinks of God in terms of bare power. Or, alternatively, that even if he imagines God in more value-laden terms, he is not entitled to attribute *goodness* to God. The most complete reply to this would, of course, require a full description of Schleiermacher's account of Christ and redemption – an exploration I hope to undertake in a future work. But for now, the divine holiness and the attendant doctrine of conscience allow us to see clearly how value-dependent Schleiermacher's account of *sin*, and thus evil, truly is.

Conscience is "not the same thing as the manifestation of the God-consciousness in humanity,"[115] according to Schleiermacher, but rather, as he explains,

> Under the expression "conscience" we simply understand all arising from our God-consciousness, and the stimulable modes of action arising through the same, as demands, not established theoretically, but asserting themselves in our self-consciousness in such a way that every deviation of our life's expressions [*Lebensäußerungen*] from them is a hindrance to life [*Lebenshemmung*], and is therefore understood as sin.[116]

We saw in the previous chapter how sin consists in a misranking of goods/ first principles with the sensuous self-consciousness vying with the God-consciousness to determine thought and action. Conscience, then, is that power (or act) which constantly claims the God-consciousness's rightful rule. Because the God-consciousness's priority is always asserted, everything which fails to follow this priority is accompanied by the pain of internal dissonance. And, in light of our inability to rectify this disorder on our own, conscience generates "the consciousness of humans' incapacity."[117] Conscience, therefore, is not the God-consciousness, but is directly related. Namely, conscience stands to the God-consciousness in exactly the same way that conscience stands to *synderesis*.[118] It is a distinct natural power (or act), alongside the intellect and the will, which advances the *just* claim of the God-consciousness upon us.[119]

Significantly, Schleiermacher explains conscience, our sense of falling short of the demands made by the God-consciousness, as synonymous with explanations of conscience as our sense of falling short of *the idea of the good*. As he says,

> We may certainly assume as a known fact that conscience is elsewhere explained by a corresponding relation to the idea of the good [*die Idee des Guten*]; here we have but to say in passing that the two ideas are in no real sense different. For if it were ever to occur that under the idea of the good the natural conscience [*natürliche Gewissen*] made other demands than in the same community are insisted on by the God-consciousness prevailing there, so that the two were in conflict, we

should simply have to attribute the fact to a defect in their development or in their application, just as we do where the natural conscience in any one region or period is not identical with that of another, or where different forms of faith differ in the demands they make. In the Evangelical (Protestant) Church, however, we are not troubled with any such conflict, for it is readily admitted that the modes of action emanating from our God-consciousness are identical [*Identität*] with those developed from the idea of the good.[120]

Conscience as a sense of incapacity to the demands made by the God-consciousness is *in no real sense different* from conscience as a sense of incapacity to the demands of the idea of the good. Indeed, according to Schleiermacher, Protestants regard them as *identical*. A likely inference to be drawn here is that the two make identical *demands* because they have identical *causes*. That is, to be conscious of God *is* to apprehend the idea of the good (and vice versa) and their *being* the same explains why they make the same demands. If what then makes the consciousness of God and the idea of the good *about* the same thing is that the two regard the same *object* – namely, God – then Schleiermacher is, in at least some respects, identifying God with the good.

Schleiermacher has more still to say on the matter which makes clear how meaningful he means his claims to be. He endorses the inference that

> insofar as evil [*das Böse*] is the object of displeasure and is opposed to the good [*dem Guten*], it also cannot exist, and therefore neither can it be posited as a thought of God; that is, there is no reality in, nor any idea of evil [*daß es kein Wesen und keine Idee des Bösen giebt*].[121]

In other words, Schleiermacher means very much for his reflections on good and evil to have ontological import. Because evil cannot be a thought of God, it cannot have any *being*. This implies that the opposite is true of the good: it is both an idea and a reality alike grounded in God, and is perhaps, as earlier, even synonymous with God.

It is, accordingly, clear that Schleiermacher means for several key notions to converge in relation to conscience: the human good (i.e., the contrary of hindrances to life), the God-consciousness, and value in relation to God. Because he identifies the idea of the good with the content of the consciousness of God, and because he also identifies the human good with the consciousness of God, Schleiermacher associates the *human* good with the *divine* idea of the good, implying that what is good for us is, at least in part, good for us *because* it conforms to an eternal standard of value.

Conscience asserts the demands of the good in such a way that "any deviation of our life's expressions from them is a hindrance to life, and therefore is understood as sin."[122] In other words, conscience champions *the* good for *our* good. But it does so by causing any *discrepancy* between the demands of the good and our actual life to become a *hindrance* to life, which is to say, an *evil* (see earlier), and, therefore, causes us to understand the condition of this discrepancy as *sin* and to experience it as misery. How the demands of the good *generate* evil and sin is a puzzle we look at ahead.

In fact, Schleiermacher claims that "apart from conscience, nothing that results from that discrepancy ['between the form of the God-consciousness as understanding and its emergence as will'] would be sin for us."[123] The "discrepancy" referred to is, of course, the arresting of the God-consciousness resulting in *akrasia* – the only admissible discrepancy between intellect and will – that we examined in Chapter 6. But what we saw in that chapter might be taken to mean that no more is necessary to account for sin than the weakness of the will itself. What could Schleiermacher think conscience adds such that without it the conditions of sin outlined previously would not yet amount to sin?

The answer is twofold: first, and most basically, conscience causes our *recognition* of our state of sin; and second, the claim of conscience prevents us resolving the discrepancy between intellect and will to our detriment – for any disparity between intellect and will can be resolved either by strengthening the will or by compromising the intellect's judgments and modifying, or debasing, them to match the will. The latter strategy *would* remove the condition of *akrasia* because the intellect and will would, in fact, be at one. But it would be a case of pernicious intellectual distortion to resolve the dissonance of a weak will in this way. Conscience, by unceasingly championing the idea of the good, prevents this kind of intellectual compromise from ever being entirely successful. It *guarantees* that some awareness of the true good is maintained and thus that any arresting of the God-consciousness is *recognized as* a genuine hindrance to life – namely, evil – however tacitly.

In doing so, conscience *causes* this state to be a hindrance to life by refusing to completely compromise the sort of *life* it is. Recall from earlier that Schleiermacher thinks the bad becomes *evil* when we exchange the "life of spirit" for the "life of sense" as our highest end because the life that natural loss hinders is now improperly ranked as our highest good – our *life* in the relevant sense. That explains how the bad becomes evil on the condition of the misranking of our natural and supernatural ends. Conscience, in contrast, explains why this misranking itself *is* evil. It does this by making claims upon us, claims grounded in *facts* about proper human ends and our genuine good. Against our own self-deception, it *insists* on our true well-being as the "life of spirit." As an ineradicable power, conscience guarantees we are always at least weakly determined to our supernatural ends. And as a power which is grounded in the divine idea of the good, the value of this end remains independent of *our* judgments about it. Whereas the bad becomes evil when we misrank our ends, conscience *makes this very misranking evil* by contrasting our disordered souls with a transcendent standard of value: the proper end of the true life for which we were made, in view of which all incapacity of the God-consciousness, all sin, is the severest of hindrances and so the greatest of evils.

The role of conscience vis-à-vis the generation and recognition of sin and the content of conscience as the idea of the good connect in an overall picture of value that runs counter to possible misunderstandings of Schleiermacher's position. Together they show that Schleiermacher assumes a notion of *moral facts*. They show this by explaining how sin and evil are dependent, at least ultimately, on the apprehension of a transcendent standard of value mediated through conscience. It is not that Schleiermacher's notion of the good ceases to be ends-relative, and even relative to *human* ends. He certainly thinks perfection is ends-relative, and sometimes those ends are human ends. Nevertheless, our *ultimate* ends are not dependent on human determination, cannot ever be fully emended or compromised, and indeed, are grounded in the idea of the good, the good whose deliverances are *identical* to those of the God-consciousness. The end to which we are ordained, the determination of human nature which norms all our thoughts and deeds, is a divine idea. And it is the *holiness* of God which necessitates that this good, our good, is proclaimed in the soul as divine command and issues forth as moral and civil law from the consciences of whole peoples.[124]

Some of Schleiermacher's account might suggest that he is disingenuous about, or at least insufficiently condemnatory of, evil, even making evil dependent on *our* states of consciousness. He might be taken to imply that evil is *merely* a state of mind. But the holiness of God once again makes clear that Schleiermacher thinks of the power of our minds principally as powers of apprehension, powers of beholding in consciousness what is, in fact, there to be beheld. Conscience works in just this way with respect to our ultimate ends by unceasingly championing what is eternally true. Through conscience we receive the deliverances of the divine idea of the good, which, "as the voice of God within the mind, is understood to be an original revelation of God."[125] Only in light of that transcendent value do we come to fully see and suffer the evil of sin.

Conclusion

Schleiermacher offers a controversial account of how sin connects to evil. Yet upon closer inspection, it is much more subtly distinguished from other accounts than first appears. Like traditional accounts, Schleiermacher thinks all evil depends on sin. Like traditional accounts, he thinks that evil is punishment for sin. Like traditional accounts, he thinks no evil goes unsatisfied by the punishment of divine justice. Like many traditional accounts, he thinks God can, at least in some senses, make *use* of evil for good (even if God does not *intend* evil for such purposes). And, finally, like traditional accounts, Schleiermacher explains evil as a privation of proper human ends, a hindrance to that life God wills for us and in which our blessedness is found.

The differences that remain are important, but specific. Although, for Schleiermacher, evil exists only because of sin, natural ills are reckoned not as instances of *evil* but only of the bad, and these are necessary features of the world which *become* evil only on the condition of sin because, apart from sin, the suffering of ills does not obstruct humans' highest ends. Moreover, as we saw in previous chapters, there never was a time when human beings were without sin. And so there never was a time when the world was altered by the introduction of evil, in the sense imagined by thinkers like Augustine – that is, by things like death, disease, and other maladies. The world, including the bad, is perfectly ordered to the attainment of humans' ultimate ends and, as we saw in Chapter 5, this constitutes its original perfection. Finally, and most importantly, Schleiermacher does not try to exempt God from causal implication in evil itself with a theory of deficient causes.

Schleiermacher's declining to shield God from evil through deficient causes is most distinctive and most controversial. It is also *the* signature move which allows Schleiermacher to place sin (and thus evil) in complete continuity with humans' evolutionary past. Thus, the greatest benefits and the greatest burdens of his account are inseparable. To place sin in continuity with the natural world *is necessarily* to make God, in some sense, the cause of evil.

Schleiermacher is unapologetic in applying his causally complete account to moral and natural evil in equal measure. Both follow from sin, which, Schleiermacher has argued, itself *must* have causes sufficient to determine it as a state *and* to determine the acts which follow from that state. Therefore, because Schleiermacher has declined the last refuge of any theorist hoping to quarantine God from evil – the deficient indeterminate will – he has no reason to sustain an indeterminist account of the will on the whole.[126]

In making God the cause of moral evil, however, Schleiermacher faces new objections in respect to God's justice, for in refusing to sever the causal link between God and moral evil, Schleiermacher is unable to appeal to an important resource in traditional accounts: that divine blame and punishment of human sinners are just because God and humans are asymmetrically at fault for sin – that we are responsible for sin, but God is not. Instead, Schleiermacher abandons damnation altogether. Although the justice of God ordains that all sin is punished by guaranteeing that evil follows from sin as a natural consequence, it never does so without limit in intensity and time, and the punishment of sin is never ordered to vengeance *simpliciter*, but always to the deterrence of sin – and hence to *our* good.

The place of sin and evil in God's teleological ordering of the universe is not one of straightforward use, but of double effect and tragic restraint. Blessedness is the ultimate divine end. Creation is developmentally ordered to that end. Given that divine end, sin is inevitable. Given sin, evil is necessary to restrain it, lest our unclouded blessedness, our highest end, fail to be attained. But since, by God's power and wisdom, God's ends cannot fail to be attained, punishment does deter; and in deterring it chastens the flesh;

and in chastening what arrests our consciousness of God, it weakens sin, which, by the same ordinance of divine justice, diminishes evil: all in the service of the divine love which wills nothing but to share itself with us.

If this account raises suspicions about Schleiermacher's notion of value, he has a reply. And what he can say is remarkably traditional: evil is a privation of a good and sin is the privative disordering of our ends which causes evil. The *good* of which sin is a privation is, for Schleiermacher, our ultimate, supernatural end – the "life of the spirit." Sin is a hindrance to *this life*, to our ultimate end. It is, of course, evil *to us*, as the good it regards is *ours*. And this evil arises only on the condition that *we* are sinners. But it is an error to think this implies that value is merely dependent on our recognition of it. No, as we saw earlier, sin does not merely make us *regard* the bad as evil, but it *causes it to be evil* by disordering the first principles of our lives, hindering the proper determination of our natures. It is, in other words, in reference to human nature, not to this or that person's experience, that sin and evil are rightly reckoned privation. And the most important measure in preventing this state is the power of conscience which champions the rightful claim of communion with God in consciousness as our highest end. Conscience *acts* to contest the distortion of our proper ends on behalf of the God-consciousness by *asserting* a standard of value that transcends any capacity of ours to distort or ignore: the idea of the good.

This means that Schleiermacher has not abandoned the priority of the good that the privation account of sin and evil depends on, nor has he abandoned the identification of that specific value – the good of which sin is a privation – with determinate *ends*, which is to say, with a *specific nature*. Once again, even though Schleiermacher discards the deficient cause tradition with respect to sin's origins, he retains a notion of privation with respect to sin's ends. Natures remain normative. Sin is a privation of the proper ends of human life. And it is the effect of God's justice and holiness to prevent the total distortion of those ends through the ordination of punishment and forgiveness, and through the unsilenceable claim of the voice of God within.

Schleiermacher's account remains controversial, but the *way* in which it is so is specific, not generic; and the *reasons* for its controversial features always connect to Schleiermacher's evolutionary account of the cosmos and human nature. Because, as Schleiermacher argues, neither human nature nor the world was *or could have been* corrupted by sin in the historical past, natural ills could not have arisen because of sin. And because the world was not and could not have been corrupted, the divine purpose must have been to order creation to salvation from the beginning. Because the world is so ordered, it must, by the divine wisdom, be perfectly ordered to our blessedness. And because it is perfectly ordered, and yet includes ills, those ills cannot be of the kind that could prevent the attainment of our blessedness. Therefore, there must be some distinction between ultimately life-hindering ills and others – that is, a distinction between the bad and evil. And because the bad and evil are, on Schleiermacher's account of nature, alike features of *creation* (as conditions or acts of creatures), they are alike traceable to God. Therefore, (1) God as the sufficient cause of sin and evil, (2) the distinction between the bad and evil, and (3) the corresponding dependence of evil on sin are all mutually implicative consequences of Schleiermacher's evolutionary/developmental account and his theological first principles. And so the aim of God's holiness and justice in regard to evil cannot be vengeance for sin, or the counterbalancing of sin with greater good. Instead, the justice and holiness of God are ordered to the disappearance of sin, and with it evil, which is to say, to the developmental completion of human nature and so to the unending enjoyment of the ultimate good for which we were made.

Notes

1 *GL* §48.1; *The Christian Faith*, 185, translation revised.
2 *GL* §48.1; *The Christian Faith*, 185.
3 *GL* §48.1; *The Christian Faith*, 185.
4 *GL* §48.1; *The Christian Faith*, 185.
5 *GL* §48; *The Christian Faith*, 184.
6 I use the term "moral evil" throughout, but Schleiermacher uses the term "social evil [*geselliges Übel*]," and explains that he prefers the term to avoid implying that "the wicked [*das Böse*] as such is subsumed under the concept of evil." However, the confusion can run both ways, and what Schleiermacher means by "social evil" is not the actions of groups in distinction from the actions of individuals but, rather, any evil "which is due to human action [*menschlicher Thätigkeit hervorgegangen*]." Hence, the term "moral evil" more clearly captures how twenty-first-century English speakers would understand the concept described. For more on how I read his distinction between the wicked (*das Böse*) and evil (*Übel*) see ahead. *GL* §75.2; *The Christian Faith*, 316. Support for this reading can be found in Gerrish's interpretation. See Gerrish, *Christian Faith*, 93–94.
7 *GL* §48.1; *The Christian Faith*, 185, translation revised.
8 *GL* §48.2; *The Christian Faith*, 186.
9 *GL* §48.2; *The Christian Faith*, 186.
10 *GL* §48.2; *The Christian Faith*, 186.
11 *GL* §48.2; *The Christian Faith*, 186, translation revised.
12 See *GL* §§54, 55; *The Christian Faith*, 211–28; see also my discussion of this in Pedersen, *The Eternal Covenant*, 116–24.
13 See Pedersen, *The Eternal Covenant*, 69–87.
14 *GL* §48.2; *The Christian Faith*, 186.
15 *GL* §48.2; *The Christian Faith*, 186.
16 *GL* §48.2; *The Christian Faith*, 186, translation revised.
17 *GL* §48.2; *The Christian Faith*, 187.
18 *GL* §48.2; *The Christian Faith*, 187, translation revised.
19 *GL* §48.2; *The Christian Faith*, 187, translation revised.
20 *GL* §48.3; *The Christian Faith*, 188.
21 *GL* §48.3; *The Christian Faith*, 188, translation revised.
22 *GL* §46, postscript; *The Christian Faith*, 178.
23 *GL* §48.3; *The Christian Faith*, 188.
24 *GL* §48.3; *The Christian Faith*, 188–89, translation revised.
25 See Aquinas, *De Malo*, Q. 1, a. 1, resp.
26 *GL* §81.1; *The Christian Faith*, 331, translation revised.

27 *GL* §81.1; *The Christian Faith*, 331, translation revised.
28 *GL* §81.1; *The Christian Faith*, 331, translation revised; Cf. Aquinas, *De Malo*, Q. 1, a. 3, resp.
29 *GL* §48.3; *The Christian Faith*, 189, translation revised.
30 This is to say, created good are, in Aquinas's language, accidental causes. See Aquinas, *De Malo*, Q. 1, a. 3, resp, and r. o. 14.
31 And Aquinas. See Aquinas, *De Malo*, Q. 1, a. 3, r. o. resp;
32 See Augustine, *City of God*, XI.18, 22; XII.4–5.
33 *GL* §48.1; *The Christian Faith*, 185, translation revised.
34 *GL* §48.1; *The Christian Faith*, 185, translation revised.
35 *GL* §75; *The Christian Faith*, 315, translation revised.
36 Schleiermacher distinguishes the wicked (*das Böse*) and evil (*Übel*). Adams is helpful on this distinction. However, I doubt Schleiermacher thinks of *Übel* as less bad than *das Böse*, but rather as distinguished as passion and action: one *suffers* evil [*Übel*] but *acts* wicked [*Böse*]. If so, this would explain the relative scarcity of *das Böse* in *The Christian Faith* as deferring the topic to Christian ethics or some other genre. Regardless, Schleiermacher also claims that God is the author (*Urheber*) of sin – that is, the source of wicked action as well as the cause of moral/social evil. And this point, combined with his teaching of the congenital and social spread of sin, shows that he does not mean to exempt the wicked, in contrast with evil, from determining causes. See Adams, "Schleiermacher on Evil," 576.
37 *GL* §75.1; *The Christian Faith*, 316, translation revised.
38 *GL* §75.1; *The Christian Faith*, 315.
39 Adams claims that evil "must refer in the first instance to obstructions to the lower or sensuous life." Adams, "Schleiermacher on Evil," 576–77.
40 *GL* §75.1; *The Christian Faith*, 316, translation revised.
41 *GL* §75.1; *The Christian Faith*, 316, translation revised.
42 As Adams puts it, "It is only sin, only obstruction of the religious consciousness, that keeps us from reconciliation with the conditions of our existence, in Schleiermacher's view; and in a sense it is only sin that is intrinsically bad." Adams, "Schleiermacher on Evil," 577.
43 "*niemals könnte in eine geistige Lebenshemmung ausschlagen.*" *GL* §75.1; *The Christian Faith*, 316.
44 This in contrast to Wyman, who portrays sin *merely* as a matter of perspective when he claims that "In Schleiermacher's theology of consciousness, evil is a matter of how you look at reality," and that "it is not hard to judge that a subjectivist reduction of the reality of evil has gone hand in hand with Schleiermacher's conceptual framework." I am not at all convinced. Sin is, instead, a privation or perfection of human nature, an ontological lack; and evil is an effect *caused* by that lack. See Wyman, "Sin and Redemption," 137–38.
45 *GL* §75.1; *The Christian Faith*, 316.
46 For more on the basis of this argument, see my chapter on divine wisdom and the teleological perfection of the world in Pedersen, *The Eternal Covenant*, 46–68.
47 See Adams's criticism of Schleiermacher's "broadly Stoical" account. Adams, "Schleiermacher on Evil," 580.
48 Once again, see Pedersen, *The Eternal Covenant*, 46–68.
49 See Aquinas, *Summa Theologica*, II–II, Q. 2, a. 8, resp.
50 *GL* §75.3; *The Christian Faith*, 317, translation revised.
51 *GL* §75.2; *The Christian Faith*, 316.
52 *GL* §75.2; *The Christian Faith*, 317.
53 *GL* §79; *The Christian Faith*, 325
54 *GL* §48.1; *The Christian Faith*, 185.

55 See, for example, Augustine, *City of God*, XI.18, 22; XII.4–5; Aquinas, *Summa Theologica*, Ia, Q. 49, a. 2, resp.
56 GL §81.1; *The Christian Faith*, 331.
57 See Aquinas, *Summa Theologica*, Ia, Q. 19, a. 9, resp.
58 GL §81.1; *The Christian Faith*, 331, translation revised.
59 GL §81.1; *The Christian Faith*, 331–32.
60 GL §81.1; *The Christian Faith*, 331, translation revised.
61 GL §81.1; *The Christian Faith*, 331, translation revised.
62 GL §81.4; *The Christian Faith*, 338, translation revised.
63 See my discussions of this in Pedersen, *The Eternal Covenant*, 62–64, 133–36.
64 See Pedersen, *The Eternal Covenant*, 147; Vogler, *Reasonably Vicious*, 22–23.
65 This should not be confused, however, with Hick's stronger claim that sin is not among the conditions of this world that are well ordered to the divine ends on the whole. As he puts it, "We have to say simply that the incomprehensible mingling in human experience of good and evil, virtue and vice, pain and pleasure, continues in all its characteristic and baffling ambiguity and ends only with death." Hick, *Evil and the God of Love*, 339.
66 Namely, that account found in the section "On Providence" in Calvin, *Concerning the Eternal Predestination*, 162–85.
67 Calvin, *Concerning the Eternal Predestination*, 169.
68 Calvin, *Concerning the Eternal Predestination*, 169, 177.
69 Calvin, *Concerning the Eternal Predestination*, 171–72.
70 Calvin, *Concerning the Eternal Predestination*, 176.
71 Calvin, *Concerning the Eternal Predestination*, 177.
72 Calvin, *Concerning the Eternal Predestination*, 169.
73 Calvin, *Concerning the Eternal Predestination*, 169.
74 Calvin, *Concerning the Eternal Predestination*, 169.
75 Calvin, *Concerning the Eternal Predestination*, 176, emphasis added.
76 Calvin, *Concerning the Eternal Predestination*, 179.
77 Calvin, *Concerning the Eternal Predestination*, 180.
78 See Leibniz, *Theodicy*, 137–38.
79 Compare this problem to Aquinas's claim that God neither sins nor causes others to sin because to do *either* would implicate God in evil, which is impossible. Aquinas, *De Malo*, Q. 3, a. 1, resp.
80 As Calvin puts it, "Of course a distinction is made between the deeds of men and their purpose or end; for the cruelty of the man who puts out the eyes of crows or kills a stork is condemned, while the virtue of the judge is praised who puts his hand to the killing of a criminal." Calvin, *Concerning the Eternal Predestination*, 180. He also appeals to proximate and remote causes, but it is not clear that such an appeal would exonerate God. It seems only to secure the status of evil as a divine *instrument*, a proximate cause sharing the remote cause's purposes, unless there is *also* a difference in intent or purpose. Calvin, *Concerning the Eternal Predestination*, 181.
81 This distinction is common among Reformed thinkers but a similar distinction can also be found in earlier figures couched in different terminology. See Aquinas, *Summa Theologica*, Ia, Q. 19, a. 12, r.o. 2.
82 GL §81.1; *The Christian Faith*, 332, translation revised.
83 GL §81.1; *The Christian Faith*, 333, translation revised.
84 GL §81.1; *The Christian Faith*, 333, translation revised.
85 GL §81.1; *The Christian Faith*, 333, translation revised.
86 See Aristotle, *Nicomachean Ethics* II.6.
87 Calvin, *Concerning the Eternal Predestination*, 180.
88 Calvin, *Concerning the Eternal Predestination*, 179.

89 Augustine, *City of God*, XII.3, 40.
90 *GL* §84; *The Christian Faith*, 345, translation revised.
91 *GL* §84.2; *The Christian Faith*, 348–49.
92 *GL* §84.1; *The Christian Faith*, 346, translation revised.
93 *GL* §84.1; *The Christian Faith*, 346.
94 *GL* §84.1; *The Christian Faith*, 346.
95 Recall too that "social" evil is Schleiermacher's term for what most English speakers would call "moral" evil as all evil due to human action. *GL* §75.2; *The Christian Faith*, 316.
96 *GL* §76; *The Christian Faith*, 317, translation revised.
97 *GL* §77; *The Christian Faith*, 320, translation revised.
98 *GL* §77.1; *The Christian Faith*, 320, translation revised.
99 *GL* §77.1; *The Christian Faith*, 321.
100 *GL* §77.2; *The Christian Faith*, 322, translation revised.
101 See, for example, Luke 13:4.
102 *GL* §77.2; *The Christian Faith*, 322, translation revised.
103 *GL* §77.1; *The Christian Faith*, 320.
104 *GL* §84.3; *The Christian Faith*, 350.
105 *GL* §84.3; *The Christian Faith*, 350.
106 *GL* §84.3; *The Christian Faith*, 350.
107 *GL* §84.3; *The Christian Faith*, 350, translation revised.
108 *GL* §84.3; *The Christian Faith*, 350, translation revised.
109 *GL* §84.3; *The Christian Faith*, 350, translation revised.
110 *GL* §84.3; *The Christian Faith*, 350–51, translation revised.
111 *GL* §84.2; *The Christian Faith*, 347.
112 *GL* §85.2; *The Christian Faith*, 354.
113 See Aquinas, *Summa Theologica*, Suppl. III, Q. 94, a. 3, resp.
114 Calvin, *Concerning the Eternal Predestination*, 180.
115 *GL* §83.1; *The Christian Faith*, 342, translation revised.
116 *GL* §83.1; *The Christian Faith*, 341, translation revised.
117 *GL* §83.2; *The Christian Faith*, 343, translation revised.
118 See Aquinas, *Summa Theologica*, Ia, Q. 79, a. 13.
119 See Plato, *Republic*, IV, 435; Irwin, *Plato's Ethics*, 203–22; Kamtekar, *Plato's Moral Psychology*, 129–85.
120 *GL* §83.1; *The Christian Faith*, 342.
121 *GL* §83.3; *The Christian Faith*, 344–45, translation revised.
122 *GL* §83.1; *The Christian Faith*, 341, translation revised.
123 *GL* §83.1; *The Christian Faith*, 342.
124 *GL* §83.1–2; *The Christian Faith*, 341, 343–44.
125 *GL* §83.1; *The Christian Faith*, 342, translation revised.
126 On this point Adams and I are in complete accord. See Adams, "Schleiermacher on Evil," 569.

References

Adams, Robert Merrihew. "Schleiermacher on Evil." *Faith and Philosophy* 13, no. 4 (1996): 563–83.

Aquinas, Thomas. *De Malo. On Evil*. Translated by Richard Regan, edited by Brian Davies. New York: Oxford University Press, 2003.

———. *Summa Theologica*. Translated by the Fathers of the English Dominican Province. New York: Benziger Bros., 1947.

Aristotle. *Nicomachean Ethics*. Vol. 2. Edited by Jonathan Barnes. Princeton: Princeton University Press, 1984.

Augustine of Hippo. *The City of God*. The Works of Saint Augustine. Part I, Vol. 7. Translated by William Babcock. Hyde Park, NY: New City Press, 2013.

Calvin, John. *Concerning the Eternal Predestination of God*. Translated by J. K. S. Reid. Louisville, KY: Westminster John Knox, [1961] 1997.

Gerrish, B. A. *Christian Faith: Dogmatics in Outline*. Louisville: Westminster John Knox, 2015.

Hick, John. *Evil and the God of Love*. Third edition. London: Macmillan, 1977.

Irwin, Terence. *Plato's Ethics*. Oxford: Oxford University Press, 1995.

Kamtekar, Rachana. *Plato's Moral Psychology: Intellectualism, the Divided Soul, and the Desire for Good*. Oxford: Oxford University Press, 2017.

Leibniz, Gottfried Wilhelm. *Theodicy: Essays on the Goodness of God, the Freedom of Man, and the Origin of Evil*. Edited by Austin Farrer, translated by E. M. Huggard. La Salle, IL: Open Court, [1951] 1985.

Pedersen, Daniel J. *The Eternal Covenant: Schleiermacher on God and Natural Science*. Berlin: De Gruyter, 2017.

Plato. *The Republic*. Edited and introduction by John M. Cooper, associate editor D. S. Hutchinson. Indianapolis: Hackett, 1997.

Schleiermacher, Friedrich D. E. *The Christian Faith*. Edited by H. R. Mackintosh and J. S. Stewart, translated by D. M. Baillie, et al. Berkeley: Apocryphile, [1928] 2011.

———. *Der christliche Glaube nach den Grundsätzen der evangelischen Kirche im Zusammenhange dargestellt*. Second edition. Edited by Rolf Schäfer. Berlin: Walter de Gruyter, [1830/31] 2008.

Vogler, Candace. *Reasonably Vicious*. Cambridge, MA: Harvard University Press, 2002.

Wyman Jr., Walter E. "Sin and Redemption." In *The Cambridge Companion to Friedrich Schleiermacher*. Edited by Jaqueline Mariña. Cambridge: Cambridge University Press, 2005.

8 Conclusion
A shadow of the good

Even those who, strangely enough, consider the great majority of his works only as play and pastime, do yet think that he is at last in this dialogue serious for once, and intends to say something that has a meaning. Pity only that this correct sentiment has never grown into a clearer insight into the work, for those on the one hand, who have in general taken a right view of its most universal bearing, have not been so fortunate in their endeavours to penetrate into the details, and super add, therefore, to the difficulty of the subject a perplexed style of expression, and confusion of language upon these points; while they who speak easily and intelligibly of the same, display little else than the narrowness of their own capacity to see the meaning of such works, and consequently a very deficient criticism.

– Schleiermacher, "Philebus,"
Introductions to the Dialogues of Plato

A central aim of this work has been to advance the thesis that a recognizably modern account of the origins of sin need not require the abandonment of traditional accounts of value. This task is possible in principle, I argued, because Schleiermacher has, in fact, succeeded in maintaining a characteristically modern account of sin's origins together with traditional axiological commitments. I not only showed how Schleiermacher sought to do this but also looked in detail at the reasoning Schleiermacher offered in support of his claims. In this last chapter, I draw together the collection of arguments and distinctions from previous chapters and explain what I take my thesis to imply for a range of topics.

This chapter is structured as follows. First, I revisit the contention that the principle of parallel priority is unnecessary. Second, I reconsider Schleiermacher's relation to traditional accounts of agency and normativity in light of his rejection of that principle. Third, I explore the implications and advantages of Schleiermacher's account of sin and nature in relating to natural science. Fourth and finally, I consider the implications of my reading of Schleiermacher for the historiography of theology.

The principle of parallel priority reconsidered

In Chapter 1 I argued that disputes over sin in the theology of the last two centuries or so have their basis in the same shared premise: the view that the logical priority of the good can be secured only with the simultaneous and parallel chronological priority of the good – what I have called the *principle of parallel priority*. Because both traditional accounts and modern accounts generally share this assumption, when moderns abandon a story of the fall, they typically (but wrongly) deem it necessary to also abandon the priority of the good, the convertibility of the transcendentals, and other correlated claims about nature and value. Instead, they find themselves, knowingly or not, embracing the notion that fact and value are severable, and denying the normativity of natures. Traditionalists refuse these axiological and metaphysical sacrifices. But because they too assume the principle of parallel priority, they judge it necessary to defend a fall or fall-like account to make good on that refusal. In the face of theological criticisms of the fall or fall-like events (like Schleiermacher's criticisms in Chapters 2 and 3, for instance) this task is not easy; and, in the further light of natural scientific claims, it is impracticable. Accordingly, little headway is made between broadly traditional and broadly modern camps because each assumes that sacrifices are required which the other will not make. Schleiermacher's account of sin aims to replace the burdensome traditional account of sin's origins with an evolutionary-developmental account, and yet do so without the sacrifice of traditional first principles.

Schleiermacher is able to pursue this third way precisely because he declines the principle of parallel priority: the assumption that the logical priority of the good and related axiological and metaphysical commitments can be secured if and only if a parallel chronological priority of the good is also maintained. By declining this principle, he is able *both* to describe the origins of sin without recourse to a fall or fall-like event *and* to appeal to the normativity of natures – that specific goodness of which sin is a privation. In turn, Schleiermacher provides a comprehensive counterexample to the assumption of the principle of parallel priority. This reveals that this principle *is an assumption*. Thus, to appeal to this assumption in criticism of Schleiermacher's position openly begs the question. And Schleiermacher's account further reveals, more importantly, that the principle of parallel priority *is not a necessary assumption*. If it can be declined in fact, it can be declined in principle. And because this principle can be declined, it is possible to *maintain* traditional claims about value and, at the same time, *deny* traditional claims about sin's origins in a fall or fall-like event. Therefore, debates over the origins of sin, so characteristic of the divide between traditional and modern theology, need not end at this impasse because at their foundation lies a false dilemma.

Chapters 2–7 each laid out a step in Schleiermacher's case for why this should, and how this can, be done. The first three chapters emphasized

Schleiermacher's critique of traditional accounts. The weight of the last three chapters was on how he thought the best of the tradition could be kept and explained. Each also introduced premises that are key to understanding Schleiermacher's account properly.

Chapters 2 and 3 laid out Schleiermacher's critique of the fall of the Devil and the fall of Adam respectively. In so doing, each more fully revealed the notions of agency, freedom, and responsibility that are at work in his arguments. In respect to both the Devil and Adam, Schleiermacher argues that a change in nature was metaphysically and/or morally impossible. Rather, their moral imperfection must have preceded their first sinful act, an act, which in any event, could not have resulted in self-reflexive violent transformation.[1] Therefore, not only was there never, in fact, a time in which the first humans were not sinners, but also there never could have been. A fall or fall-like event, of any kind, whether of one person or many, is incoherent in principle. It is *not possible*, Schleiermacher argues, to secure the chronological priority of the good. Because it is not possible, we should not seek to do so.

Chapter 4 examined the central premise of this argument: a strong version of the principle of sufficient reason explained as a causal completeness thesis. This thesis directly challenges the Augustinian deficient cause tradition, which denies that there was an efficient cause of Adam's evil will. Schleiermacher argues, instead, that there *must* have been a cause or causes sufficient to explain *why* Adam willed what he willed. To refuse the principle of sufficient reason in this case would not generate the agency and culpability required; and if we follow the appeal to deficient causes to its natural conclusion, the occurrence of such causes would ultimately imply that God is *not* that upon which all depend absolutely.[2] In its place we begin to see Schleiermacher's own account take form. Schleiermacher *agrees* with Augustine that good cannot corrupt good, but disagrees that there could be an undetermined, which is to say, causally incomplete, failure. Rather, things must be *caused* to fail – even the will. Therefore, Schleiermacher turns the Augustinian account on its head. Rather than deny Augustine's axiological commitments, he denies Augustine's historical claims: that humans *became* sinners in a past event.[3] In so doing, Schleiermacher also rejects *all* analogue accounts of a *voluntary* origin of sin, whether in two people or in whole societies.

In place of a theory of sin originating from the deficient will of the first humans, Schleiermacher believes that sin is as old as human being and that there never was a time when the first humans were not yet sinners.[4] But this raises potentially dire questions about whether sin is *natural* not only with respect to human origins but also with respect to human ends. If sin is natural, Schleiermacher cannot be committed to the normativity of natures without making the blessed in heaven sinners, and one who is not a sinner (i.e., Christ) less than, or other than, human.

Yet, despite arguing that sin is as old as human being, Schleiermacher denies that sin is natural in the normative sense. In Chapter 5, Schleiermacher explained that sin is natural only in origin – that is, only in the sense that there are causes within nature itself sufficient to bring it about. Yet sin remains specifically (i.e., with respect to human nature) unnatural, and a privation of human nature. Indeed, sin is privative in several respects, falling short of the proper ends for which humans were made, and falling short of Christ's *human* perfection.[5] As a result, Schleiermacher subscribes to the logical and metaphysical priority of the good, even, in some senses, the temporal priority of the good in that the consciousness of God must be *present but incomplete* for a condition of sin to arise. Schleiermacher can thus assuage potential worries about the naturalness of sin because he distinguishes between the natural origins of sin and the naturalness of sin with respect to proper human ends. In the latter respect, sin remains utterly unnatural and therefore a privation of a good. In the former respect, sin is "natural" only in the sense that it has natural (i.e., created) sufficient causes. Because Schleiermacher locates both origins and ends within an evolutionary-developmental account of the universe, he can make both claims without contradiction: for *every* case of incomplete development is deficient with respect to its proper ends in that it is *not yet* what it is meant to be.

In Chapter 6, we examined Schleiermacher's moral psychology of sin and saw how, at every step in his account, sin is a sufficiently caused deficiency. In the previous chapter, we saw that the God-consciousness is a natural passive potency and that sin consists in the incomplete presence of this perfection. Here we see how it can come about that this power is hindered: namely, that we find ourselves in a condition of *akrasia* caused by the competitive determining power of the sensuous self-consciousness; and that this competitive power is, in turn, explained by appeal to individual, historical, and cosmic evolutionary-developmental circumstances.[6] A state of sin is, in short, a state that creatures develop *into* as animals evolve into the kind that is ordered to, and so capable of, union with God in consciousness. As a result of the competition of the flesh and the spirit (explained by the flesh's developmental good), those in a *state* of sin are only ever weakly determined to *act* in accord with their proper ends.[7] What distinguishes Schleiermacher's account is, once again, the way he thinks deficiencies are always explained by other powers; that defects are always *caused*, and causes are always goods. This causally complete moral psychology not only is further evidence for my interpretation of Schleiermacher but also points, once again, to the greatest burden of his account, and what appears at least initially to be the chief obstacle to linking his account of sin and nature to traditional axiological commitments: namely, that God is the author of sin and the cause of evil.

Chapter 7 looked closely at Schleiermacher's claim that God is the author of sin and the cause of evil. These two claims appear to contradict traditional claims about value: that only things are causes, and only goods are things; that to author is to intend, and to intend is to cause with an eye to some end, an end which is always a good; and, most importantly, that causal implication of God with sin and evil would contradict traditional descriptions of God as goodness itself.

Despite initial appearances, however, we see that Schleiermacher, in fact, *explains* these claims in a way that is remarkably consonant with traditional claims about value. For Schleiermacher says that by calling God the cause of evil and the author of sin, he means that God is the sufficient cause of the sufficient causes of sin and evil. God can (and, indeed, must) rightly be called cause and author in light of this claim because the in-principle causally complete structure of Schleiermacher's account makes the divine causality completely transitive.[8] But God is not the proximate cause of sin or evil because God is not the proximate cause of *any* particular created effect.[9] And God is also only the cause of the *privation* of sin and evil because God is the cause of those created causes, which are themselves goods, which *cause* the imperfection of other things by virtue of their own power (which is itself a created perfection).[10] Therefore, God wills sin and evil only as tragic concomitants of the mutual determination of the world as a whole, a world ordered to the ultimate good of redemption. Sin and evil are never intentional objects of God and always fall outside God's commanding will, even if God brings both about by virtue of God's efficient will.[11] Indeed, Schleiermacher is clear that evil as such has no being, and so cannot be a thought of God.[12] And if evil cannot be a thought, it cannot be an intentional object. Therefore, on count after count, what initially appears the least traditional feature of Schleiermacher's account turns out to make use of the very axiological principles that it most calls into question.

As we have seen, Schleiermacher disagrees with a range of traditional accounts of sin and its origins in a number of ways. However, contrary to so many other modern theological options, he does so not by abandoning but precisely by *amplifying* traditional commitments. Because he shows that and how these can be maintained, while, at the same time, discarding traditional accounts of the origins of sin, Schleiermacher proves that the principle of parallel priority is not necessary. In so doing he shows much of the debate over sin and its origins in the last two centuries to have been premised on a false dilemma and, therefore, to have been fundamentally mistaken.

Agency, normativity, and tradition

The account of value underwriting Schleiermacher's account is deeply traditional. Fittingly, the tacit notions of agency at work in Schleiermacher's case are also decidedly ancient (and medieval, and early modern), which is to say, not Kantian. In fact, Schleiermacher's account relies largely on turning Aristotelian notions against a theological line that is often associated with Aristotle's adoption. And Schleiermacher fills out the gaps left by the excising of traditional elements in his own account with characteristically Aristotelian and Platonic elements.

This is an irony worth noting. But it has further consequences for Schleiermacher's constructive account (and those like it). The affirmative use of Aristotelian notions of agency and power against traditional accounts of the origins of sin shows that the abandonment of traditional accounts of sin's origins need not *also* require discarding Aristotle for Kant (or the like). Indeed, it is difficult to see how Schleiermacher's critical arguments examined in Chapters 2 and 3 could succeed on premises other than broadly Aristotelian ones, or those accounts that are very much akin. Schleiermacher's recommendation of the abandonment of the fall in important ways *depends on* ancient accounts of agency. We can, on Schleiermacher's grounds, best be modern by being yet more ancient. And this not only entitles but also recommends our use of other commitments correlated with ancient accounts, such as the normativity of natures and the priority of the good.

However, that might invite the misunderstanding that Schleiermacher turns ancient accounts of agency on a theological tradition that was simply ignorant of its own divergence from thinkers like Aristotle and Plato. In Chapter 4, we saw how this is decidedly not the case when we examined Schleiermacher's rejection of a deficient causal account of the origins of sin. Instead, we saw how the Augustinian deficient cause was explicitly proposed to exempt at least the first sinful will from the kind of causally complete account Schleiermacher thinks we must, in principle, give.[13] Schleiermacher's declination of the deficient will tradition is instructive. Against a deficient will, Schleiermacher appeals not only to an account of agency in which actions are always determined by antecedent sufficient reasons but also to higher principles. He argues that the causal incompleteness which a deficient causal account of the origins of sin implies is incompatible with the causal *completeness* entailed by the belief that everything depends absolutely on God. Therefore, we are forced, Schleiermacher thinks, to choose between a traditional account of sin's origins and what he takes to be the only adequate account of God. He unambiguously recommends the latter, with implications for our further accounts of human agency.[14] Schleiermacher's disagreement with his own Augustinian tradition identifies the true locus of dispute as the exceptionless application of the principle of sufficient reason, even to the will of the first sinner. And giving an account of a sinful will having an antecedent sufficient reason locates Schleiermacher *even further* from Kant than from the Augustinian deficient will tradition.

Even when we see that Schleiermacher does indeed reduce or reject some traditional distinctions, he does so – remarkably – on largely *ancient* grounds. For instance, in the case of God's authorship of sin he holds with Aristotle that being and activity are the same, and that form is what disposes a thing to specific acts under particular circumstances. Therefore, Schleiermacher holds that God is the sufficient cause of sin: since God preserves the things (which are their activity) in question, God is, remotely, the cause of their state of sin and their acts that follow from that state. As earlier, to describe God as the author of sin and the cause of evil amounts to an apparent disagreement with at least the majority of the theological tradition. But this line, too, blurs upon closer inspection, for we see, in comparison with Calvin – a fellow Reformed theologian straightforwardly echoing Augustinian sensibilities – that, in the end, many of the most important apparent differences in Schleiermacher's account appear minor, or even merely nominal. In fact, by the conclusion of that comparison we saw that Schleiermacher not only is happy to distinguish divine intent from the intent of the wicked in matters of sin's authorship but also holds that God's will should be distinguished as commanding and efficient will, a teaching which, in the end, not only amounts to a view shared by the Reformed tradition but also extends beyond it.[15] Thus, even with respect to *divine* agency, Schleiermacher's account is much closer to the tradition than a superficial reading might suggest, and what differences there are follow from the stricter application, not abandonment, of ancient accounts of agency.

That Schleiermacher's account of agency is largely ancient is not, however, to say it is entirely so. And the differences which remain matter greatly. Most importantly, Schleiermacher thinks of deficient states and acts of the will as, *like all natural things*, amenable, in principle, to causally complete explanation.

As I claimed in Chapter 4, Schleiermacher's innovation is to modify ancient accounts of agency to match modern physics' account of motion (or force) and rest. For Augustine there was no efficient cause for an evil will, only a deficient one; and this deficient cause was not understood as a species of efficient causality, let alone as a quasi-thing. Instead it was a sort of causal, and so explanatory, void: where causes are deficient, *there is no cause.*[16] On the grounds of Aristotelian physics, this claim was admissible in principle, for Aristotle thought that things had an innate disposition to rest, and thus required an *added* impulse to be kept in the same state of unnatural motion.[17] This innate disposition to rest was a kind of deficient cause of locomotion, an arc of natural dissolution. Therefore, it was at least plausible for someone like Augustine to conceive of the will as deficiently caused on analogy with the motion of stones and arrows.

When modern physics, culminating in Newton's dynamics, substituted modern accounts of inertia for the Aristotelian impetus tradition, it undercut the plausibility of this analogy, for, on the new account of motion and rest, an object in motion stays in motion, unless acted upon by another force.[18] Objects, in short, must be *made* to rest from without; and thus, the idea of a thing's innate disposition to rest was replaced by an account of causal opposition on the part of other things in the world. What Schleiermacher does is apply this new conception of inertia and force to the will in the same way Augustine applied the older notion.[19] In so doing, Schleiermacher renders the old deficient will account obsolete: the will, on analogy with modern dynamics, must be *made* to fail by some other, sufficient, determining cause.[20] Schleiermacher's great disagreement with the theological tradition is, therefore, not so much over the tradition's accounts of value, or agency, but over the metaphysics of causality that unites ethics and physics.

The result is that *all* deficiencies are, like the slowing of an arrow *by another force*, brought about by causes sufficient to make them so. Accordingly, Schleiermacher thinks a state of sin *and* the acts resulting from such a state are amenable, in principle, to explanation; and that a sufficient explanation will be one that completely accounts for the effects in question. Because these explanations will provide *reasons* for the state of sin and the acts that follow, and because reasons *are* causes, Schleiermacher thinks this explanatory demand applies to agents in exactly the same way: the state of sin and the voluntary acts which follow from such a state are both causally complete in principle.

Thus, Schleiermacher's account is distinguished from traditional accounts by its *exhaustive* application of the principle of sufficient reason. Crucially, Schleiermacher includes antecedent sufficient reasons for willing and acting in the total set of causes that we are, in principle, liable to give. Because so, his account, while sometimes differing from older deficient causal accounts of failure in this respect, differs *even more* from Kant's account, for Kant rejects the idea that the will and action are explained by objects in the world as determining goods.[21] And Kant's account also arguably requires that at least some species of libertarianism is true.[22] Schleiermacher's account, by contrast, holds (1) that every state or act, including whatever we count as free acts and/or voluntary acts, has antecedent causes sufficient to determine them; (2) that such acts and states are never, apart from God's will and act, the terminus of explanation, thus denying any ultimate responsibility criterion applied to human agents;[23] and, finally, (3) that God wills what God wills of *absolute necessity*, and because this necessity is transitive, there are, Schleiermacher thinks, no unactualized creaturely possibilities either.[24] Therefore, Schleiermacher denies the principle of alternate possibilities. Because Kant's account of agency apparently requires the denial of (1), it appears that Kant's account is incompatible with Schleiermacher's account of agency. Further, Kant's account arguably requires that some species of libertarianism is true. But (2), (3), or both are arguably required for libertarian accounts of the will. Therefore, Kant's account is incompatible with Schleiermacher's account on both points.

In relation to Kant, however, Schleiermacher's most dramatic divergence lies in his subscription to the normativity of natures and the priority of the good. We saw in Chapters 5, 6, and 7 how sin was a privation of a good, how what made that good *good* was its propriety to ends which are natural to human beings, how those ends consisted in a certain sort of activity (and, accordingly, how its privation consisted in a hindrance to that activity), and how not only human nature but also the entire cosmos was ordered to the developmental perfection of this natural passive potency of (at least) human being through the redemption accomplished by Jesus of Nazareth. And, therefore, we saw how sin consisted in a privation of nested norming natures: human nature specifically, and nature itself most generally – both the parts and the whole of that divinely ordered life which is the universe.

Not only are these natures normative but also they are prior to their defects ontologically and logically, though not chronologically. Indeed, the natures in question need not be historical; and the original perfection of the world (and humanity with it) is not only not *past* goods but also not necessarily even *temporal* goods. Theirs is a *timeless* perfection, just as is the divine causality that brings about their ends in a developing and ephemeral creation. In Chapter 7, we further saw how the natural final end of human beings, to which nature itself and human nature specifically are ordered, is not only *a* good but also *the* good. The God-consciousness has an object. And the goodness of this object, though indeed a specific natural good for an animal ordered to its apprehension, is not other than the communication of the goodness of the object itself.[25] Thus our *conscience*, that power or activity which commands *the* good for *our* good, makes demands which are *identical* with the *idea of the good*, demands which are, in turn, *identical* with those yielded by the consciousness of God. In short, at nearly every turn, Schleiermacher not only gives an Aristotelian account of agency, action, and the normativity of natures but also supplements and expands upon it with a Platonic account of the grounding of specific created goods in a transcendent source of value, the consciousness of which is identical with *the idea of the good itself*. And it is the good which, we find, has absolute and eternal priority over what is good and right for its creatures to do in time.

In further respect to the normativity of natures and the priority of the good, Schleiermacher's account is incompatible with a *prima facie* reading of Kant. Indeed, a principal motivation of Kant's was to seek an adequate account of ethics which does *not* appeal to the normativity of natures, or to the priority of the good and the eudaemonism it recommends.[26] On all counts, Schleiermacher pursues the opposite course. Aristotelian accounts of agency and action find their home, by way of an Aristotelian account of natures, to an account of value grounded in the transcendent goodness of God, which is our final end. Which is to say, Schleiermacher follows that well-trod path of so many theologians before him of wedding Aristotle and Plato in service of a distinctly Christian synthetic vision of agency, action, purpose, and value within which to situate an account of sin and nature. Yet, uniquely, Schleiermacher does so within a broader understanding of human nature with its distinctive activities and ends, as yet another animal kind born of evolution in a teleologically ordered world, rather than a doctrine of human nature corrupted by a historical past.

Schleiermacher's theology of sin and natural science

Schleiermacher's theology of sin is concerned with nature and the natural at nearly every turn, both nature itself (i.e., nature as a whole, the nature system) and human nature. Indeed, for Schleiermacher, human nature and the system of nature are intimately linked. Human nature stands to nature itself as part to whole, both informed and informing. Moreover, Schleiermacher's conception of human nature's relation to the natural world is not only broad but also deep. His is an account born of an interest in the *origins* of sin and the hindrance of our attainment of that good of which sin is a privation. As I mentioned in Chapter 5, and argued at length in *The Eternal Covenant*, Schleiermacher was both familiar with and clearly subscribed to the pre-Darwinian evolutionary theories of his day.[27] And apart from certain anti-teleological applications of evolutionary theory, there is no reason to suspect Schleiermacher would have been any less friendly to the developments which postdated his death. In fact, as I claimed in Chapter 1, and as I showed throughout this work, particularly in Chapter 5, Schleiermacher was actively concerned to advance an account of sin that is *in principle* coherent with, and supported by, an evolutionary story of cosmic, broadly biological, and specifically human origins. In this section I explain Schleiermacher's account of sin and sin's origins in light of evolution and remark on how it differs from standard approaches from theology-and-science specialists – especially in ways that recommend Schleiermacher's account over its alternatives.

Recall that Schleiermacher substitutes an evolutionary-developmental account of human nature in place of a story of its past corruption. Schleiermacher's reasons for doing so are manifold. He deems the accounts of agency, power, and perfection used by traditional accounts to explain this corruption unsatisfactory. He also deems some of the claims of such accounts burdensome as matters of fact. He thinks, for instance, there never was a time when human beings began to die, and that such a notion is not only false as natural history but also incompatible with finite existence as such. Schleiermacher concludes overall that sin is as old as human being; that the first humans, whoever they were, were the first sinners, not by choice but by birth.

At the same time, Schleiermacher does not concede, and indeed denies, that such a condition is *natural* – with respect to human ends. For, on Schleiermacher's view, natures norm, and sin is privative of that norm, because sin consists in an *inability* to attain to the proper activities as ends to which human nature is ordered. It is irrelevant that there were never any humans (before Christ) who were so able to attain. For *Christ* is the *normal*, which is to say, *ideal* human. At the same time, the consciousness of God is something that humans are naturally able to become able to attain through communion with Christ. Indeed, the God-consciousness must be a natural passive potency of human nature, otherwise Christ's divinity would null his humanity, and redeemed sinners could be redeemed only on the condition of a destructive transformation of their natural kind (and thus also their personal identity). No, the world is providentially ordered to redemption in Christ: not only to Christ's incarnation and saving work but also to our reception and appropriation of it *as humans*.

Schleiermacher's account entitles him to deny traditional accounts of sin's origins *and their variants* while maintaining traditional metaethical principles regarding the priority of the good and the normativity of natures. Both points differ from accounts offered by most, if not all, theologians in conversation with the natural sciences.

One major strand of theology-and-science work is concerned to maintain a historical fall or fall-like event, only to do so in a way that is compatible with the natural history of the earth. Various accounts or gestures at accounts have been proposed.[28] But all hold in common the basic structure of the traditional story of sin's origins: that by a voluntary act or acts, the first humans (of whatever number) alienated themselves from God and corrupted or disordered human nature. Of course, many of these accounts concede that there must have been more than two original humans, or that this voluntary corruption was gradual, or social, or both. And nearly all of them not only concede but also endorse the main overarching themes of evolution which entail, for instance, that humans did not introduce biological death into the world. But what these accounts do not, collectively, admit is that there never was a time when human beings were without sin, that there were causes sufficient to bring about a state of sin and the acts which follow from such a state, and that, therefore, humans and God are both causally implicated in sin, which is to say, this strand of thought retains both the principle of parallel priority and humans' asymmetrical fault for sin. And in both respects, such accounts are very traditional.

But as Schleiermacher's arguments go to demonstrate, such accounts do not really offer the benefits they appear to. In the first place, accounts that include the introduction of sin in the past by a voluntary act depend on contending over the facts of history. The consolation of champions of such accounts is that those facts are unlikely ever to be fully uncovered. But, more importantly, it isn't at all clear that modifying the details of the story of the fall addresses any of Schleiermacher's in-principle objections. What difference does it make, Schleiermacher might ask, if there were two people or two thousand? Either they all fell, or they all did not. If some did not, they do not stand in need of redemption by Christ, which is against that most basic Christian belief and amounts to the Pelagian heresy. On the other hand, if they all fell, how did that happen? How were all of them so motivated to do so? And if we suppose thousands of people collectively finding the suggestion of disobedience of God tempting, how does that guard against Schleiermacher's accusation that a person who finds such a course tempting is already in a state of sin? Would it not seem they were *all already* sinners before the first sin? And would that not lead to Schleiermacher's account all the same? In fact, the whole of Schleiermacher's line of argumentation against traditional accounts of the fall of both the Devil and Adam could simply be repeated against *all* fall-like accounts because *all* alike depend on the same accounts of agency, judgment, responsibility, power, and nature which Schleiermacher thought made their traditional forbears incoherent or eliminable without loss.

As an alternative to such accounts, other theology-and-science specialists have offered evolutionary accounts of sin which depend not on past events but on the power to will what we will freely – where freedom is most often understood in indeterminist terms.[29] Evolution, on such accounts, gives rise to human beings who are then able to freely choose to sin or not. Such accounts enjoy different benefits than their modified-tradition alternatives but also shoulder new burdens.

Above all, such accounts struggle to explain how an action can be both naturally determined and, at the same time, free. Indeed, such accounts strive, in principle, to exempt free acts from antecedent causal explanation on analogy with the deficient causal tradition, explained only in terms of, say, neurological quantum indeterminacy, or a similar appeal. But it is one of the major theses of Darwinian accounts of behavior that all animals, including humans, at least sometimes desire to do the things we do *instinctually* – including acts potentially ranging from music and dance to sex and war, to the selection of food and the enjoyment of sleep. We *want* to do what we do in such cases precisely because we have *evolved* to want to do so. Importantly, sometimes what we want to do by virtue of evolved instinct might be reckoned sin, as in the kind of group killing and sexual domination that humans appear to share in common with chimpanzees.[30] And this might be expanded, in principle, to any sociobiological explanation of bad human action.

In cases like these, theories of the origins of sin that appeal to a certain sort of free will cannot describe the acts which follow from these instincts as sins. They cannot do so because such accounts typically define freedom in a way that makes the choice between a determined and a free act exclusive, and an evolutionary account of an act sufficient to explain renders it determined enough to be incompatible with freedom so understood. There are two consequences that follow. First, such theories must deny that there are any evolutionarily explained sinful behaviors – assuming, as these accounts typically do, that freedom of a certain sort is required to secure the blame that sin implies. Second, such theories, should they wish to defend the sinfulness of apparently evolved acts, must be concerned to deny evolutionary explanations, or at least sufficient evolutionary explanations, of said acts. Counterintuitively then, sin understood in terms of freedom of this sort yields either less responsibility for sin (or less sin, all told) or a program committed to finding causal gaps. And neither seems to be what adherents to this kind of account ultimately want.

Even if such accounts were able to reply to the foregoing concerns, however, there would be other, more basic problems – namely, that, in order to secure a theory of indeterminate free choice, such accounts must be committed to this sort of freedom obtaining generally. And that leaves open the prospect that it is possible, of our own free will, *not* to sin. And that is a doctrine which seems to imply that at least some people, other than Christ, might, in fact, not sin. And that is the Pelagian heresy. And if, in an effort to avoid the Pelagian heresy, adherents of this view concede that every person but Christ *shall* be a sinner, then they simply end up with Schleiermacher's view on the matter, only without his much less burdensome (and hence much more desirable) axiological and metaphysical assumptions. Adherents of this view accrue all the burdens of modern accounts because, in fact, accounts like these simply echo, in the most important respects, Immanuel Kant.

There is not space here to settle the great debate between ancient and Kantian views, but I do wish to point out two advantages of Schleiermacher's position over and against what are typically taken to be basic Kantian positions, specifically with respect to natural scientific concerns. The first advantage is that Schleiermacher's position on evolutionarily informed voluntary action is compatible with causal determinism. The second advantage is that Schleiermacher's position on such action is compatible with eudaemonism.

Compatibility with both causal determinism and with eudaemonism is particularly pertinent in light of questions of natural determination through evolution or other processes. Natural determination is not, of course, limited to *genetic* determination (though genetic determination is one kind of natural determination). Instead it is much broader, and could, in principle, include any cause that played a part in forming an agent prior to an agent's act, such as cultural or psychological causes. Regardless of the cause or causes that ultimately determine our acts, Schleiermacher's account is compatible *in principle*. Because evolutionary causes are simply one more species of determining cause, they are equally compatible with Schleiermacher's account of agency. On Schleiermacher's position, theologians are thus freed from seeking causally indeterminate gaps in our natural determination in order to secure human freedom, for nothing about *natural* indeterminacy secures freedom more fully once we are, like Schleiermacher, free from anxieties about its compatibility with causal determinism more generally.

As for eudaemonism, Schleiermacher's account is compatible with the sense of this term given by many philosophers and theologians: that our highest good is our happiness or blessedness, and that moral obligation is compatible with, and even entailed by, our pursuit of our own highest good. This should be of little surprise given Schleiermacher's appeal to Plato, Aristotle, and traditional theological accounts of human well-being as beatitude, not to mention Leibniz and Spinoza, who also subscribed to species of eudaemonism. However, specifically with respect to matters of natural science, the compatibility of Schleiermacher's position with eudaemonism frees him from the need to identify strictly altruistic reasons for the evolution of certain traits and dispositions, where *altruism* is understood as precluding our regarding an action as *moral* when such action accrues personal advantage or is done for the sake of personal good. And freedom from this anxiety relieves Schleiermacher from the task of proposing *super* evolutionary accounts of *true* Christian charity.[31]

Instead, Schleiermacher can combine causal determinism and eudaemonism: the world is ordered through evolutionary processes to bring about

animals that can and will pursue their happiness by virtue of naturally determined causes. In contrast with much talk in theology and evolutionary ethics, Schleiermacher need not identify "selfless" acts in order to provide clear
instances of the good and the right. Instead, he can happily admit that our
acting well is always for *our* good, but not *only* for our good. And this general picture does not change with the transition from "animal confusion" to
the intermittent and incomplete consciousness of God, to its summit in the
God-consciousness of Christ. It is never that we cease to act for *our* good,
and that acting well for our good is what right action consists in, but that
our good is elevated and perfected. To our proximate personal and social
advantage is added a higher end, an end which we are capable of appre-
hending in consciousness because, and only because, of all prior evolutionary history.

Sin, nature, and the historiography of theology

Finally, Schleiermacher's theology of sin and nature has important implications for the historiography of theology. As noted in Chapter 1, Schleiermacher is often associated with the beginnings of a distinct sort of theology,
modern theology.[32] And as also noted, this distinct sort of theology is often
associated both with new developments in natural science and with the philosophy of Immanuel Kant. Sometimes explicitly, but most often by assumption or association, Schleiermacher is identified as a modern theologian *both*
by his concern for matters of science, including natural science, *and* by his
association with Kant.[33] If so, this historiographical tradition implies, or at
least has been taken to imply, that there is a line from Kant through Schleiermacher to Ritschl and beyond.[34] In this light, *modern* theology as a whole
more or less amounts to *Kantian* theology, not in the most modest sense of
working in Kant's wake but in the stronger sense of sharing many of Kant's
most characteristic beliefs and guiding principles.[35]

By exhibiting Schleiermacher's concrete claims and implicit premises,
I showed that Schleiermacher did not subscribe to, and could not have consistently subscribed to, key Kantian claims about nature, the good, human
action, the compatibility of our freedom with natural and divine determination, or the deficiency of evil's determining causes. In consequence, this
standard historiographical tale, or assumptions about Schleiermacher's
place in it, is not right. *Either* Schleiermacher is not a characteristically
modern theologian, *or* modern theology cannot be mainly associated with
the adoption of certain characteristically Kantian claims and commitments.
The former option seems implausible. Schleiermacher is rightly regarded
as at the forefront of a new epoch in theology in some respects quite apart
from his supposedly Kantian views – for instance, on matters of sin, with
respect to his treatment of traditional authorities, or his rejection or modification of traditional theological claims about the fall of the Devil and the
fall of Adam. That leaves the latter option: that what is typically regarded as

modern theology has been too narrowly construed, and that there is no *necessary* connection between distinctly modern theology and characteristically Kantian claims and commitments. Modern theology is a broader phenomenon and *on matters of nature and value does not, and need not, necessarily diverge from traditional accounts of the same.*

Schleiermacher's concrete accounts of agency, nature, privation, and the good all militate against the idea that modern theology as such is characterized by the rejection of traditional axiological and metaphysical commitments. Not only does Schleiermacher's account of sin and nature largely track traditional accounts, especially with respect to the priority of the good and the normativity of natures, but also even when Schleiermacher rejects traditional claims, he does so for mostly ancient reasons. It is Aristotelian accounts of agency and reason that rule out the Devil's fall. It is Aristotelian accounts of action, predication, natures, and powers that rule out Adam's defection and corruption. It is an Aristotelian account of *akrasia* that describes our state of sin and the acts which follow from it. It is Platonic accounts of the good, our good, and the power of conscience, as the spirited part of the soul that champions the just claim of the good, within which Schleiermacher characterizes the evil of sin. If the genuine Schleiermacher, and not a caricature, is to be remembered as the "father of modern theology," then modern theology cannot principally consist in the abandonment of Greek metaphysics and axiology.

That is not, however, to say that Schleiermacher's account *merely* amounts to, or follows from, a readoption of ancient beliefs and first principles. No, Schleiermacher is doing something different from the ancients (and even more different from Kant) with his strong version of the principle of sufficient reason. As noted in Chapter 4, Schleiermacher's strong use of this principle is most consonant with the principle as used by Benedict Spinoza. This use is incompatible with traditional accounts of sin as deficiently caused. Positively, it entails that God is (in some sense) the author of sin and the cause of evil, two theses Schleiermacher, again following Spinoza, endorses.[36] Importantly, it is this very same strong version of the principle of sufficient reason that makes Schleiermacher's account of sin, agency, and value especially amenable to explanation in ways that are, in principle, compatible with natural science. Schleiermacher's account is, then, a largely ancient account, modified by a strong version of the principle of sufficient reason, for, among other reasons, securing the in-principle coherence of Christian claims about sin with scientific claims about natural history and the development of life and the cosmos. It is, in short, an account of sin ordered to sustaining an adequate account of nature and the natural simultaneously with respect to both origins and ends.

Sin, for Schleiermacher, is a privation of a specific nature. But that ideal was never, apart from Christ, found in history. It was never a lost past, yet it is a lack – only not of our origins but of our *telos*. Sin is a "shadow of the good":[37] an imperfection of that blessed and unbroken communion

with God that was always to be ours from the foundation of the world and
which, by God's omnipotent love, shall be attained.

Notes

1 *GL* §§44, 72.2–3; *The Christian Faith*, 161–62, 293–96.
2 *GL* §§4.4, 8.2, 49.1; *The Christian Faith*, 16–17, 35, 189–90.
3 *GL* §72.4; *The Christian Faith*, 299.
4 *GL* §72.6; *The Christian Faith*, 303–4.
5 *GL* §§68.2, 61.5; *The Christian Faith*, 256, 277–78.
6 *GL* §§5.3, 5.4; *The Christian Faith*, 20–21, 23.
7 *GL* §66.2; *The Christian Faith*, 272.
8 See Pedersen, *The Eternal Covenant*, 98–126, 139–42.
9 *GL* §47; *The Christian Faith*, 178–84.
10 *GL* §48.2–3; *The Christian Faith*, 185–89.
11 *GL* §81.1; *The Christian Faith*, 332.
12 *GL* §83.3; *The Christian Faith*, 344–45.
13 Augustine, *City of God*, XII.6.
14 *GL* §§48, 79; *The Christian Faith*, 184–89, 325–26.
15 See Aquinas, *Summa Theologica*, Ia, Q. 49, a. 1, resp.; Q. 103, a. 7, r. o.
16 Augustine, *City of God*, XII.6.
17 See Aristotle, *Physics*, II.1, IV.1.
18 See Newton, *Principia Mathematica*, vol. 1, Definition III, and Law I; see also
   Leibniz, "A Specimen of Dynamics" ["*Specimen Dynamicum*"], 118.
19 Of course, this was not an utterly new thought but a more consistent application
   of an older one. See Aquinas, *Summa Theologica*, Ia, Q. 49, a.1, resp. But again,
   compare this claim to the cause of *voluntary* evils in Ia, Q. 49, a. 1, r. o. 3.
20 Leibniz attempts to explain deficient causes on the grounds of modern dynamics,
   in his *Theodicy*, but not, to my mind, successfully, leaving the greatest potential
   objections unmet and even undermining the Augustinian account in the process.
   See Leibniz, *Theodicy*, 140–41.
21 See Kant, *Groundwork of the Metaphysics of Morals*, 4:389.
22 See Hogan, "Metaphysical Motives of Kant's Analytic–Synthetic Distinction,"
   291–99.
23 For more on the ultimate responsibility criterion see Kane, *The Significance of
   Free Will*, 60–78; "Libertarianism."
24 *GL* §54; *The Christian Faith*, 211–19.
25 *GL* §168.1; *The Christian Faith*, 732–33.
26 Again, see Kant, *Groundwork*, 4:389.
27 See Pedersen, *The Eternal Covenant*, 35–45.
28 As a small sample of the most recent work, see Deane-Drummond, "In Adam All
   Die?"; Smith, "What Stands on the Fall?"; Van den Toren, "Original Sin and the
   Coevolution of Nature and Culture."
29 Again, as a small sample, see Clayton, *In Quest of Freedom*; Hick, *Evil and the
   God of Love*; Peterson, "Falling Up"; Schwager, *Banished from Eden*; Swinburne,
   "An Irenaean Approach to Evil"; Williams, *Doing Without Adam and Eve*.
30 Again, see Wrangham and Peterson, *Demonic Males*.
31 See Coakley, *Sacrifice Regained*.
32 As Brandt, for example, puts it, "Schleiermacher and Darwin were probably
   the two persons most directly responsible for the shaping of modern Protestant
   religious thought." Brandt, *The Philosophy of Schleiermacher*, 308.
33 Indeed, some have taken Schleiermacher's program of an "eternal covenant"
   between faith and science as a kind of Kantian détente between the disciplines,

what Andrew Dole calls the "segregation model." Dole, *Schleiermacher on Religion and the Natural Order*, 140. See also Brandt, *The Philosophy of Schleiermacher*, 261–62. I have argued at length that the segregation model is in most important respects (though not in every respect) mistaken. See Pedersen, *The Eternal Covenant*, 3–11.

34 For instance, Brandt describes Troeltsch's account of religion as "the Kant-Schleiermacher view." See Brandt, *The Philosophy of Schleiermacher*, 308.

35 Another exception to the rough identification of modern theology with characteristically Kantian claims and commitments could be Hegel (depending on how Hegel is read). Why Hegel's role in forming modern theology has not already amounted to a case against modern theology as more or less mostly Kantian in the sense I use remains mysterious, but I suspect it partly has to do with the resistance on the part of both philosophers and theologians to read Hegel *as a theologian*. For helpful correctives to this view, see Dorrien, *Kantian Reason and Hegelian Spirit*; Hodgson, *Hegel and Christian Theology*.

36 See Spinoza, "Ethics," IIP20, IIP48, VP18S.

37 GL §74.4; *The Christian Faith*, 314.

References

Aquinas, Thomas. *Summa Theologica*. Translated by the Fathers of the English Dominican Province. New York: Benziger Bros., 1947.

Aristotle. *Physics*. Vol. 1. Edited by Jonathan Barnes. Princeton: Princeton University Press, 1984.

Augustine of Hippo. *The City of God*. The Works of Saint Augustine. Part I, Vol. 7. Translated by William Babcock. New City Press, New York, 2013.

Brandt, Richard. *The Philosophy of Schleiermacher*. New York: Harper, 1941.

Clayton, Philip. *In Quest of Freedom: The Emergence of Spirit in the Natural World*. Göttingen: Vandenhoeck & Ruprecht, 2009.

Coakley, Sarah. *Sacrifice Regained: Evolution, Cooperation, and God*. Oxford: Oxford University Press, 2020.

Deane-Drummond, Celia. "In Adam All Die?" In *Evolution and the Fall*, edited by William T. Cavanaugh and James K. A. Smith. Grand Rapids, MI: Eerdmans, 2017.

Dole, Andrew. *Schleiermacher on Religion and the Natural Order*. Oxford: Oxford University Press, 2010.

Dorrien, Gary. *Kantian Reason and Hegelian Spirit: The Idealistic Logic of Modern Theology*. Oxford: Wiley Blackwell, 2015.

Hick, John. *Evil and the God of Love*. Third edition. London: Macmillan, 1977.

Hodgson, Peter C. *Hegel and Christian Theology: A Reading of the Lectures on the Philosophy of Religion*. New York: Oxford University Press, 2005.

Hogan, Desmond. "Metaphysical Motives of Kant's Analytic–Synthetic Distinction." *Journal of the History of Philosophy* 51, no. 2 (2013): 267–307.

Kane, Robert. "Libertarianism." In *Four Views on Free Will*. Oxford: Blackwell, 2007.

———. *The Significance of Free Will*. New York: Oxford University Press, [1996] 1998.

Kant, Immanuel. *Groundwork of the Metaphysics of Morals*. Translated and edited by Mary Gregor. Cambridge: Cambridge University Press, 1997.

Leibniz, Gottfried Wilhelm. "Specimen Dynamicum." In *Philosophical Essays*, translated by Roger Ariew and Daniel Garber. Indianapolis: Hackett, 1989.

———. *Theodicy*. Edited by Austin Farrer, translated by E. M. Huggard. La Salle, IL: Open Court, [1951] 1985.

Newton, Isaac. *Philosophiae Naturalis Principia Mathematica*. London, 1687.

Pedersen, Daniel J. *The Eternal Covenant: Schleiermacher on God and Natural Science*. Berlin: De Gruyter, 2017.

Peterson, Gregory. "Falling Up: Evolution and Original Sin." In *Evolution and Ethics: Human Morality in Biological and Religious Perspective*, edited by Phillip Clayton and Jeffrey Schloss. Grand Rapids, MI: Eerdmans, 2004.

Schleiermacher, Friedrich D. E. *The Christian Faith*. Edited by H. R. Mackintosh and J. S. Stewart, translated by D. M. Baillie, et al. Berkeley: Apocryphile, [1928] 2011.

———. *Der christliche Glaube nach den Grundsätzen der evangelischen Kirche im Zusammenhange dargestellt*. Second edition. Edited by Rolf Schäfer. Berlin: Walter de Gruyter, [1830/31] 2008.

Schwager, Raymund S. J. *Banished from Eden: Original Sin and Evolutionary Theory in the Drama of Salvation*. Translated by James Williams. Leominster: Gracewing, [1997] 2006.

Smith, James K. A. "What Stands on the Fall? A Philosophical Exploration." In *Evolution and the Fall*, edited by William T. Cavanaugh and James K. A. Smith. Grand Rapids, MI: Eerdmans, 2017.

Spinoza, Benedict. "Ethics." In *The Collected Works of Spinoza*, Vol. 1, edited and translated by Edwin Curley. Princeton, NJ: Princeton University Press, 1985.

Swinburne, Richard. "An Irenaean Approach to Evil." In *Finding Ourselves After Darwin: Conversations on the Image of God, Original Sin, and the Problem of Evil*. Grand Rapids, MI: Baker Academic, 2018.

Van den Toren, Benno. "Original Sin and the Coevolution of Nature and Culture." In *Finding Ourselves After Darwin: Conversations on the Image of God, Original Sin, and the Problem of Evil*. Grand Rapids, MI: Baker Academic, 2018.

Williams, Patricia. *Doing Without Adam and Eve: Sociobiology and Original Sin*. Minneapolis: Augsburg, 2001.

Wrangham, Richard, and Dale Peterson. *Demonic Males: Apes and the Origins of Human Violence*. New York: Houghton Mifflin, 1996.

Index

absolute beginnings 95–6

absolute dependence: on Christ 91–2; on God 74, 76; and heresy 89–90; and sufficient reason 73–6; *see also* "one single Redeemer"

absolute freedom, feeling of 74–5

absolute independence: of God 75; and relative freedom 78–81

actions: attribution of 78; grounded in natures 46–51, 72–3; and human nature 47; involuntary 40–1; motives for 54–5; and natures 47–8; non-voluntary 22–3; and thought 119–20; voluntary 132

Adam: Adam's nature and principle of sufficient reason 54–5; alteration of nature of 49–51; culpability of 40–1; direct relationship with God 44; and free will 37–8; pre-fall and post-fall 49–50; prior disposition to sin 38, 44–5; sin as voluntary act 61; sinless state 41; temptation by Devil 37–8, 51; *see also* fall of Adam

agency, normativity and tradition 182–6

akrasia 115, 123–7, 169, 181, 192

altruism 190

angels: concept of 18–19; equality of 25; and fall 19, 23–6; fallen angels 26–8; and involuntary action 21; perfection of 18–21; and voluntary action 19–20

animal behavior 189

"animal confusion" 119, 127–8, 191

appeal to deficient causes 180; *see also* deficient causes

Aquinas, Thomas: argument concerning Devil's motivation 21–2; on deficient causes 71–2; evil and principle

of sufficient reason 69–70; on fallen angels 34n24; on heresy and redemption 111n3; on nature and determined failures 69–73

Aristotelian concepts 184, 192

Aristotle: agency and power 183; on *akrasia* 124; doctrine of concrete universals 135; and eudaemonism 190

arrested God-consciousness 162, 166, 169; and sin 116–20

asymmetrical fault 161–2

Augustine of Hippo: account of sin by deficient causes 59–60, 73; account of the will 63–4; on acts, grounded in nature 73; on deficient causes 61–2; and divine justice 162; on efficient cause of evil will 67–9; on good corrupting good 93; on good natures choosing evil 68–70; on human nature 97–8; on nature and determined failures 68–72; on origins of sin 86; on possibility of corruption 108–9; Schleiermacher's approach to 110–11, 111n3, 180; on sexual desire 52–3; as theological traditionalist 2; "two men" example 63–6; on will and intellect 62

Barth, Karl 2

beautitude *see* blessedness

biological death 188

biology and culture 137

blessedness 43, 152, 171, 172

Buridan's ass example 64

Calvin, John: contrasted with Schleiermacher 184; on divine justice 162; on God as author of evil 157–61, 166